Walking
to
Forest Grove

The life and times
of the prettiest town in Oregon

By Ken Bilderback with Kris Bilderback

Table of contents

Chapter

1

Walking to Forest Grove
with Tabitha Brown

Explaining how to get to Forest Grove from Portland can be daunting.

"Take the Highway 26 freeway to Jackson School Road. Turn right on Scotch Church Road, then keep going west on Zion Church Road ..."

"Wait! I thought I was on Scotch Church Road ..."

"Oh, sorry! Scotch Church becomes Zion Church at Highway 219. So anyway, stay on Cornelius-Schefflin Road to ..."

"Back up! Do I turn right or left on Cornelius ..."

"Sorry. Zion Church becomes Cornelius-Schefflin Road, but you're going south now, not west, until you go either west or south by taking either the first right or the second right at the first roundabout and/or by taking either the first right or the second right at the second roundabout ..."

By the time one explains the public transportation route ("Take the light-rail line west until it reaches the end of the line, then take the

Number 57 bus until it reaches the end of its line ...") some people might think the visit isn't worth the effort.

Fortunately, many others are undaunted and take the time to come to town, either for a visit or to stay. Take, for example, Tabitha Brown. "Grandma" Brown didn't have directions to Forest Grove, because when she began her trip, Forest Grove didn't exist. And her journey didn't start in Portland, but rather back in Massachusetts, which wasn't yet a state when she was born in 1780.

Tabitha's life journey hit several roundabouts and detours, such as when her husband died at the tender age of 46 and she was left with two sons (Orus and Manthano) and a daughter named Pherne. Her late husband's brother, John, was a ship captain whose swashbuckling adventures on the high seas somehow had landed him in Missouri, which is where Tabitha, Orus, Manthano and Pherne soon joined him. Tabitha did not depend on a man to support her, however, and as a single mom she took up a career in teaching.

By 1846 Tabitha was 66 years old. That's retirement age even today, but considering that when Tabitha was born life expectancy was less than 40, 66 was pretty old to start a new life. But by 1846, Orus had visited the promised land of Oregon, which was not yet a state, and while Tabitha's promised land of Forest Grove did not yet exist, his tales summoned her westward as well, with her swashbuckling brother-in-law, Pherne and her grandchildren in tow.

Orus accompanied his mother on her journey as far as Fort Hall in what is now eastern Idaho. Tabitha had a horse, but as was the custom, the horse was as much for carrying cargo as humans, so she did a good deal of walking along the way. By the time they reached Fort Hall, she was exhausted. A young man, whom Tabitha described in her journals as "a rascally fellow," persuaded her to follow him on what he described as a new and better trail than the one Orus had followed in 1843. Orus protested, insisting that the established Oregon Trail along the Columbia River was the best route.

But the "rascally fellow" had what he was sure was a better idea. It seems that the same summer Orus trekked the Oregon Trail for the first time, a fellow by the name of Jesse Applegate had as well, along with his extended family and a friend named Levi Scott. For the Applegates the trip went well as far as Fort Hall in Idaho, but then two of their children died on the last stretch along the Columbia River. Certain that there must be a safer and faster route to Oregon, Applegate, his brothers and Levi Scott backtracked to Fort Hall, then mapped a route south through Nevada (which wasn't yet Nevada), through the California Gold Rush country (before the big Gold Rush hit) and then northward into Oregon. Tabitha's "rascally fellow" is believed to have been either Jesse Applegate or Levi Scott, both polished salesmen out to strike it rich off of travelers along the Oregon Trail. Whichever one it was, he persuaded Tabitha and daughter Pherne, now married to Virgil Pringle, to join the first expedition along the new route. Orus protested, but to no avail. He took the Columbia River route, wishing his mother and sister luck with their shaky set of directions. With the Applegates' directions in hand, the rascally fellow had them turn left at Fort Hall and proceed straight through the sweltering barren desert to the Humboldt River, where he took another right toward the Sierra Nevada mountains. At the mountains he could have gone right toward Oregon or left and then right and then right again when he reached the valley on the California side of the Sierra Nevada range …

Anyway, trying to find Oregon proved to be too daunting for this guide, and he abandoned Tabitha, Captain John, Pherne, Virgil, and Pherne and Virgil's children in the middle of nowhere. Being lost in the wilderness never is fun, and is even less fun when winter is closing in and you have no food or shelter. Tabitha did not want to meet the same fate as the Donner Party, although at this exact moment the Donner Party was alive and well along the Applegates' trail, having hung a left where Tabitha and Pherne had turned right, or perhaps at the next left after that (directions were confusing in 1846). Regardless, Tabitha's party needed help, and Pherne's husband, Virgil, trekked north toward where Forest Grove someday would stand.

Onward Virgil trekked as the snows of autumn fell. With no civilization in sight, he knew that his wife, children and mother-in-law were in mortal danger. Fortunately, he ran into Orus, who had headed south to find his mother and sister when they didn't arrive in Oregon on schedule. Together Virgil and Orus found their way back to Tabitha and led her and the rest of the party to safety in Salem on Christmas Day, 1846, with Tabitha making the last 50 miles or so on foot, according to legend. The members of the Donner Party had not been so fortunate, and found themselves stranded in the mountains as the flurries turned into a blizzard. It wasn't until three months after Tabitha and Pherne were reunited with Orus that the last of the Donner Party was rescued, not counting the ones who had been eaten after the rest of the party ran out of food.

Tabitha Brown's journey to what is today Forest Grove was far from over, however. In their book *Splendid Audacity: The Story of Pacific University*, Gary Miranda and Rick Read pick up her story. Tabitha spent the summer of 1847 in Astoria, enjoying the cool, coastal air. That fall, she started home to Salem, stopping in Forest Grove to visit Orus, who had settled on a donation land claim there. Orus' friend the Reverend Harvey Clarke and his wife, Emeline, invited Tabitha to stay at their house. She obliged, and when she said she was ready to continue her trip back to Salem, Harvey Clarke persuaded her to spend the winter in Forest Grove. While staying with the Clarkes, word came of the murder of Marcus Whitman and others in Walla Walla, Washington. Marcus Whitman was one of the earliest white settlers in the Oregon Territory, establishing a mission to serve the Cayuse tribe in 1836, near what today is Walla Walla, Washington. In 1843, Whitman led the first major wagon train across what would become known as the Oregon Trail. Nearly all of the earliest settlers on the Tualatin Plains had a close connection to Whitman, including Clarke, Joseph Meek, Alvin T. Smith, Almoran Hill, John Griffin, Robert Newell and William Doughty. The murder of a man who was a close friend to many on the Tualatin Plains had profound emotional impact on the settlers, and would help set in motion a series of events that would forever change the face of what we now know as Forest Grove. Most of the surviving settlers in Walla Walla fled to safer ground, which for many meant the Tualatin Plains. The list of those settlers in *Splendid Audacity* reads like a Who's Who of early Pacific University, including Alanson Hinman, Elkanah Walker, and Cushing Eells, among others.

"Grandma" Brown settled in for the winter with the Clarkes, who were young enough to be her own children, and whom she soon loved as though they were. She wrote in her journal of a conversation she had with young Reverend Clarke one day in October 1847. "Why has Providence frowned on me and left me poor in this world?" she asked Clarke. "Had He blessed me with riches ... I know right what I would do. I would establish myself in a comfortable home and receive all the poor children, and be a mother to them." The Reverend Clarke took up her cause and settled her in a log cabin, where she took in the children left orphaned by the rigors of the Oregon Trail.

In point of fact, Tabitha Moffatt Brown didn't walk all the way to Forest Grove. Her real story is much more complicated than simply that of a tough old grandma. She spent her life teaching, and loving, children, whether they were her own, her grandchildren or total strangers. The path that led her to Forest Grove was arduous and full of roadblocks and detours, but the life she created for herself as she neared the age of 70 was well worth the daunting trip. Tabitha Brown arrived in Oregon at a momentous time, one that combined almost unbearable hardship but also nearly unlimited possibilities. The city of Portland got its name just months before she arrived in Oregon, and would not actually become a city until 1851, long after Harvey Clarke and Tabitha Brown had planted solid roots in what was to become Forest Grove. Oregon was not yet a state, and Salem was not yet its capital; many cities vied for that honor, including potential metropolises such as Champoeg, not far down the road from Forest Grove on the banks of the Willamette River. Forest Grove was not yet Forest Grove, but rather a loosely defined area known as Tualatin Plains. Some people in Tualatin Plains had ambitions to become one of Oregon's largest and most important cities, while others couldn't decide whether to stay in Tualatin Plains or not. Some of the early settlers, such as Joseph Gale and Robert Newell, vacillated between the Tualatin Plains and the river port possibilities of Champoeg. Other settlers, including George Atkinson, also considered walking away from Forest Grove and establishing what was to become Pacific University in Oregon City or elsewhere. Tabitha Brown was in some ways caught in the middle. She didn't have land or money to decide the issue, and the contribution she did bring to the table was transferable almost universally. While she could have walked away from Forest Grove, Tabitha Brown chose to stay, and her legacy is her love for children and education, which planted the seeds for a great university and a great city, one that later arrivals would find well worth walking to themselves.

Chapter

2

Walking to Forest Grove with Rutherford B. Hayes

When Rutherford B. Hayes decided to become the first American President to visit the West Coast, he chose Forest Grove as one of the cities he wanted to see, in large part because of the great legacy of education that Tabitha Brown had helped to create.

Unfortunately, he chose a travel planner as inept as Tabitha's. After four leisurely days in Portland, Hayes was scheduled for an evening appearance in Vancouver, Washington, just about six miles north. His travel planners, however, squeezed in his visit to Forest Grove for his last day in Portland. The 30 mile detour to the west was lengthy back in 1880 under the best of conditions, and the conditions on Saturday, October 2, were far from ideal.

Befitting a visit by the President, a special train was assembled for the jaunt to Forest Grove. The train chugged along smoothly for more than 20 miles, but just seven miles short of its destination the train encountered a major problem: a damaged trestle over Dairy Creek and a ravine. A story in the October 4 edition of *The Oregonian* explains what happened next. President Rutherford B. Hayes, the First Lady, Lucy, their son Rutherford P. Hayes and the rest of the party disembarked and scrambled down the side of the ravine. The President of the United States and his entourage then made their way through thick brush and weeds, across the creek on "a weak foot bridge" and up the other side of the ravine. To entertain themselves, the reporter wrote, a chorus led by Lucy Hayes sang songs of the day. They walked under warm, cloudy skies for two miles until they stopped, exhausted and hungry. A group of Civil War veterans travelling with the President formed a foraging party and found an orchard, where they picked apples for a Presidential snack. By now hastily assembled railroad crews had repaired the trestle, and the train was able to cross and catch up to the hikers. After a brief stop in Cornelius, the train arrived in Forest Grove to be met by a fleet of carriages. Now too short on time to visit Pacific University, the President was taken to the home of E.R. Merriman, who had served with Hayes in the Civil War. When he finally spoke, 52 of the 310 words in his speech were devoted to complaining about the bridge that delayed his arrival and lamenting the fact that "our intercourse must be short."

His speech still found a place in Forest Grove history for decades because of his proclamation of Forest Grove as the "prettiest town in Oregon," which became the town's motto for many years. But President Hayes used 243 of his words to talk about the town's status as one of the West's top educational centers, including Pacific University, which owed its founding to Tabitha Brown, along with missionaries Harvey Clarke and George Atkinson.

There are not many reasons for a 66-year-old, 108-pound woman who got around with the aid of a cane to ride and walk half way across the American continent, but founding a great university would have been a good one. That's not why Tabitha Brown made her journey, however. In fact, when she first settled in what is now Forest Grove, Tabitha's first job was sewing gloves, according to her biography in the university archives. Then she persuaded Harvey Clarke to help build an orphanage. Neither Harvey Clarke nor Tabitha Brown had a university in mind, however, until 1848, when the Reverend George Atkinson came to town. Atkinson did not arrive on foot from across the Plains, however. When his superiors dispatched him from New York City to Oregon to establish a Congregationalist university, Atkinson left by boat. He sailed down the Atlantic Coast of first North America and then South America, then around Cape Horn and across the Pacific to Honolulu, where he learned of Marcus Whitman's death. From there he sailed onto Oregon to establish a university. On his arrival, missionaries suggested he visit Harvey Clarke and Tabitha Brown. The orphanage soon became Tualatin Academy, and then Pacific University. Tabitha died more than 20 years before President Hayes paid his visit in 1880, but her legacy was very much alive.

Hayes had come to see another indirect offshoot of Tabitha Brown's orphanage: The Indian School. By 1880, the Indian Wars had been won by the settlers, at least in the Tualatin Valley, which was named, ironically, after the Atfalati people whose lives revolved around Wapato Lake, about six miles south of Forest Grove in what today is Gaston. When Rutherford B. Hayes arrived in Forest Grove, not much remained of the Atfalatis except for the Americanized "Tuality" and "Tualatin" names that adorned schools and rivers and valleys. Nearly all of the few remaining tribal members had been shipped to a reservation near Grand Ronde, 50 miles away.

But while the battles were over, bitterness remained among many of the white settlers. Some of the area's most prominent citizens had ventured west across the Oregon Trail with Marcus Whitman, or in his footsteps, to the newly established Fort Hall. While Whitman put down stakes in Walla Walla, Washington, Joseph Meek, Almoran Hill and others continued on to the Tualatin Valley. Whitman, Meek and Hill remained close friends, however. When Meek's wife died he sent his young daughter to Walla Walla to be raised by the Whitmans, and the Whitmans visited Almoran Hill several times at his home in what today is Laurelwood, on the banks of what was then Wapato Lake. When Marcus Whitman, his family and several others, including Meek's daughter, were murdered in Walla Walla in 1847, Meek was named as the Oregon Territory's first official law enforcement officer. One of his first official acts was to hunt down and execute the Native Americans accused of committing the Whitman Massacre. Meek died five years before President Hayes came to the Tualatin Valley, but Hill and many other veterans of the Indian Wars still held prominent roles in the area.

General Phil Sheridan's Camp Yamhill was gone by 1880 as well, having served its purpose of preventing the Atfalatis from fleeing the Grand Ronde reservation to return to the land that had been taken from

8

them around Wapato Lake. Although there is great doubt that Sheridan ever actually uttered the words most often attributed to him, "The only good Indian is a dead Indian," there is no doubt that many of the settlers still held that view in 1880. Against that backdrop, the words of President Rutherford B. Hayes concerning the Indian School on October 2 were noteworthy, even if they did take second billing to his pronouncement of Forest Grove as "the prettiest town in Oregon."

"Some persons think that God has decreed that they should die off like wild animals," he told the assembled pioneers. "With that we have nothing to do. ... This country was once theirs. They owned it as much as you own your farms. We have displaced them." Of the Indian School he said: "I am glad that Oregon has taken a step in the right direction."

The direction of the school that so pleased the President was not to return any land to the Indians, however, nor even to return these Indian children to their native culture. In fact, not one of the students at Forest Grove's Indian School was from the Atfalati culture; all of the students came from tribes in Washington, purposely sent far from home to help destroy ties to their heritage. Harry Taylor, son of a teacher at the school, recalled in a November 26, 1925, *News-Times* article his dismay at seeing the young Native Americans cry upon arrival at the school, where they were stripped of their prized blankets and other tribal symbols, to be replaced with generic uniforms. The direction of the school, as outlined by President Hayes, was that "if this is so, if they are to become extinct, we ought to leave that to Providence, and we, as good, patriotic, Christian people, should do our best to improve their physical, mental and moral condition. We should prepare them to become part of the great, American family. If it turns out that their destiny is to be different, we shall at least have done our duty."

The Oregonian reporter picks up what happened next. While the presidential party dined at Merriman's home, staff of the Indian School assembled the students in a line on the lawn, where a crowd of several hundred people surrounded them. After lunch, the President came out to meet the students, where Army Captain Melville Wilkinson introduced him as "the man to whom they had been taught to call 'the Great Father.'" The Great Father then shook hands with the students, stopping to ask a couple of geography questions and to speculate on the heritage of one "black" student, whose unkempt hair Hayes ruffled. With those words and a tip of his hat, the President then retraced his journey to Portland, this time crossing the rickety bridge by train and making it to Fort Vancouver, Washington, in time for a gala in his honor. The leaders of the Indian School returned to their mission of training new members of the great American family.

Although Tabitha Brown died 20 years before the federal government established the Indian School, its siting was a result of her efforts in the 1840s to turn Forest Grove into the educational center of the Northwest. In fact, in a very real way, Forest Grove began almost as a company town for Tualatin Academy and later Pacific University. That tradition of education was what led Army General O.O. Howard to select Forest Grove in 1880 as the site for his dream of establishing an Indian School.

Howard earned his general stars in the Civil War. According to William Ferrin, a former president of Pacific University, Howard's experience in that war stirred an interest in the plight of American blacks. After the war, Howard was assigned to be commander of Fort Vancouver, the region's most important military installation, as battles with Native Americans continued to flare up. Just as the Civil War had awakened within Howard an empathy for the people he called "the Negroes," so too had the skirmishes in the Northwest created a compassion for "the Indians."

Howard was familiar with the federal government's Indian schools in Pennsylvania and Virginia, and wondered why there was no such institution in the West. Interior Secretary Carl Schurz, who was responsible for Indian affairs, also wanted a school in the West, but lacked the resources with which to establish one. In the era between the Civil War and the establishment of the income tax, the Defense Department was about the only government agency with money, but it lacked any statutory power to create schools. Together, Howard and Schurz hatched a plot to circumvent these obstacles, according to Ferrin, a Pacific professor at the time.

From his base at Fort Vancouver, O.O. Howard had become familiar with Forest Grove's reputation for education, and dispatched one of his captains, Melville Wilkinson, to the town, ostensibly to teach military science at Pacific University. There was no military science program at Pacific, and Ferrin says the whole thing was a ruse;

Wilkinson's real assignment was to create an Indian School under the guise of Pacific sponsorship. A building rose on university property, and the Indian School opened in 1880, just months before the Presidential visit. Forest Grove's reputation as the educational center of the Northwest was secure. The annual football games between the Indian School and Pacific University quickly became a tradition, but just as quickly faded. With little support from the government, the school struggled financially, and according to the Oregon Historical Society got by in part by hiring out the male students as laborers. The girls had it even rougher, according to Oregon Historical Society records. Of the 321 students who attended the school during its five years in Forest Grove, 43 died, mostly girls and mostly from communicable diseases from which they had no immunity. To add to the problems, the girls dormitory burned to the ground in 1884.

When Melville Wilkinson was replaced as superintendent by Henry Minthorn in 1884, Minthorn lobbied to have the campus moved to near his home in Newberg. The Oregon Legislature became embroiled in the controversy and decided instead to move the campus to Salem. Now called Chemawa Indian School, the school still operates today. Instead of teaching assimilation into white culture, however, it teaches its students their cultural heritage. Forest Grove lost its Indian School, one of the reasons for the first ever visit to Oregon by an American President, to the desires of a man with ties to Oregon's most direct Presidential connection. The year the Indian School left Forest Grove, a young Herbert Hoover moved from Iowa to Oregon to be raised by his uncle, Henry Minthorn, superintendent of the Indian School.

Although Forest Grove lost the Indian School, Tabitha Brown's long trek to Oregon was not in vain. Her efforts permanently cemented Forest Grove's reputation as the ultimate college town. Rutherford B. Hayes' long trek to Forest Grove had less of a lasting impact, although the story of his train trip makes for entertaining reading. Oh, and his speech cemented Forest Grove's reputation as the prettiest town in Oregon. Except for one thing. Within the 310 words in his speech, the phrase "prettiest town in Oregon" never appears. He did say Forest Grove was "beautiful," but otherwise the speech was all about extolling the virtues of education and complaining about a poorly maintained bridge that made him late for lunch.

Chapter

3

The prettiest town in Oregon

So there's no evidence that Rutherford B. Hayes ever actually proclaimed Forest Grove as the prettiest town in Oregon, and there were doubts about the claim even among those who believed that he did. "Of course," a writer in the May 1888 edition of the travel magazine *The West Shore* sniffed, "he had not inspected all parts of the state, nor may his judgment be infallible."

Still, the travel writer found much to commend for his readers up and down the West Coast, waxing poetic about the town's "gently undulating land," "charming views" and "salubrious climate." Overall, he found Forest Grove to be "of more than usual natural beauty," which "impresses the stranger with a sense of its enlightened and homelike pleasantness … so cozy a nook as Forest Grove is a gem that would be esteemed in any land where enlightened people dwell." The writer noted that "the influence exerted by the university is very noticeable here, and the action of the people in general is in unison with the best sentiments of the community," and he found little to dissuade his readers from agreeing with the alleged words of Rutherford Hayes.

Fifteen years later, editorialists for *The Oregonian* also commended Pacific University for its influence on Forest Grove, even suggesting that the town was the prime candidate to become "a city of the 'educational' type – like Evanston near Chicago, Cambridge near Boston, Princeton and several other places near New York …" that could help lure more people west to the greater Portland area. Yet while noting the town's great potential, the editorial was meant as a warning to civic leaders. Despite its great university, the editorial writer said, the town "lacks something. One who finds that he cannot go from the railroad station into the town, either winter or summer, without getting besmeared with mud or befouled by dust, is not likely to form a good opinion of Forest Grove; and a little later when he trips up attempting to pass over a broken sidewalk, he is likely to develop other motives not friendly to the town."

The Oregonian was not the first to point out the pitfalls of Forest Grove's claim to being the prettiest town in Oregon. By 1902, the town's residents had been complaining for 35 years about Joseph Gaston's railroad, which he designed to head due west out of Hillsboro before taking a sharp left about a mile before Forest Grove. The town of Gaston, about seven miles south, never prospered as its founder had hoped, and Joseph Gaston soon lost his railroad to Henry Villard, who had no interest in snubbing Forest Grove but who also had little interest in investing in a detour spur into town. So in 1902, the mud and dust of that one measly mile continued to elicit complaints. The town had survived Gaston's snub (just as the towns of Yamhill and McMinnville had survived similar snubs), but its reputation had taken a hit. Town leaders realized, however, that there were other factors within their control that were besmirching the town's image. Dirt streets, broken or non-existent sidewalks, raw sewage … the city had its work cut out for it, and at the urging of the Woman's Club in 1902, city fathers established the Civic Improvement Society. *The Oregonian* applauded the effort, which it said "will make Forest Grove what nature designed it to be, namely, one of the beauty spots of Oregon." With support from the business community and newspapers, the society set about its work.

Civic leaders already had at their disposal zoning and beautification ordinances that seem draconian by today's standards. The zoning laws often were strict, including requiring planting of only certain types of plants and flowers and using a certain amount of recycled materials in buildings, but it was how they were enforced that set them apart from today's laws: Violators could be arrested, and sometimes were. In September 1901, for example, Charles Large, Forest Grove's pre-eminent physician, was arrested for constructing a shed behind the building that housed his medical practice. After his arrest, the irascible Doctor Large tore down the shed, but railed to the judge about the unfairness of his arrest, pointing to other zoning infractions that had been ignored by police, including one by Alanson Hinman, one of Forest Grove's earliest pioneers. Hinman came west in 1844, taught at Whitman's school in Walla Walla and was, in 1901, a Forest Grove merchant and a distinguished member of the board of trustees at Pacific University. As a result of Doctor Large's protestations, Hinman soon had an arrest warrant issued for him, charging zoning violations. Forest Grove took zoning ordinances very seriously.

Members of the Civic Improvement Society knew that more than punitive zoning ordinances would be necessary to improve the town's appearance. Many large infrastructure projects would be necessary, requiring voter support for major tax levies. They had their work cut out for them, and by October 1903 had organized their first project: a flower show designed to show homeowners how to beautify their yards. Flowers would become a centerpiece of Forest Grove's beautification efforts over the decades, focusing first on roses and daffodils. Forest Grove also was a pioneer in the effort to control invasive weeds, and by 1912 the Civic Improvement Society launched a festival to wipe out a nefarious, noxious weed that was gaining a foothold in Oregon. Civic leaders turned this effort into a contest for children to see who could pick the most of these weeds and create the best flower arrangements from them, hoping that this effort would eradicate the scourge. After only two years, however, Dandelion Day had been cancelled, and today dandelions still are seen blooming within the city limits.

The proliferation of dandelions was in large part an unintended consequence of an earlier beautification effort by the city. Until the 1890s, dogs, chickens and cows ran free on the streets and sidewalks of Forest Grove. In the early 1890s the city started a crackdown, beginning with dogs, when the city marshal was empowered to "arrest" strays and jail them in a pen behind the jail. The city cut residents some slack on the chickens and the cows, because back in the days before refrigeration, most people had to produce their own eggs and milk. Still, aggressive roosters were a nuisance and chickens can be kept in coops and pens, so soon the city outlawed free-ranging fowl on city streets, allowing only cows to roam free. In 1902, however, Forest Grove landed one of the most-prized industries of the day: A milk condensery. By heating milk and canning it, stores could stock condensed milk for months. No longer did every home need its own cow, and the city wanted to encourage business for the condensery, so free-roaming cows soon were subject to arrest by the marshal as well. City beautification advocates were thrilled to finally get the "breachy and vicious" cows and their manure off of the city streets. By the next summer, however, a new problem arose. Without the ravenous cows wandering the avenues, weeds sprang up all over town.

Daffodils also still are seen blooming in and around Forest Grove, although not nearly in the quantity that some early Grovers foresaw. In the early Twentieth Century, daffodils were touted as an easy to grow and care for spring blossom. A century ago Americans considered daffodils exotic, with most bulbs imported from the Germanic countries of Europe. Daffodils were less exotic around Forest Grove, however, because within a few miles of town there were a number of bulb farms. A few miles east of Forest Grove lies a small community that originally was known as the German Settlement, for obvious reasons, because it was settled by Germans. In the early 1900s many of the residents still spoke German as their everyday language. The German settlers brought more than their language with them from their native land to America, however, including daffodil bulbs, which they grew in abundance. The blooms became so abundant, in fact, that when the German settlers desired a name other than German Settlement for their community they chose "Blooming" as the obvious choice. Forest Grove residents eagerly bought up Blooming's daffodil bulbs, and soon the town was awash each spring with blossoms, months before most other flowers arrived. Soon Forest Grove once again was drawing notice from other towns for its beautification efforts, for which daffodils earned much of the credit. Before long, the story of Forest Grove's daffodils had spread all the way to Washington, D.C., and talk turned to making the bulbs into a major industry.

By the 1920s, the Industrial Revolution had given American workers more leisure time than they ever had enjoyed when farming ruled the economy. Freed from farm chores, more people took up hobbies, including, ironically, gardening. With more disposable income, exotic bulbs became available to common people. That created an economic problem, however, because at the time nearly all bulbs had to be imported from Europe, driving up the cost and creating a balance of trade problem for the United States. To add to the problem, animosity toward Germany still lingered from World War I, so most bulbs now came from France. The Department of Agriculture created a unit charged with finding regions within the United States where tulip, daffodil and other bulbs could flourish. David Griffiths, touted as the nation's foremost authority on bulbs, was hired to lead the effort.

Griffiths quickly set his sights on the northwest corner of Washington, from Seattle to the Canadian border, as the region most likely to share the climate and soil of Holland and Germany, and the unit was headquartered in Bellingham. Griffiths heard of the daffodil farms in Forest Grove, Canby and other western Oregon towns, but was skeptical. At least he was skeptical until he spent some time in the rich humus soil of the Tualatin River and Gales Creek watershed. The *Washington County News-Times* of September 3, 1925, breathlessly reported his findings in a Page 1 story, including an all-capital headline "SUCCESS IS POSSIBLE" and a lead paragraph that exclaimed "It is possible to supply approximately one half of the American demand for bulbs from plantings here." Griffiths placed the value of Forest Grove's potential bulb harvest at as much as $8 million a year, or more than $100 million in 2014 dollars. And David Griffiths wasn't done. Little unincorporated Blooming had the potential to become a worldwide financial powerhouse. The soil in Blooming and other local zones was the equal of that in Bellingham or even Holland, the good doctor told the assembled crowd, but the Tualatin Valley held a potential advantage over both: the area's "salubrious climate" could be equally salubrious to local bulb growers' bottom lines. Oregon's hot, dry summers dried the bulbs much faster and better than any other region in the world with equal soil. But alas, daffodil mania did not last long in Forest Grove because other parts of America, such as Michigan and the rest of the upper Midwest, enjoyed almost equally salubrious climates and had better transportation options to reach the major population centers of America. Forest Grove's dream of becoming Daffodil Town never came to fruition.

16

Back in 1902, when the city's beautification efforts started, cars were not even a factor in sleepy Forest Grove. Horses and trolleys were the preferred forms of transportation. That is until 1910, when the Woman's Club went to the City Council for relief from the unsightly problem created by the growing number of these loud, foul-smelling contraptions, which people left willy-nilly on the streets or on front lawns. The solution suggested in a proposed ordinance was to mandate "parkings" between the street and the homes of automobile owners, each disguised and decorated with a uniform planting of flowers and shrubbery along each. The Council chose instead to pass a resolution strongly urging the motorized public to obey the guidelines, but to little avail; a century later, cars parked willy-nilly on streets and lawns remain a principle complaint of Forest Grove residents. Records don't indicate whether daffodils were among the proposed mandatory botanical selections.

Another new-fangled invention also was on the minds of Forest Grove's beautifiers in 1900: electricity. No matter how pretty the city was, the founders of the Civic Improvement Society reasoned, the effort was wasted when the sun went down. Street lights were the obvious answer, and Forest Grove had an obvious solution. In 1895, the city had created a public utility district to produce electricity, one of the first of its kind and today one of the longest continually operating public utilities in the West. Power was created by pulling water from Gales Creek at B Street, which was then boiled to create steam that powered turbines that created electricity. The system created enough power for the few buildings that had electric lights in 1895, but only during the day when the city had people on hand to stoke the furnace that boiled the water to create the steam that turned the turbines. Frustrated by the lack of street lighting, business leaders demanded that the city stop generating its own electricity and instead buy it from local businessman and State Senator Edward W. Haines, who already was producing power at his grist mill just outside town and who planned a major dam on the headwaters of the Tualatin River. Haines promised city leaders that in no time at all he would be turning out enough power to light up Forest Grove throughout the night. Haines never made good on that promise, and before long business leaders were demanding that the city break its contract with Haines and generate its own electricity.

City beautification efforts sputtered through the first decade of the 1900s. Outdoor lighting remained elusive, as did a sewer system to keep human waste off of city streets. The city always had touted its inherent beauty; "There never was a spot more ... consecrated to the Muses than our chosen Forest Grove," proclaimed the first issue of the *Forest Grove Monthly* in 1868. Yet while Forest Grove had avoided the reckless development that blighted Portland, Oregon City and other regional towns, it had done little to create beauty within the town. The city lacked a significant park, athletic field or central square. Forest Grove had no tree-lined boulevards or public green spaces. The burden of beautification always had been placed on individual property owners, often under penalty of law. Throughout the nation, the Progressive Era was putting pressure on municipal governments to use public works projects to enhance urban livability.

That message hit home for Forest Grove when August Lovegren announced plans for a Utopian village south of Forest Grove. Lovegren laid out his plans for Cherry Grove in great detail, exceeding even the grand schemes of Forest Grove's founders. Cherry Grove would be a bucolic society with ordinances drawn straight from the Holy Bible. Temperance was mandated, as were all types of uniformity. Lovegren built streets, stores, hotels, restaurants and more, threatening to eclipse Forest Grove as the most important city in Washington County. Lovegren built parks and athletic fields and, remembering the beauty of the mountain lakes in his native Sweden, he dammed the Tualatin to create a recreational lake in Cherry Grove. Hotels thrived, and a community grew. Cherry Grove was on track to supplant Forest Grove as the region's prettiest and most important town. One of the byproducts of Lovegren's dam was electricity, making Cherry Grove one of the first small rural towns in the West to enjoy electric power, including the street lamps Forest Grove craved.

Up in Forest Grove, the race to beautify the city shifted into high gear. Three stories atop Page 1 of the July 31, 1913, *News-Times* illustrated some of the many efforts city fathers had put into place. One story had to do with paving city streets. Lovegren had built a railroad right into the center of Cherry Grove and was paving the carefully plotted streets in his town. Forest Grove, on the other hand, was plotted long before the automobile was conceived. The grid was a hodgepodge of muddy, dusty

18

streets that in some cases didn't even connect with each other. The summer of 1913 saw a flurry of road work that included paving Pacific Avenue, the main street into and through town. Another Page 1 story that day urged city residents to prepare their babies for the upcoming state eugenics championship. "Oregon has the proud distinction of developing the highest scoring child in the United States," the paper reported, "and we cannot afford to go backward." The practice of eugenics was designed to produce a genetically perfect baby, as defined by a panel of judges. The editors urged Forest Grove to win the state contest, because "babies are rapidly becoming known as our best product." A third story on Page 1 focused on the natural beauty and salubrious climate that Forest Grove offered to less fortunate children from the big city of Portland. The city of Silverton had embarked on a program called "Fresh Air Children," in which youngsters from Portland would stay with local families for two weeks. The *News-Times* wanted Forest Grove to take up the cause, which "should have the strong support of all who are in the position to care for one or more of (Portland's) waifs. Surely we will be amply repaid to know that we have brightened the lives of these poor children who so seldom have a glimpse of the beautiful in Nature." Even people who didn't want to house the waifs were urged to participate. Noting the lack of transportation, the paper sought "those who will volunteer the use of their machines to carry the children to the places assigned to them."

The following week's paper reported that while Forest Grove couldn't match Silverton's total of 50 Fresh Air Children, it had found homes for 35. The paper reported that one of the children in the Silverton program had never been outside of the basement in which he was born and "cried continuously when taken in the party to Silverton because of the bright sunlight." The August 7, 1913, paper also had several Page 1 stories about the street paving project, including an account from the city of The Dalles, Oregon, which was slightly ahead of Forest Grove in this exciting adventure. "Already the automobiles go blithely gliding over the smooth 'bitucrete' wherever the finished streets have been thrown open," the story reported. "Many a driver ... will find a part of his previous, perhaps necessary, vocabulary rapidly decreasing, for the better the roads the less will the swearing be." Finally, another Page 1 story had even more good news for the city. A new private electric company was trying to drum up business and offered Forest Grove a 20-day free test of its "juice," as the story called it. "The 24-hour light service certainly would be a great benefit," the paper concluded, but the offer of free "juice" eventually fizzled. Forest Grove streets would remain dark.

Meanwhile, down in Cherry Grove, August Lovegren's dam went into service in October 1913. His sawmill, larger than any of Forest Grove's, churned out lumber and the street lights lit the city. For several months it appeared that Cherry Grove was indeed destined to supplant Forest Grove as the region's prettiest and most prosperous city. In January 1914, all that had changed. Lovegren's dam burst under the strain of western Oregon's brutally wet winters, taking with it Lovegren's power plant and plunging Cherry Grove into decades of darkness.

Forest Grove's next battle over beauty came along in 1915, sparked by the enraged editors of the *Washington County News-Times*. On September 30, a Page 1 headline blared "What are you going to do about it?" The lead paragraph set the dire tone for the story. "Quietly and without warning, but not the less destructive in the insidiousness of the attack, Forest Grove was invaded last week by a modern-day Attila and his Huns."

"And if these latter day Huns and Vandals do not put to the torch our homes and put to death our people, they nevertheless would slay what should be dear to us – our pride and our self-respect, and the beauty of our city." It was not until the third paragraph that we learn what this horrible threat was. "We refer, of course, to the invasion of the billboard menace."

It seems that the Kelly Advertising Company had, in recent days, begun erecting "huge, glaring monstrosities that they are pleased to term 'artistic' sign boards." The story raged against the hideous scars the signs were inflicting on the beauty of Forest Grove and against the messages they carried. "They may desire to develop our artistic sense by displaying in glaring lines the merits of some medicine concern that will be able to tell the people of the nasty horrors that only exist in the minds of harpies that fatten on the credulity of sick people."

"Is it fair," the editor demanded, "to compel our citizens and taxpayers to rebuild walks, lower grades, remove trees, cut weeds and often at an expense that they can ill afford, in order that the city may be made more beautiful and attractive, and permit this menace to invade the city, disfigure its beauty and distress and outrage the sensibilities of its people with the pictured nightmares that usually adorn these 'artistic' billboards?"

The story raised countless objections to allowing billboards in town, but omitted one obvious concern of the newspaper's owners: until now, newspapers had enjoyed a virtual monopoly on advertising sales in Forest Grove. The citizens were not nearly as distressed and outraged as the editors, and billboards were still in town a year later when the Woman's Club met to provide an update on beautification efforts.

When Dr. Mary Farnham, the Woman's Club president, addressed the assembled crowd on October 9, 1916, her address was printed in full at the top of Page 1 of the *Washington County News-Times,* although not until the reporter gave a rave review to a Miss Goldie Peterson, who opened the meeting with an apparently stirring vocal rendition of "Three Little Green Bonnets" and "You'll Get Heaps of Lickings." The address on beautification efforts mentioned neither the presence of billboards nor the absence of streetlights, but did again lament the lack of mandated uniformity in "parkings" and shrubbery. The address laid out the club's revised plans for improving the appearance of the city, starting with what was seen as a way to improve the appearance of women on the streets. The Forest Grove club endorsed an effort by the national leadership of the Federation of Women to impose a national dress code. "There is no question," Dr. Farnham said, "that freak costumes have somewhat belittled our dignity as intelligent women." Preserving women's dignity had a purpose beyond beauty in 1916, because while Oregon had granted women the right to vote in 1912, the Nineteenth Amendment, extending that right nationwide, still was four years in the future. Women's clubs across Oregon were fighting to preserve and extend that right, in no small part to pass more laws protecting the beauty and health of America.

As such, the Forest Grove Woman's Club was launching an effort to take the local beautification effort back to its roots: flowers. This new campaign, however, was far different from the one a decade earlier, and marked a turning point in the way Oregonians viewed their environment. Instead of encouraging the cultivation of imported bulbs, this generation of women wanted the focus to be preserving the native flowers and overall natural beauty of the state. For the first 70 years of Forest Grove's history and first 50 years of Oregon's, the forests and valleys of Oregon were where people worked, planting crops and cutting down trees to erect buildings in the burgeoning towns and cities. The land was so vast and the air and water so pure that little thought was given to preservation. But the efforts of conservationists such as John Muir, coupled with the progressive Republican politics of Theodore Roosevelt, were beginning to have a profound effect on many people. Not surprisingly, the staunchly progressive Republican populace of Washington County was beginning to take up the cause of nature.

By 1916, the Woman's Club was calling for efforts to protect native plants threatened by extinction, including the Oregon grape and rhododendron. Stopping short of curbs on agriculture and logging, however, many of the proposals were modest, including discouraging children from picking bouquets of wildflowers. Instead, the group suggested, wildflowers such as the rhododendron should be welcomed into the city, not ripped out as weeds, with the seeds carefully cultivated to be spread along the sides of roads leading into town. The group also called for paving more of those roads, in addition to city streets, to control the dust and mud kicked up by the ever-increasing number of automobiles. Another wish was a city park to provide recreational opportunities and a place to preserve nature in town.

The list of hopes and dreams in Dr. Farnham's address was long; her list of accomplishments from the previous decade was much shorter, beginning with nascent efforts to create a sewer system to cut down on disease and foul odors. Befitting the town's origins as an education center, however, most of her praise was saved for the public schools. In the previous few years, Forest Grove had been on a school building spree. The result was beautiful buildings with beautiful grounds and a high school that on a per capita basis was doing a better job than any other in the state of enticing children to stay in school past the eighth grade, rather than dropping out to work in the forests, farms and factories.

On balance, the address concluded that despite much work yet to be done, Forest Grove once again finally had earned the right to call itself "the prettiest town in Oregon."

Chapter

4

Unless you're walking, you can't get there from here

"Forest Grove was in one corner of the settlement, and was almost inaccessible by reason of bad mountain roads," Sidney Harper Marsh was quoted as saying of his first look at the town in the 1850s. "Within a radius of 10 miles there were scarcely 50 voters ... Forest Grove could scarcely have been called a village."

But the reason for Marsh's arrival also is the reason Forest Grove became a city. He was hired to be President of Pacific University. He made his recollection in 1878, according to the authors of *Splendid Audacity*, and two years later, Rutherford B. Hayes would still have trouble making it into town.

Typically throughout history, cities have risen along strategic transportation corridors (rivers, bays, railroads, stagecoach routes, highways, etc.). Forest Grove is not typical. Tabitha Brown and President Hayes are only two of several people throughout history who found transportation to Forest Grove so difficult that they resorted to making part of the journey on foot. Natural beauty, civic pride and an almost mystical dedication to education are a few of the reasons that Forest

Grove has bucked the odds by flourishing despite being off the beaten track.

In its earliest days, Forest Grove was particularly isolated. It really wasn't on the way to anywhere, and getting to the town from nearly any direction meant having to traverse rugged hills and mountains. Then, as each new mode of transportation developed, planners plotted routes tantalizingly close to town, but never quite close enough.

While the Tualatin River once supported small steam ships coming upstream from the Willamette River, the ships could make it only as far as Cornelius, a few too many miles away to be of use to Forest Grove residents.

With its location due west of Portland, Forest Grove seems like the natural route to the coast, but several factors worked against it. First was the fact that early steamships headed to Portland had two coastal inlets in which to dock safely, at Astoria and Tillamook. The overland route from Astoria was simple: a path along the Columbia River. The overland path from Tillamook was not at all simple, but the rough topography west of Forest Grove was more treacherous than the somewhat more gentle route along the Trask River from Yamhill and Gaston, which meant that those towns benefited from a stagecoach route long before Forest Grove did.

When Joseph Gaston built his Westside Railroad, freight and passengers made the trip due west out of Portland all the way to Cornelius, where the rail took a sharp left turn toward Gaston, leaving Forest Grove a rugged mile or more from the nearest station.

When U.S. Highway 26 finally provided a fast automobile route from Portland to the Oregon Coast, the highway paralleled the railroad, headed out of Portland due west toward Forest Grove. About halfway to Forest Grove, however, the road shifts to a northwest route, skirting Forest Grove by several miles.

In the 1980s, Forest Grove got one more chance to be a transportation hub, as planning started for the MAX light-rail system. The commuter rail line parallels Highway 26 for much of its way west, but unlike the old railroad and Highway 26, the tracks do not bend either south or north to avoid Forest Grove. They simply end in downtown Hillsboro, a few miles east of Forest Grove.

The town's history is full of tales of dreamers yearning for more convenient transportation routes. Most of those dreams have gone unrealized, so it's a testament to the town's other charms that it has thrived. Forest Grove doesn't have almost anything that most cities need to grow, whether it be strategic location, unique natural resources or one major industry.

More than happenstance led to Forest Grove being settled away from a major river or seaport, which were the primary paths of transportation in 1840. Many Oregon towns of the day, including Astoria, Portland, Oregon City and Salem, were settled by intrepid pioneers who had made their way west from the seaports of the East Coast, from the Great Lakes region or from the cities along the Missouri and Mississippi rivers. For these men, the banks of the Willamette and Columbia rivers felt like home and were the natural places to build their towns.

The pioneers who settled on the Tualatin Plains were a different breed. Men such as Joseph Meek, Almoran Hill, William Doughty and Joseph Gale cut their pioneer teeth as trappers and hunters in the Rocky Mountains before the fur trade collapsed and they sought greener pastures farther west. For them, the region around Forest Grove seemed ideal. The flat plains provided excellent farming opportunities, while the slopes of the Coast Range and Chehalem mountains provided a familiar wooded wilderness for them to continue to hunt and trap, although for most, those activities were now more hobbies than careers.

It's somewhat ironic, then, that when a group of Portland and Oregon City settlers devised a plan for the *Star of Oregon*, the first sailing ship to be built in the territory, they asked Forest Grove's own Joseph Gale to lead the effort. Despite his reputation as a mountain man, Gale's love affair with water began long before Forest Grove's main water source, Gales Creek, bore his name. Caroline Dobbs picks up Gale's story in her classic 1932 history of Oregon, *Men of Champoeg*. Gale was born near Washington, D.C., in 1800, and his first career was not as a trapper but rather as a sea captain up and down the East Coast. But after a few years aboard sailing ships, Gale gave up the high seas for the Rocky Mountains and high Sierras, settling near what would become Forest Grove in the late 1830s. Still, Gale agreed to help with the planning and building of the *Star of Oregon*. For one thing, he loved ships, and the group was not asking him to return to the seas for long, because for them, the ship was just a means to an end. Their real mission was to bring cows to the Oregon Territory.

Considering that Oregon today is a major dairy producer, the absence of cows in 1840 might seem odd. However, cows are not native to America, instead having been imported from Europe, landing at the ports of the East and Gulf coasts. Cows spread west with the American settlers, but the Rocky Mountains were a natural barrier to bringing herds to Oregon. Cows also were spreading northward with the Spanish settlers of Mexico, and eventually the flat plains of Texas would provide a trail up the western edge of the Rockies. With that hurdle overcome, the Sierra Nevada and Cascade mountains still impeded migration into the Oregon Territory. The Spaniards also brought cattle with them west of the Sierras as they settled California, but the east-west range of the Siskiyous blocked the last leg of the trip into Oregon.

The settlers looked at the herds of California cattle and concocted a plan to bring them the rest of the way to Forest Grove and to the rest of the Northwest, and that plan involved the *Star of Oregon*. The plan was not to try to bring the cattle north along the treacherous seas and mouth of the Columbia aboard the ship, however. The plan was to build the ship, sail it empty to San Francisco, sell it, use the money to buy cows, and then use the skills of Oregon's mountain men to herd them across the Siskiyous. Gale's skills on land would be of as much use as his skills on the sea.

This all made sense to the *Star of Oregon* dreamers, but not to the bankers of Portland and Salem who had the money the dreamers needed to build their ship. It seemed as if the cattle trail, like so many other trails since, would bypass Forest Grove. Joseph Gale was equally skeptical, so while he helped design the ship, he told the group he would not participate further until the group could prove that they could secure materials and build a seaworthy vessel. Doing so was not easy, however, and *Men of Champoeg* details the litany of problems that befell the ship builders over the ensuing months on Swan Island in the Willamette River. At first things went smoothly. Finding wood for the ship was no problem in Oregon's forests, and the Hudson's Bay Company in Vancouver agreed to sell the party nails. But then the troubles began. Hudson's Bay Company officials said that Gale's friends had ordered the nails under false pretenses, saying they needed them for buildings. When he learned the true mission, the Hudson's Bay Company's Fort Vancouver leader, John McLoughlin, refused to sell the group the sails they would need. To add insult to injury, he said the ship would never make it across the treacherous Columbia River bar and into the high seas, and would be considered a pirate vessel and seized even if it did.

Still, Joseph Gale now was a believer, and when the group was able to move the ship upriver to Oregon City, Joseph Gale moved with it, devoting full time to the project, even moving his family to the burgeoning river port of Champoeg, a few more miles up the river. As the only member of the group with sailing experience, Gale met with the commander of the meager American Navy presence in the Northwest and convinced him to provide sails and official government papers for the ship. Finally, in August 1842, Joseph Gale sailed the ship down the Willamette to the Columbia and docked the *Star of Oregon* defiantly across from Fort Vancouver. He then sailed it down the Columbia to the Pacific with a crew of four, none of whom had ever been on the ocean, and made it across the bar and all the way to San Francisco, where they traded it for 350 cows.

Gale knew, however, that he and his four fellow mountain men could not possibly herd that many cattle over the mountains alone, so they wintered in San Francisco and Gale worked tirelessly to encourage California ranchers to migrate to Oregon. By the spring of 1843, Gale had rounded up 42 men, 1,250 cattle, 3,000 sheep and 600 horses. They managed to traverse the Siskiyous, and Gale arrived back to his family in Champoeg just in time for the most momentous moment of his already momentous life.

The growing seaport of Champoeg had been selected that year as the location of the first "Wolf Meeting." The ostensible purpose of the conclave was to create a bounty system to eradicate the wolves that threatened the meager livestock holdings of the settlers. At the time, the Oregon Territory had no official government, its protection split in an uneasy truce between the British and Americans. Champoeg was chosen for the meeting because it was about halfway between the major population centers of Portland and Salem.

Champoeg also was chosen because it was part of the narrow "French Prairie" along the Willamette River from Champoeg to Charbonneau, making it somewhat neutral territory for the hidden agenda of the 102 settlers who convened for the Wolf Meeting: A firm choice between the rule of the British or the Americans. After several more meetings and much debate, the Americans won by the narrowest of margins, 52 to 50, the balance tipped by the few French settlers who attended. Joseph Meek often is referred to as the leader of the effort, and he was rewarded by being named the first marshal of the Territory. Joseph Gale, in large part because of his *Star of Oregon* success, received an even higher honor, being selected as one of three men who would share leadership of the new provisional government. Although he never held the formal title of Governor, he asked for the rest of his life to be addressed as Governor Gale.

The rest of his life did not include a move back to Forest Grove. Champoeg held allure for him, in part because it was the potential capital of Oregon and in part because of its role as a river port. Ultimately, however, he was lured back to the wilderness, living out his life near what is today Baker City in Eastern Oregon. His choice to leave Champoeg proved fortuitous, because it lost out to Salem for the site of the new capital and saw its position as a transportation hub stripped by the arrival of the railroad, which bypassed the town in favor of a more direct line between Portland and Salem. Then in 1861 Champoeg succumbed to the nemesis of most river ports, a flood. This was no ordinary flood, however. Before it crested, the Willamette River rose nearly 50 feet, obliterating nearly every trace of Champoeg, leaving it a ghost town.

By 1861, Forest Grove's lack of a river port was looking more like a blessing than a curse. Joseph Gale's creek floods, but never has buried the city's downtown under feet of water, a fate well-known to the major Willamette and Columbia port cities. In addition, the railroads that bypassed Champoeg were destined soon to roll right into downtown Forest Grove. Joseph Gaston had won the right to build the railroad from Portland to Eugene, and helped plot the route that bypassed Champoeg. While Gaston was back East securing financing, however, the nefarious Ben Holladay, one of Portland's wealthiest but most despised residents, took the stagecoach to Salem and passed around enough money in those days to bribe the entire Legislature; somewhere between $15,000 and $35,000, depending on who did the counting. Joseph Gaston was stripped of the lucrative Willamette Valley route and given instead the much less lucrative Hillsboro to Corvallis line to build.

Undaunted, Gaston set out to build the first leg of his Oregon Central Railroad, often referred to as the Westside Railroad, from Hillsboro through the Wapato Gap that separates the Chehalem and Coast Range mountains and on to McMinnville. That route made Forest Grove or Yamhill logical towns to host the construction crews, but Gaston had other ideas. He found a spot that seemed like the ideal location for a railroad camp and primary whistlestop for this first leg. The spot was along the Tualatin River, providing an excellent source of water for steam with which to power his locomotives. It was about seven miles south of Forest Grove at the north end of the Wapato Gap, which could help him control virtually all transportation between the Tualatin and Yamhill valleys. The spot also sat beside Wapato Lake, a sacred site for the Atfalatis before they were run off, but now dismissed as a swampy, disease-bearing miasma. Joseph Gaston had the clout to be given the lake under the terms of the federal Swamp Act in return for the promise to drain it and convert it to fertile farmland. Gaston took the lake, bought 40 additional acres from local donation land claim owners, and created his own town, appropriately named Gaston.

Forest Grove and Yamhill lost out on hosting the construction camp, but that did not diminish enthusiasm in Forest Grove. In June 1868, the first issue of the *Forest Grove Monthly* focused on the promise of the railroad. "Thanks to the Oregon Central Railroad Co., of which Mr. Gaston is President," the *Monthly* said, "we are soon to have removed the only objection to our location that the most critical have ever mentioned. We shall be as accessible as any spot in Oregon." That rosy assessment never came to pass. Gaston steered his railroad south before reaching Forest Grove, in part because of topography and in part for the same reason it skirts Yamhill further south: to steer more business into his own enterprises in his new town. In his book *The Saga of Ben Holladay*, Ellis Lucia writes that Joe Gaston assured Forest Grove leaders that once the line to McMinnville was finished, he would construct a line through Forest Grove, over the Coast Range and down the Nehalem River to connect Portland with the deep-sea ports of Astoria, Tillamook and Newport. Under his plan, Forest Grove would become one of Oregon's most important transportation hubs.

Forest Grove's station ended up in what became the unincorporated community of Carnation, which once stood on what is now Elm Street, just south of what is now Highway 47. That mile doesn't seem very far today, but in the 1870s that mile had to be traveled on foot or by horseback or open carriage. That mile, Joseph Gaston hoped, would be enough to entice travelers and businesses to bypass Forest Grove and settle instead in his own town. For a short period in the early 1900s, Carnation prospered, but today you won't find it on most maps. Still, the railroad's detour to avoid Forest Grove took its toll, so much so that in 1909 it was Forest Grove that could not be found on the map, or at least on that year's official map prepared by the federal government. Carnation was on the map, as was Gales City and Dilley. In fact, every town with a Post Office was supposed to be on the map, but alas, there was no Forest Grove. This especially rankled city leaders because they had been financing a publicity campaign in New York and Washington, D.C., to promote the region's beauty, while cities such as Hillsboro contributed nothing, yet every other town got star billing on the map.

Gaston never really managed to drain Wapato Lake and gave up on farming. He managed to build the first leg of his railroad, although not without years of overcoming obstacles. One of the biggest problems in Gaston's plan was in the middle of Wapato Gap. Almost immediately after the railroad opened, Joseph Gaston's planned route began to sink into the earth for no obvious reason. Engineers were certain that the sinkhole was shallow, but it proved to be voracious, swallowing all the rock Gaston's crews could dump into it. For the next hundred years, long after Gaston gave up on railroading, crews dumped more rock and eventually tons of concrete from demolished buildings into the hole, but never fully stabilized it. The rail lines sometimes sank noticeably between the time a train passed south on its way to McMinnville and its return north later the same day.

In fact, if you believe the persistent rumors in the taverns of Gaston and Yamhill, it sank so fast one day in about 1894 that it swallowed an entire locomotive in a matter of hours. The legend of the sunken locomotive is a matter of faith to many bellied up to the bar, swapping stories. In 2005 the legend took on new life when railroad historian Gordon Zimmerman wrote *A Song of Yamhill*, which included the story his father had told him of being an eyewitness to the sinking of the locomotive, along with a fellow nine-year-old boy, as cranes tried desperately to pull it from the quicksand-like sinkhole. Unfortunately, the

30

account from the two little boys is all the known evidence of the catastrophe, and other railroad historians discount the possibility of such an occurrence. If there is a locomotive in the sinkhole, most reason, it was intentionally scuttled for stability, not lost to accident.

Before rails even were laid over the sinkhole, Gaston lost interest in his sinking railroad, and his partners bought him out. In fact, according to Ellis Lucia, Gaston was forced out by his partners, in large part because of his vision for a spur line into Forest Grove and over the mountains to the Coast. His financial backers, most notably Henry Ainsworth, just happened to have made their fortunes in the Columbia River steamship business. They were fine with the thought of railroads carrying freight from Portland to the inland valleys, but they were not about to surrender their transportation monopoly along the Columbia. Deeply stressed and nearly bankrupt, Gaston relinquished his share of the railroad in exchange for Ainsworth and others agreeing to assume his debt.

By 1896, Gaston also abandoned his stubborn swamp, and in fact his entire town, and packed up and moved to one of Portland's most spectacular homes, with magnificent views of the city, Mount St. Helens and Mount Hood. The town of Gaston never was able to capitalize on its strategic transportation attribute. Forest Grove didn't get its promised coastal route, but neither did it perish because of the railroad snub. That's not to suggest that Forest Grove's railroad problem didn't exact a price, however, if for no other reason than the region's two most ambitious sawmills, Stimson Lumber and Lovegren's Cherry Grove Lumber, were situated near Gaston because of the ability to run spur lines up Scoggins and Patton valleys to haul logs from the vast forest.

Joseph Gaston remained bitter for the rest of his life about the loss of his railroad, but he became even more bitter in 1873 when archrival Ben Holladay finagled his way into a controlling interest in his lost prize. Exactly how bitter became the topic of speculation in the April 8, 1873, edition of *The Oregonian*, which contained a dispatch from Gaston with the headline "A Most Dastardly Attempt." It seems that Holladay was taking a victory lap of sorts on his new railroad, passing through Gaston to thumb his nose at his rival. A crew on a handcar went ahead to check on the unpredictable Wapato Gap sinkhole, but was stopped in its tracks before it arrived. Rounding a curve just south of Gaston, the handcar crew was stunned to find a large boulder and downed tree on the tracks. They stopped the handcar in time to avoid hitting this bizarre mess, but Holladay's locomotive would have been unable to stop, and would have derailed. Whether Joe Gaston was responsible for this obstruction remains a mystery, as does whether he would have made good on his pledge to extend the railroad into Forest Grove.

By 1897, Forest Grove still was looking for a good way to get to town from Hillsboro and points east. Things got so bad that *Washington County Hatchet* editor Austin Craig promoted an idea submitted by a reader that walking to Forest Grove might be the best answer. Specifically, the reader urged that a wooden boardwalk be built from Hillsboro to Forest Grove for use by pedestrians only. Decrying the muddy "slough used as a road," she suggested that walking was a safer and perhaps faster means of conveyance. The *Hatchet* championed the cause in an editorial headlined "Worthy Suggestion." Soon Forest Grove merchants were soliciting subscriptions and donated materials with which to build the boardwalk, but alas the plan never came to fruition.

The lack of a boardwalk did not discourage pedestrian traffic into town, however. Take the example of Alvin Brown, whose story was told in the September 29, 1904, *Forest Grove Times*. Brown was one of the city's earliest pioneers, having walked across the Plains from Missouri in 1846 at the age of 17. That was not why he made the paper nearly 60 years later, however. This story was about what he did on Monday, September 26, 1904, while on a visit to Portland. That morning he saw the path he had walked the final 30 miles of his 1846 journey, and decided to walk along it for a while before boarding the train back to Forest Grove. Along the way, he reported, he ran into an old acquaintance and rested his 75-year-old legs for a spell while chatting. Rejuvenated, he decided to keep walking. After a time he saw the house of another old friend and again rested and chatted before catching the train the rest of the way home. Again refreshed, he continued to amble along until he realized that he was almost home but that it was getting dark, so he picked up the pace and finished walking to Forest Grove at about 7 that evening. Although he said he had no intention of walking the entire way when he left Portland, the deed was no fluke for Mr. Brown. Four years earlier when he turned 71, he realized that the digits of his age were reversed from his arrival on foot at the age of 17. Wondering if he could still make the walk, he hopped the train into Portland and walked back to Forest Grove. He told the reporter in 1904 that he was beginning to feel his age, because his trek at 75 took noticeably longer than the one he made at 71. In 1909, Alvin was 80, and wondered again if he could accomplish the feat one more time, so at 6:30 a.m. on Saturday, July 17, he left his Forest Grove home and headed east, stopping for breakfast in Hillsboro at the home of his son, the county Coroner. Bidding adieu, he hit the road again and easily beat his time from five years previously, arriving at his daughter's home in Portland by 3:30 in the afternoon. Alvin Brown didn't need transportation in 1846, and 63 years later he was not going to worry about muddy roads and a railroad that bypassed his adopted hometown. He loved Forest Grove, and he didn't care how much effort it took to get there. After all, Alvin had made his original trip to Forest Grove from Missouri with his grandmother, Tabitha Brown.

The rival *Forest Grove Times* took up a different campaign, dismissing the *Hatchet*'s boardwalk effort. The *Times* favored that new-fangled wheeled conveyance, the bicycle. On July 6, 1899, the paper noted that a dirt path from Forest Grove to Hillsboro "would be pretty good if it were not so bumpy in spots." The path, it seems, turned to mud in the winter, then hardened into a rollercoaster ride under the summer sun. The paper noted another obstacle for cyclists: "The cow that roams the lanes is no respector of paths." Still, the *Times* saw bicycles as the future of transportation, and after a bright day in February 1900 brought out the town's cyclists, the paper's editors started a campaign. Many townspeople considered bicycles to be dangerous, and ordinances had been passed to keep them off the sidewalks. But this beautiful day illustrated the problem with the ordinance; although the sun was shining, it still was February, which meant that most of the streets were muddy morasses, rendering bike riding nearly impossible except on the sidewalks. Some townsfolk wanted bicycles banned altogether, but where others saw only problems, the *Times* saw opportunity. An editorial suggested creating bicycle paths into and out of town so people wouldn't have to walk to Forest Grove. The first paths, the editors suggested, should go north a couple of miles into the bustling community of Greenville and to the Catholic Church in Verboort, but others could extend to other towns. "There are some difficulties in the way of keeping these paths up, of course" the *Times* acknowledged, "but none serious." The paper urged community leaders to go to the county Courthouse to demand action, but Forest Grove didn't get its fancy bike paths for about a century, when a resurgence in interest made bicycling more popular than ever.

Forest Grove residents were just as frustrated by the lack of a good way to go west to the Coast. In 1892, residents took a break from lobbying for a railroad and went back to accomplishing the lesser dream of a stagecoach line to carry passengers and mail to coastal communities, which still lacked a good overland route. A stagecoach route along the Wilson River watershed had been a dream of Oregonians since the earliest settlers arrived. Finally, in 1890, W.S. Runyan of Tillamook started blazing a trail that, three years later, proved to be viable for stagecoach travel. In fact, a reporter for the *Forest Grove Times* made the journey with Runyan before the route formally opened and found the trip more than viable. In a little more than six hours, the writer marveled, the stage had traveled 24 miles, beyond the logging camp of Idiotville, named because only an idiot would venture that far into the wilderness. Runyan was no idiot, but his company never got off the ground and he went into receivership.

Despite Runyan's failure, dreams of a stagecoach to the Coast soon lured one of early Forest Grove's most colorful characters into giving it a try. Theodore McNamer made a name for himself as a butcher, becoming the town's primary purveyor of meat and seafood. In 1895, however, Theodore launched a stagecoach to Tillamook. McNamer scoffed at the 12 to 15 hours that it took for Runyan to make the 56-mile trip to Tillamook, vowing to cut the time to 10 hours. He built two waystations along the way, promising travelers meals of his finest meats. At one of the waystations, McNamer rented camping supplies for those who chose to break the arduous trip into two days. It took McNamer a couple of years to get his stage line fully functional, but when he did he got rave reviews, proving that the 56-mile trip could be completed in as little as eight hours in perfect conditions. "Mc is a good feeder," the *Washington County Hatchet* raved on May 27, 1897, "and knows how to feed his passengers, and the public may depend on the anticipation of every want."

Unfortunately for "Mc," there were not many people who wanted a bumpy eight- to 12-hour ride from Forest Grove to Tillamook. Less than a year after the 1897 *Hatchet* story, Theo McNamer was making front-page news for his new adventure, taking sheep and pigs up Alaska's Yukon River to feed the Gold Rush miners. Theodore and his brother,

Converse, who went by "Conrad," herded the livestock as far north as they could, then loaded them onto scows for the treacherous journey up the Yukon River. The brothers' adventures enthralled the McNamers' friends back home until a tragic dispatch in the November 25, 1899, edition of *The Oregonian*: "The two brothers who were drowned ... from a scow in the Yukon River were Theodore and Conrad McNamer of Forest Grove."

The shock was felt statewide. In the decades since Joseph Gale had risked his life to bring cattle and sheep to the Tualatin Plains, Forest Grove had become a major supplier of meat to Portland, Salem and elsewhere, and Theodore's fame had spread. Then on Christmas Day, *The Oregonian* ran another surprise story. "Theodore McNamer remarked yesterday that he had no idea of his popularity until he read his obituary," the story said. It seems that the McNamers had been part of a fleet of scows headed up the Yukon in November, battling dangerous ice floes to deliver one last load of goods before winter made travel impossible. When the convoy reached an island, all of the scows followed one channel, while the McNamers veered the other way. When the other adventurers got to the end of the island, they realized that the McNamers were missing. A search of the area turned up nothing, and they were presumed lost in the treacherous current. As it turns out, Theo and Con McNamer had chosen the better channel, and shot ahead of their colleagues, reaching the mining camps first. The McNamers' friends back in Oregon were thrilled to learn the truth, but Theodore was chagrined. It turns out that by the time the laggards from the convoy reached the mining camps a few days later, desperation at the thought of a long Alaskan winter had pushed prices for meat sharply higher. Theodore believed that he lost several thousand dollars by getting there first. In the end, Theodore McNamer joined Joseph Gale as a successful ship captain and livestock herder, but he also joined the list of several others who failed to create a successful overland route from Forest Grove to the Coast.

Theodore McNamer's departure for the Klondike didn't end the dream of a Forest Grove-Tillamook stagecoach route. In 1902, his half-brother, John, revived the route. John McNamer had earned his stripes as a stagecoach driver on October 24, 1876, while working for Wells Fargo in California. The stage that he was driving along the Weaverville Road that day carried just three passengers, but also a strongbox with $6,800 in cash. When a robber confronted the stage, pointed his gun and demanded the strongbox, John McNamer obliged. McNamer drove the stage around a bend, then stopped and turned over the reins to one of the passengers. Creeping back toward the scene of the crime, McNamer spotted the robber and cried out for him to stop. When the thief didn't stop, McNamer fired his revolver several times, killing him. John McNamer recovered the $6,800 for Wells Fargo. In fact, McNamer said he found an additional $1,300 in the robber's pockets, which was donated to the California public school fund, according to his obituary in the January 26, 1922, edition of the *News-Times*. Wells Fargo gave John McNamer a gold watch for his heroism; his half-brother Theodore gave him the Forest Grove-Tillamook stagecoach route, which lasted only into the first few years of the Twentieth Century.

The lack of a stagecoach or rail route did not prevent people from journeying between Forest Grove and Tillamook, however. For example, Pacific University Mathematics Professor Henry Price decided to go to Tillamook to visit his friend Thomas Robinson over Christmas Break in 1909. The Trask River stage from Yamhill was grounded by four feet of snow in the Coast Range mountains. One option was a 30-mile train ride to Portland and a 150-mile steamship journey up the Columbia River and down the Coast from Astoria to Tillamook, which is barely 40 miles from Forest Grove as the crow flies. Henry Price chose a different route. He set out on foot along Gales Creek, and up into the Coast Range. At the summit he found the head waters of the Wilson River, which he followed down the densely forested western slope and into the pastureland of the valley around Tillamook. After a few days there, he reversed course, making his way through feet of snow while walking back to Forest Grove.

Adding insult to injury, while Forest Grove awaited a measly one-mile spur into town, work began in the 1890s on a rail line from Hillsboro to the Coast. Rather than heading toward Tillamook, however, the line was destined to connect farther north in Astoria. To reach the northernmost point in Oregon, the rail line would once again bypass Forest Grove. Forest Grove's loss appeared to be a boon for the tiny town of Buxton, and speculators snatched up timberland and built houses in a suddenly booming Buxton. The boom quickly went bust, however, when the railroad ran out of money. Buxton boomed again in 1905 when

Elmer Elm Lytle and his Pacific Railway and Navigation Company announced plans to build a line through town. Unfortunately, at the same time that Buxton residents were looking for ways to secure a little piece of railroad wealth, a group of speculators back East was scheming to corner the world's copper supply; when their scheme imploded it took with it the nation's economy. The resulting financial panic brought capital projects, including the railroad through Buxton, to a screeching halt. Work resumed later and the railroad opened to Tillamook in 1911, with another line north to the logging town of Vernonia. Buxton had what Forest Grove always had dreamed of, but reality didn't match the dream. A 1949 history published in the *News-Times* told of the problems passengers encountered. The story quoted a Mrs. Reuben Kelly, who lived in Buxton when the railroad finally opened. The first problem was that the railroad did not have a set schedule, so passengers would simply wait by the tracks until a train happened along. The second problem was that the trains did not have passenger cars, so travelers rode the freight cars. "We held umbrellas over us to keep cinders from the locomotives out of our eyes," Mrs. Kelly told the newspaper.

The Hillsboro to Tillamook railroad came to another small town north of Forest Grove as well. Or to be more specific, the town came to the railroad. The tiny hamlet of Banks was established in the 1890s but never flourished. Finally its Post Office and other businesses packed up and moved about two miles south to the larger town of Greenville, leaving Banks a virtual ghost town. Although it is difficult to imagine today, in the 1890s Greenville was an important city in the county. For example, it had telephone service and a bank before Forest Grove. Then, when the Pacific Railway and Navigation Company announced its plans for a route to the Coast in 1905, the line cut right through the former townsite of Banks. The *News'* Banks correspondent was giddy in the May 24, 1906, edition. "Railroad! Railroad! Is all the talk!" the correspondent wrote. "The construction train is here and the track is graded. After waiting all these long 20 years we have the roaring engine reverberating from mountain to mountain." The writer took special glee at the fate of rival Greenville. "Greenville is dead – the railroad went two miles east of the place, and left the town high on the beach, deserted, wrecked, stranded." The Moore family, Greenville's founders, immediately packed up their store and Post Office and moved to Banks. "Greenville picked up and moved almost bag and baggage to the former site," the *News* reported. Greenville became a ghost town. The news only added urgency to Forest Grove's railroad boosters when they saw that while they had heretofore survived being one mile from a railroad, being two miles from a railroad could destroy a town overnight.

Forest Grove finally caught a break that same year, however. Plans were announced for an electric passenger trolley from the railroad depot into town, courtesy of Edward W. Haines, who also had a contract to supply the town with its electricity. Haines wasn't beholden to the major New York banks because in addition to the electric utility, he also owned his own bank. Sadly, the Haines electric utility was plagued by problems that sometimes cut all power to the city for days, so his electric trolleys had a lot of down time. A couple of years later the Oregon Electric Railway built its own spur into town. Haines threw in the towel, but hopes again soared that Forest Grove someday would become a railroad hub. The town buzzed with excitement on May 23, 1913, when the Forest Grove Commercial Club hosted all of the top executives of the Oregon Electric Railway. The point of the visit was to sell the railroad on the idea of providing passenger service to areas such as Gales City, several miles west of Forest Grove. But the true prize sought by the Commercial Club was to create passenger service to the booming city of Cherry Grove at the headwaters of the Tualatin River.

Cherry Grove didn't exist three years earlier, but by 1913, the Lovegren Lumber and Land Company had built a city of 400 with amenities that Forest Grove lacked, including nearly all paved streets and sidewalks, parks, athletic fields and dependable electricity. Better yet, Cherry Grove's reason for being, the giant Lovegren Lumber Mill, hadn't even opened yet, because the giant dam across the Tualatin would not be finished for several months. The Commercial Club wanted to make sure that all roads to Cherry Grove led through Forest Grove.

The sales pitch itself probably should have served as a warning to both the Commercial Club and the Oregon Electric executives. The executives toured the area in a convoy of automobiles. The trip was arduous. The drive six miles south to Gaston and six miles west to Cherry Grove took most of the day by the time the weary travelers returned to Forest Grove. Yet they made their trip by automobile, and highways were only going to get better. Within a year, Cherry Grove's dam and dreams both collapsed, and within a few years, automobiles had overtaken trains as the dominant means for transporting people. Once again, Forest Grove was bypassed by history.

Ironically, while Forest Grove always felt slighted by the railroads, it has the misfortune of being linked to one of the worst rail disasters in Oregon history. At 5:48 p.m. on Tuesday, February 11, 1908, a passenger train left the Forest Grove station, about a mile east of town, to continue its trip south toward McMinnville. As the passengers who got off in Forest Grove still were waiting for the trolley into town, the train rounded the curve south toward Gaston. The trip from Portland had been smooth, with the train departing the station east of Forest Grove about a minute early. The sun had set about 10 minutes earlier as the train was sitting at the station, so by now darkness was descending on the remaining passengers, most of whom were bound for Gaston, McMinnville and Sheridan. As the train crossed the trestle over Gales Creek everything seemed fine. The engine crossed the trestle, along with the cars carrying baggage and mail for residents of the Yamhill Valley. But as the passenger cars crossed, the rails beneath them gave way. The first two passenger cars plunged over the embankment, while the third was left hanging over the abyss on its side. The passengers in that third car were lucky, the February 13 edition of the *Washington County News* reported. Young Grace Harding of Gaston, returning home from her studies at Pacific University, was tossed from the car into the creek below, landing feet first with only minor injuries. Passengers in the first two cars were not as lucky. John McDonald, a brick mason from McMinnville, died at the scene. Mrs. J.E. Bates of Gaston also perished, her death made all the more painful by that of her 5-month-old son Howard, who left this Earth cradled in his mother's arms. At least 26 others were injured in the train wreck, including Howard Bates' 6-year-old sister, left with severe lacerations on her face and head and without her mother to raise her.

Oswald West was Oregon's railroad commissioner at the time. He was charged with investigating the disaster but never laid blame. When the accident occurred in 1908, newspapers were focused on the dangers of automobiles, reporting fatalities from throughout the West. Railroads still were king in Oregon, so danger be damned, Forest Grove still wanted the rails to extend into the city. Oswald West, meanwhile went on to be elected governor of Oregon, known for introducing women's suffrage,

Prohibition, and the initiative and referendum system to the state. He is best remembered, however, for protecting public access to every inch of Oregon's coastline. That groundbreaking law was a direct result of the automobile. West declared the beach a public highway right of way.

In 1908, a few months after the Forest Grove train disaster, Oregon finally developed an automobile route from the inland valleys to the Coast. Not surprisingly, that route did not include Forest Grove. Instead, it loosely followed the stagecoach route up the Trask River from Yamhill to Tillamook. What did surprise motorists, however, was just how fast this route was. "From the Valley to the Coast in Just Six Hours," the headline in the August 16, 1908, edition of *The Oregonian* exclaimed. To reinforce just how fast this nearly 40 mile journey had become, the subhead expounded: "How the automobile has annihilated space."

Yet while six and a half miles per hour felt to a reporter in 1908 like "annihilating space," Forest Grove residents held out hope for even better. Finally, on July 28, 1910, the *Washington County News* announced a breakthrough: A road from Forest Grove to Tillamook. This road was "ideal for automobiles," the story said, except for a couple of minor problems. First, the road had not been "graveled," so driving in either of Oregon's two seasons (Dusty Season and Muddy Season) would be difficult. Second, there was a four-mile gap in the route that had to be figured out before any Ford or Cadillac could complete the journey.

By April 24, 1913, the *Washington County News-Times* was running Page 1 stories about Forest Grove residents who had succumbed to what the paper called "Fordtitis" and "Cadillactitis," listing automobile purchasers by name. At the same time that Forest Grove was finally getting rail service directly into the center of town, its residents were falling victim to what the newspaper termed "automobile fever." Even two years later, on November 11, 1915, the *News-Times* harbored ambivalent feelings toward the automobile. Lamenting what they saw as the folly of those who chose the automobile over the train, the editors wrote that "the railroads will always continue to be the great Democratic highway for the mass of the people," the paper concluded. "Long tours in a motor car have zest for a time. But in time it ceases to be a novelty." Fearful that railroad rights of way were becoming prohibitively expensive, the editors urged further rail expansion into and out of Forest Grove. Yet the city remained at the dead end of service for either type of transport.

Forest Grove was, it seemed, about as far west as one could go by land on the American continent.

The years dragged on, with neither trains nor automobiles establishing solid transportation options for Forest Grove. By the 1920s, the railroads were feeling the heat generated by trucks and buses that were sapping their business. In January 1922, railroad executives demanded city ordinances to thwart intracity buses from carrying passengers that might otherwise take the train. The railroads were rebuffed. In April 1923, railroad executives were back, demanding government protection against the trucking industry in the form of mandated shipping rates. The railroads were built on government handouts, from land grants to cash payments from towns to avoid being bypassed, so additional demands seemed likely to be met. They were not, however, and truckers gained a foothold in moving cargo, and without further government handouts, the railroad companies lost interest in Forest Grove.

The automobile, it seemed, had won the war, but for Forest Grove one battle remained; how, civic leaders wondered, can we traverse the Coast Range mountains and establish our city as a transportation hub? For the past decade, a Wilson River Highway had been promised. The answer to their question came, it seemed, in the same month that the railroads asked for relief from buses. The plan came in the form of a toll road to be built mostly at taxpayer expense and then turned over to a private company that would turn a profit by collecting tolls. Washington and Tillamook counties approved the plan, but some in the state Legislature objected to this huge gift of public funds to the private company, which coincidentally was headed by state Senator A.G. Beals. This plan for a Wilson River Highway, like so many more before it, never got off the ground. The pressure for such a road kept building, however, because U.S. Highway 101, nicknamed the "Roosevelt Highway" in honor of Theodore Roosevelt, who pushed for its creation, now extended along the coast from San Diego to Seattle, creating a major route that bypassed not only Forest Grove but also Portland and nearly every other major Oregon city. Lawmakers from all those cities now joined in the effort to create a convenient route from the Roosevelt Highway to the population centers of the Willamette Valley. Forest Grove stood to be the big winner in this battle.

Year after year the battle for a Wilson River Highway raged until March 1928, the same month that Gordon Burlingham and William Forbis brought the first airplane to Forest Grove. Finally, now that the prospect of air travel over the mountains arrived, Washington and Tillamook counties approved a Wilson River Highway. In reality, however, the plan wasn't for a highway. It was more of a road. It was not even a year-round road, mind you, but nonetheless a trail that the most robust cars could travel on a good day in the summer. The road roughly followed W.S. Runyan's stagecoach route, the one abandoned years earlier. This iteration soon was abandoned as well, as mudslides routinely obliterated large chunks of the road.

So after decades of battling for a Wilson River Highway from Forest Grove to Tillamook, pretty much everyone had given up on the dream as the Great Depression took hold, or at least until two simultaneous lucky breaks finally came along in the early 1930s. "Lucky," as usual, was in the eye of the beholder, especially in this case. The first lucky break came in November 1932, when Franklin Roosevelt was elected on the promise of a New Deal stimulus package to jumpstart the economy, which he promised would include bridges and highways. The second break came in August 1933, when the first of the Tillamook Burns raged across the Coast Range, devastating everything in its path, which tended to follow the Wilson River from Forest Grove to Tillamook. Roosevelt's Works Progress Administration offered up the cash to build the highway, and the Tillamook Burn cleared a path for construction.

The Tualatin Valley Highway took advantage of the straight east-west bearing of Portland and Forest Grove. When the long awaited Wilson River Highway finally opened a trail between Portland and the Coast in 1940, it appeared that at long last Forest Grove had caught a break, because the new highway was an extension of the old Tualatin Valley Highway. Winding west of town along Gales Creek, the highway would stretch about 50 steep, rugged, winding miles to Tillamook. The path was a little too rugged, however, and constant slides and deep mud kept the highway from fully opening until 1942. By then World War II was underway and folks in Oregon were facing gasoline and tire rationing, which kept most travelers off the road, further delaying Forest Grove's chance to become the gateway to the Oregon Coast. By the time the war ended, the Wilson River route no longer was seen as the best route to the

Coast, however. That honor now fell on a route that roughly follows the Wolf Creek drainage, and drops down out of the Coast Range far north of the Wilson River Highway, directly into the tourist mecca of Seaside and much closer to the Coast's major city, Astoria. Like the Wilson River Highway, the Wolf Creek Highway also was a New Deal era project, started early in the Great Depression. Although the Wilson River route opened first, the Wolf Creek pathway was the one that garnered the most attention from the federal government. By the time it opened in 1949, the Wolf Creek Highway had been renamed the Sunset Highway in honor of the Forty-first Infantry Division of the Army, also known as the "Sunset Division." It also was known as U.S. Highway 26, and as the fastest and best route to the Coast. Although Highway 26 heads due west out of Portland, aiming directly at Forest Grove, just like the railroad, it takes a sudden turn before reaching town. The bend in this road sends motorists sailing far north of Forest Grove through open fields at highway speeds.

The 1950s ushered in an era of unprecedented mobility as cars and freeways became firmly entrenched in American society. On the west side of Portland, the Sunset Highway was a freeway; by contrast, the Tualatin Valley Highway, the one arterial that passed through town, was a local road with dozens of stoplights. Forest Grove, once again, was bypassed. To add insult to injury, in 1957 the Wilson River Highway was rerouted north near Glenwood to intersect with the Sunset Highway near Banks. Now Forest Grove was bypassed by both major routes to the Coast.

Perhaps Tabitha Brown, Rutherford B. Hayes and the lady who proposed the boardwalk had the right approach, hoofing it into town. After all, there's never been a good way to get to or from Forest Grove by car, by train, by ship, airplane or stagecoach. Yet people keep coming to this once self-proclaimed prettiest town in Oregon, to this educational center, to this beautiful grove of trees on the Tualatin Plains.

Chapter

5

A city of trees

The Great Depression and the great forest fire of 1933, dubbed the Tillamook Burn, combined to create a potentially devastating blow to the city on the fire's eastern edge, blocking out the sun and burying under ash and soot the streets of the town named for the vast forest.

Or, more to the point, the town *might* have been named for the vast forest. Then again, it might have been named for the groves of trees in the Tualatin Plains. Or, perhaps, the trees in Oregon might have nothing to do with how Forest Grove got its name; maybe it just took the name of a town back East, the way Portland and Salem got their monikers. At any rate, the town is named for trees.

Until about 1850, the informal name of the town was "West Tualatin Plains," to distinguish it from another fledgling community a few miles east, which fittingly was described as "East Tualatin Plains." East Tualatin Plains had taken the name Hillsboro, after pioneer David Hill. West Tualatin Plains, on the other hand, still struggled for a name. In *Splendid Audacity*, authors Gary Miranda and Rick Read explore the origins of the name, pointing out that "Forest Grove" can be seen as an oxymoron. After all, by definition, a grove is a small stand of trees, while a forest is, well, a very large stand of trees. Sidney Harper Marsh, the university's first president, refused to use the oxymoronic name, the authors write, instead referring to the town always as "The Grove." A century later in 1952, the wife of then University President Walter Giersbach wrote a brief history, arguing the name was chosen because the town marked the spot at which the forest ended and groves of trees began. Regardless, there's a surprising amount of uncertainty about the naming of this city of trees.

For most of the town's history, Rosannah Lancaster was credited with naming the town after the one in Pennsylvania in which she grew up. That legend was repeated in newspaper accounts and history tomes up to and including Mrs. Giersbach's in 1952. Rosannah Lancaster was the wife of Columbia Lancaster. Judge Columbia Lancaster is known best for his role in establishing what now is the state of Washington, but before that he was the "supreme judge" of the Oregon Territory, and lived in Forest Grove. Columbia Lancaster's name was so synonymous with "judge" that many people did not even know his real first name, and nearly all references to the person credited with naming Forest Grove refer to her as "Mrs. Judge Lancaster." For example, the *Forest Grove Times* told the legend of "Mrs. Judge Lancaster" in its July 27, 1899, special edition about the history of the town. The writer tells of a meeting in 1850, in which residents of the town got together to choose a name. Their decision would carry no legal authority, because in 1850 the community was not officially a city and was governed informally by town elders. Although no formal records of the meeting were kept, legend has it that the attendees took their task very seriously, and a lively debate ensued. Many names were proposed, including Vernon, but most included the word "grove" in one form or another. Like so many others, this writer said that Mrs. Judge Lancaster prevailed, and the name of her hometown in Pennsylvania was selected.

Mrs. Judge Lancaster's obituary in 1903 also says that she is credited with naming the town, but the same obituary says that she was born and grew up in Mahohing County, Ohio, before marrying Columbia Lancaster and moving to first Centerville, Michigan, and then on to Oregon. There is no mention of time spent in Pennsylvania, but indeed there is a Forest Grove in that state. Oddly, it's about 400 miles from where Rosannah grew up, and according to *Place Names in Bucks County Pennsylvania* by George MacReynolds, the town was called Forestville until

45

it was renamed Forest Grove in 1877, a quarter of a century after the naming of Forest Grove, Oregon.

The naming of Forest Grove is of more than trivial interest, however. The process of naming the city speaks volumes about the political tensions involved in the formation of the town, and it also illustrates how difficult it can be to trace history. There's little doubt that Rosannah Lancaster was an advocate for the name Forest Grove, or that the people present at the community meeting supported her proposal. But the next year, the trustees of Pacific University felt that the authority to name the city rested with them. George Atkinson, who was sent to the Oregon Territory to establish the college, had taken to referring to his adopted town as Vernon, after a widely used place name in his native Massachusetts. The community meeting in 1850 had favored Mrs. Judge Lancaster's "Forest Grove," but Atkinson had not given up the fight. As the trustees met on January 9, 1851, he asked that Vernon be selected as the town's name. Trustees were underwhelmed and elected to sleep on it. The minutes of the next day's meeting reflected the final decision thusly: "Moved by Mr. Atkinson and seconded to call the town 'Vernon.' Rejected. Moved by Mr. Thornton and seconded to call the town 'Forest Grove.' Passed." Like most aspects of Forest Grove's history, the story wasn't quite that simple. Power, personalities and politics each played a part in the final outcome.

The Reverend Myron Eells filled in some of the gaps in a history of the town that he wrote for the November 6, 1895, edition of *The Oregonian*. Eells was a son of pioneer Cushing Eells, who would lead the school for a time before returning to Walla Walla, Washington, to found Whitman College, named in honor of his dear friend, Marcus Whitman. There were many powerful men at the trustees' meeting who had settled the community and wanted a name that reflected its unique location, rather than pick a name of a town back east. Thomas Naylor, one of the area's largest landowners, lobbied for "Naylors Grove," the name he had given to his Donation Land Claim. Equally powerful Quinn Thornton preferred the name he had given to his Donation Land Claim, "Forest Grove." Local pride won out.

The city was established by a university, and could have been named "College Town" or "Educationville." Instead, the university chose trees as the town's theme, and a city's destiny was cast. Ash Street, Birch

Street, Cedar Street … the north-south streets of Forest Grove bear the alphabetical names of trees, at least to Oak Street. As the city annexed eastward in 1961, it created a committee to come up with new names for other streets. The suggestions were Nutmeg or Noble Fir; Quince; Redwood, Rose, Rosewood or Rhododendron; Sequoia, Smoketree, Spruce or Sycamore; Tamarack, Torchwood or Tuliptree; Vermillion or Vinemaple; Walnut, Willow, Witchhazel or Waxmyrtle; Yew or Yellowwood; and Zebrawood. Martin Road became Quince, which later became the Highway 47 bypass around town. Most of the other names, including Waxmyrtle, failed to take root in the hearts of citizens, and the city abandoned the streets-named-for-trees concept.

Elsewhere around town the tree theme flourished. The campus of Pacific University includes magnificent Marsh Hall and an ultramodern library, but what visitors tend to notice first are the gigantic oak trees that shade the park-like lawns along College Way. Here and there around town are giant sequoias with trunks wider than trucks, and in some cases nearly as wide as the houses they shade.

Forest Grove wasn't built for the same reason as the other pioneer cities of Oregon. It wasn't a gateway to the vast land giveaways in the Willamette Valley. It doesn't have a river and as such never enjoyed the riverboat craze. It only barely had a railroad, so it missed out on that boom as well. It didn't have gold, or at least very much. Sure, there was the legend of the Lost Indian Gold Mine, which the eccentric Frank Watrous believed he finally had found, on the very day that the first Tillamook Burn started just a few miles away. The fire not only burned trees but also exposed the mountainsides, triggering mudslides that rerouted creeks and rivers and buried the Lost Indian Gold Mine that Watrous claimed to have found. The quest for gold threatened to make Forest Grove a ghost town before it ever got started, as many of the rugged mountain men who chose the Tualatin Plains packed up and headed south to find their fortune during the California Gold Rush of 1849. None of them found much, if any, treasure and returned empty handed. Well, with one exception. Johnny Porter, who returned with booty that forever changed Forest Grove: cones that sprouted into those giant sequoias around town and at his family's farm on Porter Road and on the lawn of the Washington County Courthouse in Hillsboro.

Forest Grove didn't have a lot of things, but it had a college and trees, trees that stretched from the western edge of town to the Pacific Ocean, creating one of the world's great forests. It seems odd today, but in the early days of white settlement in rural Oregon, the concept of a "timber industry" hadn't entered the minds of most people. There was no need to ship timber to other cities in the region, because they already had more trees than they knew what to do with. When Tualatin Plains people were deciding on a name for their city, many people called a community along the Willamette River "Stumptown," for the remains of the trees settlers were cutting to make way for agriculture. That town soon became Portland, but still didn't want any more trees than it already had, so no one in Forest Grove had any incentive to do large-scale logging. In fact, there were those in Forest Grove who foresaw and welcomed an entire state virtually free of forests. In 1868, for example, the *Forest Grove Monthly* outlined the challenges faced by Washington County, cut off as it was from Portland, the ocean, and the Willamette Valley by steep hills. The *Monthly* editors saw a hero, however, in Joseph Gaston, who was plotting a railroad that would link Forest Grove to Portland and to the Coast. "It is forty miles from Forest Grove to the coast, and at least seventy-five to Astoria," the editors wrote, but once the railroad was finished, "*All this country will be settled.* These forest-crowned hills will be clothed with flocks. They will yet wave with grain" (emphasis in original). For the next 65 years, that vision of wheat fields from Forest Grove to Astoria seemed impossible. The forest remained virtually impenetrable, and the trees seemed like they would be there forever.

By 1868, when the *Monthly* was pining for amber waves of grain, home construction had changed in the eastern part of the country from log cabins and rough-hewn timber to frame construction requiring finished lumber. The idea of an industry built on trees was becoming feasible, though still not yet in Forest Grove. Small-scale milling operations sprang up throughout the region, but only to meet the needs of neighbors who had missed the donation land claims and had no trees of their own. By 1868, Portland had grown enough that it needed more timber than it could produce, and when Gaston finally laid his railroad tracks, they went east from Forest Grove toward Portland, not west to create farmland in the mountains. Over the next couple of decades, the railroad would spur a modest timber industry by finally providing a means to ship lumber the 30 miles or so to Portland. At the same time, steam ships were replacing sailing ships. Bigger and faster than their predecessors, steam ships made it feasible to ship timber to other fast-growing cities along the West Coast.

The *Monthly's* 1868 dream of a railroad into the Coast Range didn't become a reality for nearly 40 years, so Forest Grove got a late start in reaping the benefits of the vast, impenetrable forests to launch the timber operations that would be the cornerstone of its economy throughout most of the Twentieth Century. Even then, the forest remained too remote to conquer fully, so loggers in other regions of the Northwest were able to undercut Forest Grove timber operators, who peered with envy up into the magnificent forest, worried not about ever running out of trees, but rather whether they would be able to make more than a small dent in their numbers.

That all changed in August and September 1933 with the first Tillamook Burn. From the perspective of many people in town, that impenetrable forest was gone. With their forests devastated, most of the timberland owners walked away after the inferno subsided, taking with them many of the small, family owned logging companies that fueled Forest Grove's economy and the county income taxes that paid for roads and other improvements. Because its economy had remained mostly small scale and agrarian, Forest Grove was not hit by the Great Depression with quite as much ferocity as many other cities. But now, in September 1933, all that had changed. Help came from an unexpected source: Washington, D.C. The proud pioneers of the Tualatin Plains had benefitted tremendously in the 1840s and '50s from federal largesse in the form of hundreds of thousands of acres of free land and protection from forts in Yamhill, Astoria and Vancouver. But when the land rush was over and the threat of Indian Wars receded, the federal government largely disappeared from Forest Grove, which was the way most people wanted it.

While most of the land had been free, the people who came to own it wanted as little interference from bureaucrats as possible. They fended for themselves until they got too old, when their children took them in and cared for them. That independence suited Forest Grove just fine for about 80 years, but now things were different. The entire region's economy lay charred and smoldering in a mess too large for a small town to clean up on its own. In 1933, Franklin Roosevelt's New Deal was just getting started, but most of the money for Oregon was going to the Columbia River Gorge to build the Bonneville Dam and to create a transportation corridor to connect the state to the Midwest and East Coast. In 1935, just as it looked like New Deal money might start spreading to other parts of the state, Charles Martin, a virulent enemy of the New Deal despite being a Democrat, became Governor. While serving in the Army at Fort Vancouver, Martin had married into one of Oregon's largest fortunes. After he retired from the military he was elected to the U.S. House of Representatives. Ironically, it was Martin who had spearheaded funding for Oregon's largest and most significant federal project to date, the Bonneville Dam, but he did so with the hope that it would be turned over to his friends to operate as a private enterprise. When the rest of Congress objected and declared that the electricity belonged to the public, Martin withdrew into an angry war of words with Roosevelt, black people, labor leaders and almost everyone but his wealthy neighbors in Portland and Salem.

Still, in the months and years after the Tillamook Burn, federal stimulus continued to flow into Oregon despite the Governor's objection. Much of the money flowed first into Portland, but also into massive public works projects along the Coast. The majestic bridges in Newport, Waldport and elsewhere created the technological marvel of the Roosevelt Highway, hugging the coast from San Diego to the Puget Sound. The Works Progress Administration, Civilian Conservation Corps and other New Deal agencies hired unemployed Forest Grove residents by the truckload to replant the Tillamook Forest, work on the coastal bridges and to finally build a highway from Forest Grove to the Coast, at long last making the town a transportation hub. When the Wilson River Highway, now known as Highway 6, came to fruition, Highway 8, the Tualatin Valley Highway, ran right through the center of Forest Grove, skirted David Hill, wound through the village of Gales Creek and connected to the new Highway 6 to Tillamook. Unfortunately, planners later routed that traffic over Highway 26 to Banks, not Forest Grove, where tourists could decide to turn off toward Tillamook or go straight to Seaside and Astoria. It seemed like Forest Grove had been snubbed once again.

In reality, however, the road through Gales Creek eventually would prove to be a major victory for Forest Grove, and the reason was, not surprisingly, trees. Many of the lumber mills of the early 1900s had

50

sprung up south of Forest Grove in Dilley and Gaston, including the most ambitious projects in Cherry Grove and at Stimson's Scoggins Valley operation. One major reason for the choice was Joseph Gaston's railroad, which created cheap, easy transportation of the finished lumber. Most of the raw logs were dragged down the valleys by teams of mules or oxen. When most of the lumber was just a few miles from the mill, draft animals did the trick. The village of Gaston, with its railroad, creeks and rivers and a blanket of trees that spread into town, was the ideal timber town.

Technology improved along the way, of course, but as Walt Wentz wrote in *Bringing Out The Big Ones: Log Trucking in Oregon*, Coast Range loggers were slow to adapt. Part of the reason was cost. With such a huge supply of lumber at their footsteps, the major operators saw little incentive to invest in anything more than draft animals and cheap manpower. Another reason loggers were reluctant to use the first large logging machines in the 1890s, Wentz writes, was the steep, muddy terrain of the Coast Range. These first bulldozer-like behemoths were extremely powerful, capable of hauling huge loads, albeit at about the speed of draft animals. They worked well in flat forests, but had a serious drawback for loggers in the steep Coast Range: They used steam power. Essentially, they were huge wood burning stoves with a tank of boiling water on top. Such machinery by its nature needs to be built vertically, so the driver rode on a platform atop the tank of boiling water, nearly 12 feet from the ground. This put most of the weight near the top, giving the haulers a high center of gravity and making them prone to tipping over. Anyone who has driven on even a modern Coast Range logging road knows that the terrain, mud, obstacles on the road, ice and other factors pose a serious risk of tipping over. When one of these enormous haulers did tip over, the probable scenario went something like this: The machine tips over onto its side, or just as often onto its top. The operator likely would be crushed, but if he avoided that fate he probably would be fatally scalded by the hundreds of gallons of boiling water. With the operator now incapacitated, the roaring fire from the wood-burning stove was free to spread through the forest.

The next great advance was the truck. Wentz quotes historian Nelson Courtland Brown that the first use of log trucks in Oregon was in 1913, although that was 100 miles from Forest Grove along the much more accessible slopes of the Cascades around towns such as Eugene and Silverton. Coast Range lumber barons again were slow to adapt, partly because they had low-cost options, but mostly because the Coast Range was just too rugged for early, not very powerful, trucks. By the time of the first Tillamook Burn in 1933, truck technology had improved dramatically, but with no roads into the Coast Range, that was of little value to anyone in Forest Grove, or even Gaston. The Tillamook Burn and the Great Depression changed all that. First, the burn, as devastating as it was to the timber industry, had cleared the way to build a highway into the deepest regions of the Coast Range forest, or what was left of it. It also made it possible to carve logging roads from those roads to reach the even-more remote stands of unburned timber. Because of the Depression, federal stimulus money poured in to help make that all possible. Destitute Forest Grove residents suddenly had paychecks from the Works Progress Administration or other agencies. Meanwhile, residents with ready cash or credit suddenly had a new private-enterprise option: Owning or driving log trucks.

At first these trends still favored Gaston, because the state and federal governments gave Stimson Lumber, about the only giant left standing and with enormous political clout, permission to haul downed timber to its new, state of the art mill, which went into operation about a month after the fire was out. But Forest Grove had more people and money than Gaston, so many of the trucks that hauled the timber belonged to Grove residents. Within a few years, the aftermath of the Tillamook Burn and New Deal turned things to Forest Grove's advantage. By 1935, draft animals and railroad spur lines no longer were the cheapest or most efficient options for hauling logs; trucks with nameplates such as Ford and Dodge and Mack and Autocar now held that honor. The new Wilson River Highway wouldn't be finished until 1940, but reached deep into the forest years before that. The Tualatin Valley Highway through Forest Grove and Gales Creek became the fastest route for log trucks. Suddenly even many of the logs destined for Gaston's mills had to pass through Forest Grove first.

The railroad still was the most attractive option for hauling finished timber long distances, so most of Forest Grove's many mills, including Gales Peak, Larkins and Carnation, located south of town in Carnation and Dilley, but the jobs they created benefitted Forest Grove's previously unemployed residents. The Raines family's Carnation mill was particularly well-positioned to benefit from the opening of the inner reaches of the forest, having been rebuilt after a devastating 1929 fire into a larger, more modern facility that supplanted Cherry Grove's Alder Creek mill as the second-largest in the county, behind only Stimson's Gaston mill.

The Tillamook Burn and the rise of corporate timber in the region during the Great Depression radically changed Forest Grove culture. For the first 75 years of its existence, with the exception of those who worked for Pacific University, Forest Grove had been populated largely by people who owned their own farms or small businesses. Railroad construction had not brought many jobs for locals, because labor was imported from elsewhere in the country and from China, among other places. City government was very small, as were public schools. Grocery stores and pharmacies were mom-and-pop operations, as were the small mercantiles. For a brief time a flour mill employed dozens of people, but a fire wiped out the business in 1895 and the owner could not afford to rebuild his uninsured building. A milk condenser rose from the ashes of the mill, and for a few brief years the city expected an economic boom, until the condensed milk industry went bust. The Carnation lumber mill rose at the site of the departed flour mill and condenser, but was relatively small and family owned, like dozens of other lumber mills. Most of the logging companies that cut the timber to supply those mills were mom-and-pop operations as well, although more often they were in reality brother-and-pop or son-and-pop companies. Still, as the Depression spread across the Tualatin Plains, the area was nearly devoid of corporate influence.

August Lovegren had tried to create a corporation in 1910. His Cherry Grove Land and Cherry Grove Lumber companies were larger than anything the area had seen before, but both companies were paternal and religious, with employees handpicked from mostly outside the area. When Lovegren's dam burst in 1914, so did his corporations, which were replaced with smaller family run operations. Then, in 1929, the area's first real major corporate player, Stimson Lumber, announced plans to alter the landscape of the local economy.

Stimson's business model was unlike that of most of the local timber industry. The company bought huge swaths of its own timberland, built its own railroad and planned a mill of enormous proportions. Instead of buying its logs from the family operations like most mills did, it would cut its own. Instead of paying contractors to haul the logs to its mill and finished lumber from the mill to market, Stimson planned to control most of its own transportation. Instead of sustaining dozens of small firms, Stimson would put dozens of people on its corporate payroll. As it turns out, Stimson's timing could not have been much worse. Just as it completed the purchase of its timberlands and broke ground on its mill in 1929, the stock market collapsed. Backed by one of the West Coast's largest personal fortunes, C.W. Stimson was able to persevere and pressed ahead with the mill, setting an opening in October 1933. In August 1933, the Tillamook Burn tore across the forest and threatened to burn the mill. The fire did not destroy Stimson, but it did wipe out most of the smaller timberland owners and many of the independent logging operations. The government came to Stimson's rescue, giving the company permission to salvage charred and fallen trees at a deep discount before they rotted. To process all of the fallen timber, Stimson hired many of the surviving small timber falling firms and new trucking operators to help as well. It seemed like nearly everyone whose business survived the fire was prospering again, with one notable exception: Stimson's employees.

In Forest Grove's agrarian society, people were accustomed to riding economic booms and busts together. When lousy weather ruined a growing season, every farmer suffered more or less together; when the weather was good, everyone benefitted together. When timber prices were high, everyone shared in the bounty. Stimson's arrival changed that dynamic. As the Gaston mill boomed, newspapers ran stories of C.W. Stimson sailing the world on his yacht, while his employees saw their work weeks expand and their meager pay stagnate. When employees lost a limb in one of the giant saws, an all-too-common occurrence, they simply were cast aside in favor of an unemployed man desperate for any job during the Depression. In 1935, just as everything looked rosy for Stimson, a new problem arose: labor unrest. Once again, Oregon's Governor Charles Martin stepped into the fray, intent on thwarting any assistance for the workers. If Martin hated anything more than Social Security and other New Deal programs, it was labor unions, which he considered the work of "Bolsheviks." He declared war on the timber workers. "Beat the hell out of them," he ordered the state's sheriffs.

"Crack their damned heads. These fellows are there for nothing but trouble ... give it to them!" Forest Grove-area workers would end up bearing the brunt of his anger and violence because of the Stimson mill's strategic location and stunning success.

Union leaders from throughout the Northwest targeted Stimson. Local employees were confused, because they were unaccustomed to and suspicious of unions, corporations and government programs. Some went on strike, while others kept working. Forest Grove and Gaston became the eye of the storm for another reason. While other sheriffs around the state balked at cracking the damned heads of their neighbors and the people who elected them, Washington County Sheriff John Connell welcomed the fight. In May 1935, Connell organized a group of heavily armed vigilantes, who moved in to arrest those picketing at the Stimson mill. They did not use the machine guns they had been given, but did use nightsticks and baseball bats to subdue the workers, who were then marched to jail in Forest Grove. The episode backfired on Martin, because it galvanized the public against him and turned more local workers against Stimson. Martin was defeated in the next primary and several years of protests led to the unionization of workers at Stimson and other local mills. The Industrial Age finally had arrived in Forest Grove, and it was only natural that it was all because of trees.

The Tillamook Burn and subsequent reforestation effort had another lasting effect on Coast Range logging interests, and once again Governor Charles Martin found himself overwhelmed by a tidal wave of change. "We turn to our forbears in a sense of deepest reverence and greatest affection," he wrote in the *Oregon Blue Book* during his first year as governor. "They builded (sic) well. They dominated every element that undertook to thwart their way." Chief among elements Martin wanted to dominate as governor was Oregon's timber, "of which," he said, "we have scarcely availed ourselves." The Tillamook Burn changed everything. When most of the private owners walked away and dumped their lands into the lap of county and state governments, perspectives changed. The state viewed the lands as a long-term, sustainable source of both revenue and recreation and sought strategies to preserve forest land. Ultimately, however, the remaining timber operators were as responsible as anyone for changing forestry practices. Many of the Northwest timber barons, including famous names such as Stimson, Weyerhaeuser and Miller, came west from Michigan and other Great Lakes states after that region's once vast forests had been depleted. When the Tillamook Burn hit in 1933, Oregon's forests still were far from meeting that same fate, but the devastation was a wake-up call nonetheless. The damage and subsequent reforesting efforts became a real-life laboratory to study the emerging science of forestry, and sustainability became a concern even for loggers raised on the slash-and-burn style of clearcutting. A public-private partnership was born to sustain Oregon's timber industry.

In addition, when the private landowners walked away and abandoned the forests, the state reluctantly took control of the land. Although lawmakers remained under heavy influence from timber interests, many in the large urban areas also were listening to those in the nascent tourism industry, destined to rival the timber industry in importance. With the advent of better automobiles, the Roosevelt Highway, major east-west continental land and air routes, more and more people were coming to Oregon to hunt, fish, or even to just gaze at the trees, the likes of which never had been seen by tourists from the Midwest or East Coast. The concept of multiuse forests came into play.

Today, 80 years after the Tillamook Burn, debates still rage between timber interests and environmentalists, but the duration of the debate is itself testament to the advances that have been made. It took 80 years or less to wipe out vast forests in Europe and the American Midwest, but 80 years after the Tillamook Burn, logging families still can legitimately expect to pass along their livelihood, in some form, to their children and grandchildren, and environmentalists can expect to have forests left to protect for generations to come.

People in Forest Grove always have loved trees, but trees also have been a source of conflict since the fight over naming the city. Once there were just too many trees, preventing farmers from cultivating amber waves of grain. Then the Tillamook Burn came, and there were too few trees, until people realized that the fire actually opened up the forest for more logging than crews could handle. That spirit of abundance disappeared when tourism and environmental forces combined to restrict logging, and suddenly everyone agreed that there weren't enough trees to go around. Naming streets "Elm" and "Maple" made sense to everyone, but "Waxmyrtle" and "Zebrawood" seemed like too much of a good thing.

Trees were the reason behind Forest Grove's name. For decades, trees were the basis of Forest Grove's economy. Trees remain a major reason that Forest Grove still can argue that it's the prettiest town in Oregon. Throughout its history, Forest Grove has been a city of trees.

Chapter

6

Trial by fire

Fire has shaped Forest Grove throughout its nearly 175-year history. While the Tillamook Burn was the most famous, many other smaller infernos have left scars as well. Many of the scars are psychological, because throughout Forest Grove's history, fire has been used as a weapon to quite literally inflame political passions.

For about 50 years after Harvey Clarke, Alvin Smith, Tabitha Brown and others started building what would become Forest Grove, the town did not have a fire department. Even in 1872, when civic leaders finally got around to creating a formal charter, the document made no provision for formal fire protection. The fact that there was no fire department, however, does not mean there were no fires. On June 8, 1878, *The Oregonian* reported on what it called the first fire in the city's history. That's a dubious claim, but difficult to disprove because there was no fire department and only sporadic local newspaper coverage to record any previous blazes. Regardless, this fire was a disastrous one, and sadly it set a precedent for many future fires in the Grove.

"Last night about midnight," the story began, "the alarm of fire was given, which caused a general rush to the business part of our little city." As was the custom of the time, townspeople rushed to the scene, not so much to extinguish the fire, but rather to save whatever belongings they could, and in this particular case there was little to save, because the fire was raging in several buildings simultaneously. The worst fire was in R.P. Wills' general store, which had flames coming from both the front and back of the store. Both the front and back doors were wide open. It did not require a trained fire investigator to suspect a cause. This appeared to be Forest Grove's first case of arson. Any doubts were eliminated a few minutes later. As nearly the entire town was busy hauling goods out of the four buildings that were ablaze, including the shop of Forest Grove's first mayor, John G. Boos, someone noticed suspicious activity down the street, as someone was trying to set fire to pioneer Alanson Hinman's dry goods store. Townspeople gave chase, with several stopping at their homes to grab their guns. Bullets started to fly, but the arsonist made good his escape into the midnight blackness. By sunrise, much of the small downtown was ashes. Only one of the store owners had insurance, and his was not enough to cover most of his loss.

Former Mayor J.G. Boos was one of the uninsured and was especially hard hit. The fire, which occurred on his sixth wedding anniversary, wiped out his tinsmith shop just as he was getting back on his feet financially after a series of setbacks. In 1878, tinsmithing was an important skill, because nearly all coffee pots, pans and other implements were made locally. A 1932 biography of Boos in the *News-Times* reported that townspeople immediately took up a collection and raised $240, enough to rebuild the store. Within a year, Boos and the others were back in business. The Wills family had rebuilt its store, although not yet its home, so the family was renting a home just two doors down from the store. Between their rental home and new store stood a shop owned by H.J. Barrett. Life had returned to normal in Forest Grove.

Then just before midnight on October 19, 1880, Mrs. Wills heard the crackling of flames. She looked out and saw flames consuming Barrett's shop next door. She screamed for help and townspeople came running. By now, citizens had organized a bucket brigade. "The ladies assisted in carrying water," *The Oregonian* reported on October 22, "as well as the men and boys, and deserve great credit in extinguishing the fire when they did." Unfortunately, by the time the bucket brigade extinguished the flames, they had consumed Barrett's shop and everything in it, and had jumped next door to destroy the Wills' rental home. The flames had spread the other way as well, and the Wills' new store was reduced to ashes. The fire kept spreading to John Williams' rooming house, and the bucket brigade watched in horror as it, too, fell to the flames. The fire wasn't done yet, and spread to the butcher shop and to J.G. Boos' new tinsmith shop. By now the bucket brigade was beginning to get the upper hand, and while both stores were heavily damaged, they could be repaired. The bucket brigade was not the only change in Forest Grove since the 1878 arson. By 1880, volunteer night watchmen now roamed the streets looking for trouble, and now most of the storeowners had fire insurance to mitigate their losses. Regardless, for the second time in a little more than two years, Forest Grove had lost most of its downtown to fire.

The next major fire was limited to just one building, but ultimately might have damaged the city even more than the downtown fires. Forest Grove was fighting to keep the Indian School as others sought to move it to Salem. The school was facing financial hardship and concerns about the fact that nearly 15 percent of the students had died from infectious diseases. On the morning of December 18, 1884, the girls' dormitory went up in flames. Most of the male students, some younger than 10, formed a bucket brigade from the school's well while a couple of others raced into the inferno to look for two girls rumored to be trapped inside. The rumors were false, and everyone escaped, so the blaze did not add to the student death toll, but within months the school was in new quarters near Salem.

Early settlers were so resistant to taxes and government, however, that it would be another 10 years after the Indian School fire before citizens would accept a rudimentary organized fire department, and even then it was all volunteer and financed with donations. Although fires were seen as a purely personal loss, early Forest Grovers always had been eager to fight fires without a formal organization. Sometimes too eager, in fact, which is part of what eventually led to the department's creation. In the middle of the hot Saturday afternoon of September 3, 1892, smoke was seen billowing from behind Johnson's livery stable in downtown. The flames were coming from a shed which housed the "Chinese laundry" operated by Sam Lee, or "Sam Washee" as the newspapers of the day called him. With wood-frame buidings built next to each other, the fire threatened to destroy downtown, including the popular Vert's Dance Hall.

Townspeople were not about to stand by and watch a conflagration develop, so they flocked to the scene, numbering more than 500, according to the next week's *Times*. Without hydrants or an engine of any kind, the hundreds of intrepid citizens grabbed every bucket they could find and started pumping water from every well in town. Despite the chaos, only the laundry was a total loss. Vert's Dance Hall caught on fire, but men clamored to the roof to save it. After this fire and another one a few months earlier, a group of business owners decided that having a dedicated core of about 10 volunteers was preferable to the chaos of 500. They lobbied, with the support of the town's newspapers, to form a department. Their wish was granted in February 1894. It would be another year, however, before the city would build a water system, and two years before the town installed its first five fire hydrants. The hydrants were tested for the first time at 2 in the morning of Tuesday, April 6, 1897, when flames broke out inside the drugstore owned by Charles Miller, one of the town's most outspoken advocates for the sale of alcohol in dry Forest Grove. The hydrants passed their test with flying colors. Although the contents of the building were a total loss, a nearby hydrant provided enough water to save the structure, no small feat considering that the flames were fed with an accelerant spread by an arsonist.

Not every fire in Forest Grove has been arson, of course, and most didn't directly shape history. Few fires have resulted in lost lives, but many have resulted in lost buildings, many of which tell the city's history as much as any one person's biography. A fire in 1959 helps illustrate that reality. The person who started the blaze that sent dense black smoke billowing into a bright blue July sky in 1959 had no political motivation, but the fire left a gaping wound in the middle of town. The 1959 fire was not the first time flames had ripped through the structure, which long had been one of Forest Grove's most-storied buildings, but it would be the last. Within hours, demolition crews were hauling away the charred debris of the Hotel Oregon. The 1959 fire was set by the demolition crew to reduce the cost of hauling away the wood from the building to the dump. There wasn't much market for used lumber in 1959, even for the exquisite hand-cut fir from Gales Creek used to build the hotel back in 1904. The lumber used to rebuild portions of the building after the hotel's earlier fires was newer, but still nearly 50 years old, cut from old-growth trees before the first of the Tillamook Burns.

Back in the early days of the Twentieth Century, the hotel was known as "The Laughlin." Its builder, Bedford Laughlin, made his fortune selling horses to Alaska Gold Rush dreamers, and he invested much of it in a dream of his own. Laughlin's dream was to build a grand hostelry. He succeeded. The structure that rose on A Street was an ornate wooden building, with rooms for weary travelers after a long day of riding trains and carriages from Portland or McMinnville, the finest restaurant in town, and meeting rooms for civic organizations. The hotel commanded perhaps the premier location in downtown Forest Grove, on the northwest corner where A Street meets Pacific Avenue. For many years the picturesque trolleys rounded the corner from Pacific to A, stopping to let men in their suits and top hats and women in their silk dresses and gloves glide on or off the car for afternoon tea or formal dinner at the hotel. By 1922, when Laughlin sold the hotel and it was renamed the Hotel Oregon, it had lost some of its glamour, but continued to play a vital role in downtown Forest Grove as a place to eat, a place to stay, and when commercial bus routes came to town it served as the bus depot. By 1959, however, the once grand hotel was unwanted and unloved. The new owners lit a match and a crowd gathered as it burned to the ground.

The fact that the old hotel survived at all until 1959 is something of a miracle, because this was not the first time a crowd had gathered to watch flames rip through the structure. In fact, the hotel was the scene of two of Forest Grove's larger commercial fires, just a few months apart, one of which remains a mystery. The first fire was described in the November 12, 1914, *Washington County News-Times*, written in the reporting style of the day: "The fire bell aroused many sleepy denizens of Forest Grove from their flowery beds of ease Monday morning about 6:30 o'clock," the story began. "Laughlin Hotel was on fire and quick strokes of the fire bell brought Forest Grove's gallant volunteer fire department to the scene in short order, and the boys soon had three great streams of water plying on the maddening flames, quickly bringing them into subjugation, but not before the splendid three-story hotel was practically ruined, the whole upper story being burned off ..."

The story went on to chastise the hotel guests and hotel manager, who "were so deeply engrossed in saving life and property from the hotel that the alarm was not sent in as quickly as it might have been, and the fire had made great headway before the fire company arrived." The question of whether the panicked guests should have paused to find the fire bell aside, the reporter certainly was justified in praising the firefighters for managing to save any of the all wooden structure, let alone enough for reconstruction to begin almost immediately. The cause of the fire was easy to determine, and it was what caused many structure fires in the early days of Forest Grove: A defective flue in one of the fireplaces. There was no mystery to solve yet about the hotel, but within months there would be two.

Reconstruction work began immediately, but without the hotel's 22-year-old manager and part owner, L.O. Roark, who left town after the fire. Construction crews worked frantically to repair the structure as the winter rains fell, and by January 20 much of the work had been completed. Carpenters finished up their work for the day and headed home. A few hours after they left, however, the gallant volunteer firefighters had been summoned to the hotel for the second time in two months, and once again performed a near miracle. The fire started in the basement stairwell, and was poised to spread quickly up the stairs to engulf all three floors. Because the fire was in the basement at the center of the vacant building, it could have raged beyond control before anyone spotted it in the middle of a gloomy night. Astonishingly, however, a passerby did see the flames and rang the fire bell. The volunteers arrived and had the blaze extinguished before it destroyed the building. Once again, it was easy to pinpoint where the fire started, but this time the volunteers were mystified as to how it started, finding no ignition source anywhere near the stairwell. Arson was presumed.

The mysterious origin of the fire soon paled in comparison to the mystery of young Mr. Roark, the hotel's manager maligned for his slow response when the first fire started in November. After the first fire, Roark moved to Portland, and in April 1915 he travelled to the Panama-Pacific International Exposition in San Francisco to represent several large West Coast hotels. The *News-Times* picks up the story from there, reporting that his ad sales were doing well at the expo and everything seemed normal, until one evening he told an associate that he suddenly had come into a large sum of money and had made arrangements to meet someone in Chinatown. As mysterious as this sounded, the associate let the matter drop, until the next morning, when his friend failed to show up at his expo booth. Hotel employees did not find Roark, but did find that he had left his suitcases and other personal effects in his room, as though he planned to return soon. Friends speculated immediately that he had been shanghaied in Chinatown, but with no evidence to support this speculation, the trail soon went cold and the mystery deepened. Perhaps coincidentally, next to the Page 1 story of Roark's disappearance, the *News-Times* ran another story reporting the completion of the Hotel Laughlin's renovation, noting the second fire and other troubles for the remaining owners as they rebuilt.

By late summer, Roark's friends had all but given up hope of ever seeing him again. But then, on September 9, L.O. Roark once again was the subject of a story on Page 1 of the *News-Times*. Roark had turned up safe, but not in San Francisco, nor in Portland nor in Forest Grove. He was in New York City, and his story now was spread across that city's newspapers in addition to the *News-Times*. What a story it was. It turns out, he said, that his friends' speculation from the day he disappeared was right on target, at least as far as he could remember. The first five days after his disappearance had, he explained, been lost to a combination of illness and a sharp blow to the head, which he suffered after being wrapped in a quilt by unknown assailants as he passed a dark alley in Chinatown back in April.

When he finally awoke, he said, he had no idea where he was, other than that he was on a ship. His large sum of money was gone, as were his clothes, replaced now by rags. After finally finding a member of the ship's crew who spoke English, Roark learned that he was aboard the Norwegian freighter *Callus*. When the ship's captain heard about the young man's presence aboard his ship he was furious and accused Roark of being a stowaway. So while Roark insisted that he had been shanghaied, he had not been taken to be used as forced labor as most such victims were. Instead he was on a ship whose crew wanted nothing to do with him.

A month later, Roark told New York reporters, the ship sailed into a mysterious port, where he was unceremoniously tossed onto the dock with no food or money. Unable to speak the strange language, he wandered the docks for days before learning that he was in Balboa, Peru. Finally, he had a chance encounter with the captain of an American vessel, the *Wilmerson*. The rugged sea captain did not believe Roark's story, either, but reluctantly agreed to let him work as his cabin boy on the *Wilmerson's* voyage to New York. Upon arrival in New York he learned that authorities there didn't believe him, either, and he was thrown into the brig. He was eventually released, however, and according to the *News-Times*, "his story is entirely credited by his friends in Portland and is published as authentic in the New York papers." The reporters at those papers did not know about the Hotel Laughlin or its recent fires back in remote Forest Grove, so they never asked Roark about any of that. The *News-Times* reporter, by contrast, did know about Roark's connection to the Laughlin, mentioning it in passing in the last paragraph of his lengthy story. So what, if anything, the bizarre saga of L.O. Roark had to do with the fires at the Hotel Laughlin has been lost to history. Lost, as well, is the storied hotel that survived not one but two major fires, only to fall victim to one intended for its demise. The fires at the Hotel Laughlin would not be the last in Forest Grove to involve both high drama and mystery, and they hastened previous efforts to mandate "fireproof" brick buildings in the downtown core, which was undergoing a building boom. After the second hotel fire in 1915, all downtown buildings were made of brick, and thus deemed "fireproof."

Any illusion that brick buildings were fireproof, however, disappeared less than four years later on the hot, dusty, windy afternoon of July 20, 1919, along Main Street, the site of the city's recent building boom. Many of these new buildings were made of brick and mortar, up-to-date with every fire code. Several had been built by the city's larger-than-life doctor, Charles Large, and one contained his office. Other new brick buildings on the block housed a range of businesses familiar to any rural western downtown, and some modern enterprises as well, such as Miss Belle Darling's photographic studio and gallery. Less than a block away was the site of what many considered to have been the city's most-devastating fire to date, the one that destroyed the Congregational Church, the legacy of city founders George Atkinson, Harvey Clarke, Tabitha Brown and others in 1901. A new, much grander church had risen in its place, but before the laws requiring the use of fireproof materials, so it was made entirely from wood. The church remained one of the city's most important social institutions, buzzing with activity throughout the week, but especially on Sunday mornings.

July 20, 1919, was a Sunday, and had the flames that were about to devastate the town started in the morning, the fire might have been spotted and stopped quickly. Unfortunately, the fire started about noon, which the *Washington County News-Times* lamented in its July 24 edition, was "an hour when the streets of the city were more nearly deserted than at any other time." Most churchgoers already were home by now, and the church's heavy hand in the governing of early Forest Grove made certain that Miss Darling and the other merchants were home as well. The missionaries who founded the church, and Pacific University, had deeded the land on which the city sat about 70 years before this "holocaust of flame," as the *News-Times* headline called it, with some very significant covenants, including enforcement of the "Blue Laws," which forbade the opening of stores and other businesses on Sunday. By noon, the streets of downtown Forest Grove were as close to deserted as they could get. Not entirely deserted, because some of the last to leave church still were leaving after cleaning up. In fact, one of the last to leave, Mrs. Ernest Brown, said she thought she saw wisps of smoke emanating from the back of O.M. Sanford's secondhand store across the street from her home, but dismissed it as the remnants of a fire in the woodstove and went on about her business. "Imagine her surprise," the *News-Times* story continued, "when H.W. Danielson knocked at the door and informed the family that the Sanford building was on fire ..."

Ernest Brown and H.W. Danielson leaped into action, breaking down the door of the Sanford building and lugging the roll-top desk, undoubtedly containing valuable business records, out of the now-blazing store. Mrs. Brown sprang into action as well, ordering her small son, Wendall, to mount his bicycle and spread the news to neighbors that a holocaust of flames was threatening their neighborhood. Acting on the instructions of his mother, little Wendall Brown pedaled furiously about town, and soon caught the eye of another of the town's doctor's, S.E. Todd. Dr. Todd listened to the little boy's harrowing tale and hastened to the fire bell several blocks away on Ash Street to summon the town's gallant volunteer firefighters.

As it happens, a few neighbors with the still rare telephone service already had heard little Wendall's cries for help and had called the operators at the exchange's office on Ash Street, next to the fire bell. A young T.M. VanDyke was at the telephone office, stopping on his way home from church to flirt with his girlfriend, one of the two teen-aged operators manning the switchboard on this sleepy Sunday afternoon. The two young operators had taken a couple of calls about the fire, but had been given no training on what to do in such an emergency. VanDyke lived on a rural farm and was unfamiliar with city customs, but leaped into action, racing the several blocks to where the callers said the fire was. He wrote about that day 55 years later in a history story for the *News-Times*. He confirmed that the second-hand store was indeed on fire. "I went back to the telephone office and told them what I saw, then went back to the fire." As he ran back to the fire the second time he heard Dr. Todd frantically ringing the fire bell, which stood next door to the telephone office. "Had I known," he recalled years later, "I could have rung that bell at least 15 minutes sooner."

By the time VanDyke saw the galloping horses approaching the scene pulling the fire cart, things were looking rough. The flames, he said, were 30 feet high. A brisk, dry wind was hurling embers toward the new downtown commercial buildings. Several of the older wooden buildings were by now goners, so the volunteers focused their efforts on stopping the holocaust's advance by turning their hoses on the Caples Building, built to fireproof standards and a certain firewall against further damage. The windows of the Caples Building exploded in the intense heat, but the structure held its ground. Unfortunately, while the small volunteer department assigned all of its resources to defending the Caples Building, embers had ignited Miss Belle Darling's photography studio. Even worse, the yard of the Copeland-McCready Lumber Company was now ablaze. The young telephone operators were in tears as their boss ran to the office and told them to call the Cornelius fire department, then in turn the Hillsboro fire department and finally every other department east for 30 miles, all the way to Portland. Had the Forest Grove fire been a few years earlier, Portland could not have responded, because it had no motorized pumpers. In fact, it did not have any motorized vehicles until 1910, Brian Johnson and Don Porth tell us in *Portland Fire & Rescue*, when the chief bought a car in which he could respond to fires, chauffeured by his personal driver. In 1919, the chief was leading his crews to the Forest Grove fire in his car when it collided with another at Seventh and Clay streets in Southeast Portland. The chief's car was demolished and he never made it to Washington County. In retrospect, the fact that any crews from the Portland Fire Bureau were able to scale the Tualatin Mountains with their primitive trucks and arrive in time to fight the flames that now engulfed Forest Grove pretty much tells the story of what happened on July 20, 1919.

The volunteers continued to spray water on the Caples Building and managed to save at least part of it. But the wind from the north blew embers from the fire to either side of the Caples Building, and once the Copeland-McCready lumberyard was involved, all bets were off. The windows of Charles Large's new fireproof brick buildings exploded in the intense heat. The buildings' fireproof bricks withstood the embers, but the wooden frames and wooden floors quickly succumbed. When the wooden frames collapsed, the bricks soon followed. Building after building erupted in flame, including the town's library. Crews poured every ounce of water they could muster on the beloved Congregational Church, but swirling embers soon entered the exploding windows of that structure as well. As crews watched helplessly, the church exploded in flames for the second time in 20 years. "When the fire burned the rope on the faithful old bell of the Congregational Church Sunday, it rang its own funeral knell," the *News-Times* story continued.

As it turns out, the fire of July 20, 1919, did not ring the death knell for the city. It did, however, leave some unanswered questions. For example, would volunteer firefighter F.W. Jones be reimbursed for his $12 bicycle, which he rode into the inferno to take the nozzle of a hose pointed at the Caples Building? As he valiantly tried to save the town he loved, the flames consumed his bicycle. When he asked the City Council to reimburse him, members just shrugged. The answer was clear: volunteer firefighters were on their own for losses they sustained while protecting others.

There was another much larger question that remained a mystery, however. How did this fire, one that burned 16 buildings, most of the downtown commercial district, start? Firefighters could not find a likely cause, although they knew that the mass destruction might have obliterated evidence of the origin. Within 24 hours, they were ready to chalk up the fire to unknown causes. But then an even bigger question emerged. Who, the town wondered, was the person who wrote an anonymous letter to a former mayor, claiming to have started the fire and threatening to strike again until the town was destroyed? Finding the answer to that question became much more urgent on the evening of October 22, three months after the conflagration.

Just before midnight, a night watchman at a warehouse storing the autumn's harvest of wheat from local farmers spotted a fire under a stairwell. Fast action from the volunteers kept the fire from spreading to the thousands of bushels of wheat, preventing a catastrophe, but nonetheless revealing an urgent problem. There was no doubt that this fire was arson. A week before Christmas yet another fire rocked downtown Forest Grove. The International Order of Odd Fellows had lost its new brick building in the July conflagration and was renting space above a grocery store. Just before the store opened on the morning of December 18, a fire erupted near the back door. Before firefighters arrived, the grocery store was engulfed in flames, and before the morning was over, the Odd Fellows had lost their second lodge in six months. An official cause never was established for this blaze, but many townspeople, still on edge from the two recent fires, were certain that it was arson.

The Forest Grove fire department never figured out exactly what, or who, caused any of these three fires in such rapid succession. The December fire in the grocery store was unsolved. The October fire at the wheat warehouse was minor, but the arsonist who set it obviously hoped for more damage. The July fire had left downtown Forest Grove in ruin. When Pacific University students returned to school that fall, the blocks across College Way from campus consisted of piles of rubble. Had it not been for the lush green lawn in front of Marsh Hall, the university might well have fallen victim to the flames as well, as the brisk wind had them headed toward campus.

The fires had a lasting impact on the city and on the way the fire department battles blazes in Forest Grove. The state fire marshal's office sent a team of experts to recommend ways to prevent and fight future fires. Some recommendations involved building codes. Ironically, in a town known for tough zoning ordinances concerning lawns and the outside appearance of homes and sheds, the city had yet to create ordinances concerning electric wiring, which was spreading through town. The fire marshal suggested that the city devise a set of suggestions for how these live power lines wrapped in cloth should be installed in the bone-dry wood frames of the city's homes and businesses. The team also urged the city to buy a fire truck to respond to fires.

The City Council considered these options, and Fire Chief Joseph G. Lenneville sprang into action. Rather than buy a truck, however, he found a good deal on a used Cadillac automobile and outfitted it to pull what had been a horse-drawn "chemical engine." A chemical engine consists of tanks to carry water and smaller tanks of acid and bicarbonate of soda, which when dumped into the water tanks creates a chemical reaction causing carbonation that forces the water through hoses to douse the fire. The technology was old, but new mechanical pumps were expensive and unreliable. Lenneville, whose day job was blacksmithing, saw no reason to buy a new pump, and used his skills to make the old chemical engine work with the used Cadillac. The new vehicle went into operation on Thursday, March 31, 1921, during what had been a welcomed lull in fire activity. The following Thursday, a Page 1 story in the *News-Times* explained what happened next. "Last week the *News-Times* expressed hope that Forest Grove's new firefighting apparatus would never be called into action. Vain hope! Ere the sun had set on the second day after the hope had been expressed, the boys were given a run." By the time the Cadillac arrived at the fire, neighbors had extinguished the flames, but Lenneville judged the run to have been a success. Just a few hours later, the fire bell again summoned.

"Sunday morning at about 3:20 when all the city was in the arms of Morpheus," the *News-Times* reported, "the fire bell sent in its clanging, terrorizing peals, clamoring through the stillness of the morning air." Rushing from their homes, volunteers knew that this call was for real, because tall flames were lighting up the sky. Less than three days after blacksmith Lenneville had finished work on his new motorized engine, it was being called into action to fight a fire raging inside one of the town's grocery stores. His "volunteer laddies," as the *News-Times* was fond of calling the firefighters, knew that the grocery store was a goner and followed Chief Lenneville's orders to concentrate on preventing the fire from spreading to the building next door. They did, and Chief Lenneville's blacksmith shop, where he had finished the fire engine days before, was saved from the flames.

Joe Lenneville's name does not often appear among those of famous Forest Grove pioneers, but like Joseph Gale, Tabitha Brown, Alvin Smith and others, he had crossed the Plains, albeit much later, arriving in Forest Grove in 1902. At each stop along the way, he added to

70

his credentials as a pioneering firefighter. In the 1880s paid, career firefighters were virtually nonexistent in the Northwest; even Portland relied on volunteers to fight the frequent fires that plagued the woodframe buildings heated by fire and lit by candlelight. Paid crews were more common on the East Coast and Midwest cities, such as Dubuque, Iowa, where at the tender age of 17, J.G. Lenneville signed on for a life of firefighting. Lenneville spent three years battling blazes along the banks of the mighty Mississippi River, until the call of the wild drove him westward.

Lenneville headed to the mining towns of North Dakota, not to strike it rich in the gold mines but rather to make a living as a blacksmith serving the gold trade. North Dakota did not yet have paid firefighters, but for the next nine years Lenneville volunteered with the departments in Bismarck, Mandan and Dickinson, before packing up and moving on to Forest Grove. When Lenneville hit town in 1902, the volunteer firefighters felt as though they had struck gold and within a few months elected the experienced firefighter to be their unpaid chief. The fire department had been an official branch of the city only since 1894, and had little equipment or training. Lenneville set to work to make the Forest Grove fire department a professional organization, developing formal training and drills for the volunteers.

As it happens, Lenneville arrived at a crucial time in Forest Grove history. About a year before he came, the Congregational Church burned to the ground. The fire was a defining moment in the city's history, not only for the loss of one of its most important buildings, but also for the loss of innocence the fire created in the peaceful, idyllic community. The fire started in the predawn hours of Saturday, July 13, 1901. How it started is a mystery, but the *Forest Grove Times* of July 18 adds some tantalizing details. It seems that the city was abuzz about the fire for a number of reasons, with speculation that the fire was arson, intended to destroy the church that controlled the city's tough religious laws, most specifically the citywide ban on alcohol. Although no cause was evident, many signs pointed to foul play. The first clue was that the church's bell was rigged to ring if fire cut its rope, but the alarm failed because the rope had been cut to silence the bell. When the first citizen to see the fire ran to the nearby First Christian Church to ring its bell, the department's official alarm, he found that bell wouldn't ring either. By the time people made it to the Methodist Church to ring its bell it probably already was too late, but the volunteers sprang from their beds and responded anyway. They pulled the chemical cart to the church and mixed the soda and acid, at which point any doubts of foul play were silenced. The chemicals created their explosive carbonation, but all the pressure was released through a safety valve, not through the hose. When the pressure was released sufficiently to unscrew the nozzle, the volunteers discovered that cloth had been stuffed into the hose, rendering it useless. The church was reduced to a pile of rubble. Why, the *Times* raged, was it necessary to burn a church in protest of liquor laws when spirits were available just over the city limits east of town, close enough that imbibers could stagger back to Forest Grove?

The arsonist never was caught, and for the next year and a half, Forest Grove returned to an uneasy peace. Most church and civic leaders urged peace, but a handful demanded retribution against those believed responsible for the church fire. Then, not long after midnight on the morning of March 1, 1903, Forest Grove residents again were awakened by a devastating fire. This time the flames were rising just across the city limits in the no-man's land between Forest Grove and Cornelius. Unlike the deeply pious founders of Forest Grove, Thomas Cornelius was a rough and tumble merchant, and his namesake city had an equally rough and tumble reputation for gambling and fights at its two saloons, both built at the edge of town within walking distance for imbibers from dry Forest Grove. On this chilly, foggy pre-dawn morning of March 1, both saloons burst into flames. Cornelius had gambling and drinking, but no fire department, and the two buildings were reduced to smoldering ashes in no time. No one questioned the origin of these fires. Arson was the cause. Obeying the law, Lenneville, elected chief just two months earlier, and his volunteer fire laddies had not crossed the city limits to fight the fire. Sitting idly by while tragedy struck, however, rankled the chief and rekindled his pioneer spirit.

That spirit was evident two years later on the afternoon of August 31, 1905, when a huge column of smoke rose in the sky south of Forest Grove from the unincorporated village of Dilley. Dilley had a busy railroad depot, a huge hay warehouse, another warehouse that stored firewood for the railroad, and several committed civic leaders, including Harald Hansen. Like Cornelius, however, it did not have a fire department. The lack of a fire department was a problem on this sizzling, dry afternoon of August 31, because the railroad's warehouse with its more than 400 cords of Douglas fir was on fire. Harald Hansen summoned his threshing crews from the fields and organized every able-bodied person in town to form bucket brigades. Some citizens pumped the handles of wells as others passed pails of water from hand to hand toward the now raging inferno, which was about to spread to the hay warehouse, train depot and the town's store. From there it would be a quick jump across the street now known as Bantam Avenue to Hansen's home, now site of the semi-annual Storybook Lane Christmas show. As hard as the bucket brigade worked, things looked grim ... until the horse-drawn chariots of the Forest Grove fire department descended from the north, defying formal restrictions against crossing city limits. This time Chief Lenneville and his boys had decided to take the law into their own hands. Soon the cordwood warehouse was toast, but the rest of Dilley was saved.

Lenneville served as chief for more than 20 years after the Dilley fire, presiding over many other historic blazes, but his legacy as a pioneer in the field of firefighting was sealed at the 1905 Dilley inferno. When the state fire marshal sent in a crew to investigate the 1919 fire that wiped out much of downtown, he was struck by Lenneville's devotion to serving those outside Forest Grove's city limits. In his 1922 opinion, the ensuing report urged the city to purchase a second chemical engine, his suggestion based on how often Forest Grove's engine was outside the city helping people in the unincorporated portions of Washington County. "It is only fair and just that the country population should have a large part in the purchase of this engine," the fire marshal said. Four years later, rural farmers in Dilley and elsewhere voted to form the Forest Grove Rural Fire Protection District, contracting with the city for protection. Twenty years would pass before many other rural communities would follow Forest Grove's lead in establishing rural fire districts. Joe Lenneville spread his firefighting knowledge from Iowa to North Dakota to Forest Grove, so spreading it to Dilley, Banks, Gaston, Gales Creek and beyond was only natural.

Lenneville was a tough act to follow when he resigned suddenly in March 1925, after nearly a quarter century as chief. For the next few years several men held the title of Chief for a few months or so, until in

December 1928 Walter Vandervelden was elected chief. For a few weeks, Vandervelden enjoyed a quiet start to his long career, but all that changed at about 3:30 on the morning of Sunday, January 13, 1929.

Vandervelden was jolted from his sleep by a phone call from a friend who had heard what he thought was an explosion at the Farmer's Feed and Supply warehouse, one of several rundown buildings that filled the block bounded by Main and Council streets and what are now Nineteenth and Pacific avenues, directly adjoining the downtown business district only recently rebuilt from the catastrophic 1919 fire. While the groggy Vandervelden was on the phone, he heard the piercing sound of the fire siren. He pulled on his clothes and set out on his first call as the volunteer chief of the 17-member department, 14 of whom had by now heard the siren and headed to the scene.

When they got there in the frigid morning air, flames were shooting through the roof of the feed warehouse. Looking into the windows of the adjoining transfer and storage company and a woodworking factory, the volunteers could see flames already spreading inside those structures as well. Within minutes an entire city block was ablaze, and for the second time in less than 10 years, Forest Grove's downtown was threatened with destruction. Realizing quickly that the three rickety wood-frame buildings were a lost cause, Vandervelden told his men to direct every ounce of energy and water they could muster into preventing the fire from crossing the street into the business district. As flames lit the night sky, the *News-Times* reported, Vandervelden was stunned to see a well-known local minister, Arthur Stook, race into the blazing storage warehouse, emerging moments later carrying a box, which Vandervelden learned contained all of the records of historic Forest View Cemetery.

The volunteers struggled in temperatures so cold that their hoses froze to the street despite the intense heat from the fire. Before the flames consumed the power and telephone lines, an operator was able to call the county seat of Hillsboro for help. As the lines snapped, the entire city was plunged into darkness. Vandervelden was receiving, as the *News-Times* reporter put it, a "baptism of fire ... his initiation was strenuous and a real test of his ability as a leader." It took nearly half an hour for help to arrive from Hillsboro, and by the time that city's firefighters arrived the streets were blanketed in a thick coat of ice as water from the hoses froze on contact with the frigid ground, and windows of buildings in the business district were exploding from the intense heat. The arrival of the Hillsboro department turned the tide, however, and the flames were kept to the one square block. Fueled by the hay, paper, gasoline and wood stored in the three warehouses, the stubborn fire was not entirely extinguished for nearly 10 hours. By then, the *News-Times* reported, the ranks of Vandervelden's volunteer crew had been drained, with nearly every man either injured or suffering from exhaustion. The new chief had survived his baptism by fire, however, and apparently passed this test of his ability as a leader.

Vandervelden's skills were put to the test again just six months later on July 17. By 1929, Forest Grove was in the middle of its daffodil mania and had rebuilt its downtown from the 1919 fire. The new buildings had been built under strict new codes as a result of that fire, including the use of brick firewalls. The town's new hotspot, the Daffodil Lunch Room, was not in one of these new buildings, however. While it had a brick façade, the rest of the building was made of wood. When the Daffodil caught fire just after midnight on July 17, its old wooden frame erupted in an inferno that once again threatened to destroy much of downtown, including its neighbors on Pacific Avenue, the Star Theater on one side and the town's hardware store with its volatile stock of solvents and other flammable chemicals on the other side. For more than an hour, the volunteers battled the stubborn fire, hampered by a false ceiling that made getting to the flames difficult. In the end, the town's tough new fire codes had passed their first real test. The brick firewalls of the hardware store and theater had confined the blaze to the Daffodil, of which only its brick façade remained. Vandervelden passed this latest test of his abilities as well, but his first year as chief would offer even bigger challenges before it was over. By the end of August he had endured perhaps the roughest year of what would be a 35-year career.

The lead paragraph at the top of the August 22, 1929, edition of the *News-Times* tells part of the tale: "A bandsaw and edger supported in thin air by charred timbers above a smouldering mass of ashes and debris was all that remained this morning of the main building of the Carnation Lumber Company after a disastrous $35,000 fire last night."

As firefighters in a timber town, the volunteers were no strangers to fires in lumber mills. In fact, they had been to one at the Carnation mill just three days earlier, but wrestled that one under control with little damage. This fire was different, started as it was by a millworker's worst nightmare, the miasma of sawdust that hovers in the air. When enough sawdust collects in an enclosed building, it can become as explosive as flammable gas. By 9 p.m. August 21, there was about as much dust in the air as you would ever find at the Carnation mill. Nearing the end of the day's second shift, the saws had been kicking up dust for more than 12 hours straight, running at full speed to meet the needs of a building boom in Roaring Twenties America. At about 9 p.m., the breakneck workload proved too much for a large pulley and its metal belt, which snapped under the strain. When the resulting sparks ignited the cloud of sawdust it created an explosion that blew the half-ton pulley wheel through an exterior wall. A worker told the *News-Times* that the massive edger, a machine weighing several tons, was lifted into the air by the force of the explosion. The fireball badly burned one of the workers, but amazingly he was pulled to safety and all of the other employees escaped with only minor burns and bumps and bruises from being tossed about.

By the time Vandervelden and his men arrived, the fireball had long since destroyed the six-month-old building, and with it the jobs of one of the area's largest employers. But the volunteers still had their work cut out for them. The mill yard was full of stacked, dried lumber, which could have burned for days had it fully ignited. A train sat on a siding inches from the building, half loaded with timber and railroad ties to be shipped the next day. Forest Grove firefighters were joined by colleagues from Cornelius and Hillsboro as crew after crew raced to the brewing disaster. They managed to keep the fires in the lumberyard under control, but the train cars soon were engulfed in flames that by now were threatening Carnation's smaller planing mill, the Bagstadt Brothers fuel company garage filled with five trucks and stacks of firewood, and the home of Mrs. L.F. Bouthillier.

C.M Bagstadt saw the flames and arrived with two of his employees in time to drive his five trucks, three of them filled with heavy cargoes of wood, out of the garage and, they hoped, out of the reach of the fire. Meanwhile, firefighters focused much of their effort on saving the Bouthillier home as the fire raged well past midnight. When the flames were extinguished and the sun rose the next morning, Chief Vandervelden and the mill's owner, Waldo Raines, surveyed the damage. Besides the main mill, the inferno had claimed six railcars, even melting some of the metal.

Mrs. Bouthillier's home had been spared, as had the planing mill. The Bagstadt trucks survived as well, but the garage and all of its contents were nothing but ashes. As the two men walked through the lumberyard, which had survived remarkably unscathed, they looked for the pulley wheel that had been blown through the wall. At four feet in diameter and weighing 1,000 pounds, it should have been easy to spot, but what they found instead were just twisted shards of metal strewn among the lumber. Vandervelden also had to consider the toll this fire had taken on his volunteers. They had spent all of Wednesday night fighting one of the worst fires in city history. To make matters worse, they had just spent much of Tuesday battling a wildland fire near Gaston, only to be called out again on Tuesday night to a fire in the remote village of Cherry Grove. Before they were done with that fire early Wednesday morning, the flames had consumed a house, a woodshed and a small barn.

Vandervelden's second year as chief was marked by three fires that together tell one of the darker times in Forest Grove history. The city was built by religious missionaries and educators, and strict laws kept it a quiet, peaceful place to live. Against that backdrop, the events of November 1930 seemed out of place in Forest Grove. Just about midnight on November 20, with Thanksgiving just one week away, neighbors in the small farming community of Hillside saw flames coming from the farm of Clifford Thompson, who had moved to the town of Banks and was now ready to rent out his vacant farmhouse and barns. By the time Vandervelden arrived, the house had been consumed by fire, and flames were coming from a barn a good distance from the home. Turning their hoses on the barn, firefighters managed to save it with relatively little damage. It didn't take Vandervelden long to answer the two questions this fire posed: How did the vacant house catch on fire, and how did the fire spread to the barn? The answer was obvious, because the remains of the house reeked of gasoline, and the inside of the barn was covered with accelerants that for some reason had not ignited. In reality, Vandervelden would have guessed that this was arson even without those clues.

On Thanksgiving Day, the *News-Times* laid out the story and came to a startling conclusion. It seems that a few weeks before the fire at the Thompson place, flames had consumed another nearby vacant farmhouse and barn. Although he suspected arson, Vandervelden didn't find enough clues at the earlier fire to confirm it in that case. But then a few days after the Thompson house fire, crews were called to another raging middle-of-the-night barn fire in the same area. This time the farmhouse was occupied by its owner, Karl Schaefer, and was untouched. The fire, however, consumed not one but two of his large barns, which also were occupied, one with horses and one with cattle. This time Vandervelden was certain that arson was the cause. First, someone had released the livestock into the field. Second, the rubble smelled of gasoline. Third, Schaefer had a pretty good hunch about why he was targeted; he had just rented much of his acreage to Japanese berry farmers and he knew that some neighbors were unhappy with him for doing so. Vandervelden called in veteran Washington County Sheriff John Connell, but Connell dismissed Schaefer's concerns.

But when the *News-Times* talked to Clifford Thompson about this latest fire, he told the reporter that he, too, had just rented the farm to Japanese berry farmers. The vacant farm in the first of the arsons had been for rent, although the owner said he had not found a tenant at the time of the fire. Still, the *News-Times* uncovered racial animosity in the Hillside area, not far from where in 1923 the Ku Klux Klan had held its state convention, which featured a 70-foot-tall cross, illuminated by electric lights instead of flames. The recent influx of Japanese farmers had rekindled animosity, and the editors concluded that racism was indeed the cause of the arson spree. By now Connell agreed, but there's no record that any arrest was ever made. Regardless, the string of Hillside arsons ended at three, and the Japanese farmers went on growing berries, at least for 10 years, when they were sent to internment camps after Pearl Harbor was attacked at the start of World War II.

After 1930, fires in Forest Grove became less political and for the most part less tragic. New building codes helped to dramatically reduce structure fires over the years, but no city can ever afford to become complacent when it comes to fire. Building codes from the 1920s and 1930s required brick firewalls between downtown buildings. Many downtown buildings had such firewalls because they were built to replace ones lost in the infernos of 1919 and 1929, but other blocks built in the Nineteenth Century still remained, untouched by fire. One such block was the west side of Main Street south of Pacific Avenue. Two of the town's most important food stores stood on that block, in buildings dating back decades. Grocers Sid Hardy and Fred Kuenzi were friendly rivals, sometimes sharing supplies with each other. Their stores shared something else in 1948: A common wall that was not fire-resistant.

Early in the morning of Sunday, December 19, 1948, a small fire started in the back of Kuenzi's store. It burned slowly enough at first that employees were able to get to the store and save merchandise from the fire, although those efforts ended when the roof collapsed, injuring one of the employees. The stubborn blaze soon spread next door to Hardy's market, and Forest Grove Fire Chief Walter Vandervelden issued a call for help from Gaston, Hillsboro and as far away as Beaverton, fearing that the flames would engulf an entire block of warehouses and offices, just as in his "baptism by fire" 19 years earlier on the other side of Main Street. This time would be different, however.

The side by side grocery stores sent smoke into the sky that could be seen for miles as the sun rose. Owners of other buildings in the block frantically pulled valuables into the street to save them from the spreading fire. By the time the fire was out, it had become the costliest in Forest Grove history, as long as one didn't adjust for inflation. Yet as the embers cooled, it became apparent that the lessons learned in the 1919 and 1929 fires had paid off. Except for the two groceries, all the adjoining buildings had been constructed under stricter building codes, and all had firewalls that stopped the flames from spreading beyond the two stores.

If the 1930s started a trend toward fewer commercial structure fires, however, the opposite was true in the case of wildland fires, which became more common and more destructive as illustrated by the Tillamook Burns in 1933, 1939, 1945 and 1951. But after 1951, wildland fires became tamer as well, and Forest Grove, along with the rest of the nation, was riding a wave of post-war prosperity. The post-war boom fueled a homebuilding frenzy of suburban development that had Forest Grove mills churning out lumber at a pace not seen for 23 years; not since 1929 when the Carnation mill exploded in flames while trying to meet demand.

On August 21, 1952, exactly 23 years since the fire that destroyed the Carnation mill, the city again was under tight fire restrictions because of hot, dry weather. Logging operations were curtailed, but the Carnation mill was churning out lumber at full strength, just as it was on August 21,

1929. In 1952, the frenzied activity inside the mill created a cloud of sawdust in the air, and on August 21, 1952, exactly 23 years since the last great Carnation mill fire, a spark ignited the dust. Suspended fine-particulate sawdust was every bit as flammable in 1952 as it was in 1929, and the spark created an explosion. The resulting inferno was Page 1 news in *The Oregonian* and other newspapers. A Page 1 story in the *News-Times* focused on the personal, pointing out that while the 1929 fire was one of Vandervelden's first as chief, the 1952 inferno was the first major fire that Vandervelden ever had missed in his 23 years at the helm, because he was confined to a hospital bed after an emergency appendectomy. Despite his condition, Vandervelden eagerly waited for his colleagues to deliver word of the incident along with some much-anticipated cigarettes. "The veteran fire-eater got his information," the paper reported.

The fire had eerie similarities to the 1929 blaze. Just as in 1929, the main mill was leveled, and just as in 1929, the flames claimed the nearby fuel company plant and its supply of firewood, but spared Carnation's planing mill. Fortunately no one was injured in the 1952 fire, but in other ways the damage was even worse. The flames consumed more of the lumber yard than the 1929 fire, and this time the flames spread to an adjoining 600-acre barley farm; with engine crews from Forest Grove, Gaston, Cornelius and Hillsboro tied up fighting the structure fire, the mill's 65 employees went to work in the barley field and kept the damage to about three acres, *The Oregonian* reported. The financial impact on the employees was softened compared with 1929, because by now unemployment insurance helped cushion the short-term pain. In other ways, however, the economic pain this time was even greater than in 1929. In 1952, Carnation was the second-largest mill in Washington County, behind only the mammoth Stimson operation in Gaston. Another major Forest Grove mill, owned by Larkins Lumber, had burned the previous year, and the dramatic loss in production capacity caused by the two fires seriously damaged the local timber industry. Many timber firms had to shift their supply of logs to mills in Canada, raising shipping costs and depressing prices for the raw logs. Carnation's owners, Ralph Raines and the widow of his father, Waldo, debated whether to rebuild, but within months began construction of a new mill, this one made from steel instead of wood. Within months, however, Waldo's widow, Bertha Channel, decided she wanted out of the lumber business and sold her

80

interest to logger Axel Erickson. Erickson and Raines struggled to rebuild the company, but this time market forces were against them. Just as things were beginning to return to normal, the region's millworkers walked out on strike. For Raines and Erickson, the strike was the last straw, and they put the mill up for sale to concentrate all of their efforts on their logging operations.

They didn't have to wait long for a buyer. On June 15, 1954, a shift was ending at the Gales Peak Lumber Company, another large Forest Grove mill, when a spark ignited the wood dust hanging thick in the air. Favorable winds blew flames away from the finishing end of the mill, but damages were devastating nonetheless. As the millworkers' strike began, Gales Peak owner Fred Paget kept his union employees on the payroll to rebuild the mill, but when the nearly new Carnation plant came on the market, he decided to buy it as well. Paget also had bought the loyalty of his employees by paying them through the strike. He offered his employees and the union members at the Carnation mill a five-cent per hour raise and agreed to raise their pay again if unions at the other mills settled for more. The workers jumped at the offer, and while Stimson and most of the other mills remained closed, the Carnation mill roared back to life once again, although not for long. In 1957, Paget found the Carnation site too big to handle and closed it, eventually selling it to a consortium of local timber industry veterans. Paget kept his old fire-damaged Gales Peak mill and rebuilt it. One year later, on October 1, 1958, Paget was awakened by a call a little after 3 a.m. His mill was engulfed in flames, believed to have started when a transient's warming fire got out of control.

The 1950s were a time of dramatic changes in American society, and in Forest Grove, many of those changes can be told through the fire department. The post-war boom had created a frenzy of suburban development, with houses, roads and shopping centers rising at an astonishing pace. Better roads meant that Forest Grove residents could take high-paying jobs in Portland. Shopping centers pulled retail customers out of downtown in favor of bigger, more-modern stores with large parking lots. Since its beginning in the 1890s, the Forest Grove fire department had been all volunteer, relying on men who lived and worked in and around downtown. Many owned their own businesses and could respond from work during the day or from home on evenings and weekends. But as the downtown stores closed and more men took jobs in Portland, Chief Walter Vandervelden found it increasingly difficult to round up crews on weekdays. In 1954, the city decided to solve the problem by hiring its first paid firefighters. About 75 years after Joe Lenneville left his paid firefighting job in Iowa to serve Forest Grove as a volunteer, Forest Grove finally would have a paid chief. Naturally, the man chosen for the job was Walter Vandervelden, who in turn hired two other volunteers, including his son, Ray. The three men would work from 7:30 a.m. to 5:30 p.m. Monday through Friday while the other volunteers were away at their jobs. This was before fire departments responded to medical calls and there weren't nearly enough fires to keep the men busy all the time, so their job descriptions also included such things as repairing the city's police cars, emptying parking meters and doing janitorial work at City Hall.

City residents agreed to the tax hike necessary to hire the crew in large part hoping to reduce fire insurance premiums, which were much higher than in most similar cities in part because there were no paid firefighters. Other factors also played a part in the high cost of insurance, however, and nearly all of them came into play on the night of April 15, 1953. A local homebuilder was constructing a warehouse for his company on the edge of town. In fact, according to a story in the April 23 *News-Times*, he had been constructing the building for seven years. He would get some work done, then run out of money or materials and let it sit idle for months at a time, falling into disrepair. The building had become a landmark of sorts with its mismatched doors and windows and plywood signs proclaiming the owner's evangelical religious beliefs. Finally in 1953, the city inspected the building and found numerous fire and building code violations. So many, in fact, that the builder was ordered to tear down the unfinished warehouse. He refused, and was fighting City Hall as the sun rose on Wednesday, April 15. A little after 10 that evening, a motorist flagged down the city's night police officer, Phil Wessels, and told him there appeared to be smoke coming from a building on the edge of town. Wessels sped to the scene to investigate, and found flames now coming from the builder's unfinished warehouse. With no dispatcher on duty and with no fire radios with which to rouse the volunteers, Wessels had no choice but to drive to the nearest fire alarm, which in 1953 was Forest Grove's *only* fire alarm, downtown at the fire station. By the time he got to the station, rang the alarm, and waited for volunteers to show up to tell them where the fire was, there wasn't much of the warehouse left to save. When the volunteers arrived, the building's angry owner was on scene to watch their futile efforts to save his building. The next day, he complained to the *News-Times* that the volunteers "didn't try very hard" to extinguish the fire, and threatened to sue the city for the cost of his uninsured warehouse. Portland resident Ivan Lehaie, who lived near the ramshackle building at the time of the fire, remembers that "the fire department didn't get there real fast, but no one was too sorry to see that old building go."

Many of the fire department's woes dragged on for another decade, but by 1963 Forest Grove's property owners finally got a little relief in their premiums when the insurance industry's rating service bumped the city's rating from 6 to 5. The business community still was not happy, but Vandervelden told them that the cost of additional fire alarms was prohibitive and that the shortage of volunteers was only getting worse, pointing out that the vast majority of downtown workers were now women. Hugh McGilvra, crusading owner of the *News-Times*, asked Vandervelden why he didn't recruit some of those women to be volunteers, but he reported that Vandervelden greeted his suggestion with a chuckle. "'We've never seriously considered it,' he added, nor does he expect to." Vandervelden did admit, however, that "a short little Irish woman has been chief for years" in a California town he couldn't name. Society was changing, but changes come slowly to fire departments. A few months later Vandervelden announced his retirement for the third time since taking the reins 35 years earlier. This time he was serious, and his long career came to an end at age 68. Vandervelden presided over many changes in his decades as chief, but he retired just a few years before revolutionary advancements that would shape the Forest Grove fire department as it exists today. Those changes would include the introduction of the 9-1-1 emergency system in the late 1970s and the introduction of medical calls in 1970, which today comprise the vast majority of the department's calls.

But while the number of fires has been in steep decline since the Vandervelden era, flames have continued to change the face of Forest Grove. One of the first major blazes for Vandervelden's successors came about noon on Tuesday, November 4, 1969, in a place very familiar to

Walter Vandervelden for a number of reasons. The fire started near the boiler of an apartment building owned by Walter's brother, Joe, who owned many of the apartment units in the college town. Joe Vandervelden had owned this particular building for only a few years, but had made major upgrades to the 1904 structure, which he called the Colonial Apartments. One thing he had not upgraded, however, was its ancient steam furnace, which was fueled by sawdust, which was in abundant supply from the building's neighbor, the Forest Grove Lumber Company mill. Forest Grove Lumber operated the old Carnation Lumber mill built by Ralph Raines after the devastating 1952 fire. In fact, the Colonial Apartments had been built originally as the Carnation Hotel, but the building wasn't named for the lumber company. Instead, it was named for the company that occupied the site before the mill, the Carnation Evaporated Milk Company. Evaporated milk, or "condensed" milk as it's called when sugar is added to inhibit bacteria, once was Forest Grove's major industry after Joseph Gaston's railroad helped other towns capture most of the timber trade. The process of condensing milk was developed in Carnation, Washington, in 1899 and revolutionized the milk industry. Before electricity and refrigeration, storing milk was very difficult. People without cows of their own had to buy fresh milk daily. The Carnation Company, however, figured out a way to heat milk, removing much of the water and reducing pathogens, and canning it so that it could be shipped and stored without refrigeration. Cities throughout the country quickly lined up, asking the Carnation company to build plants in their cities. Forest Grove was one of the first to have its request granted, although the condenser ended up being built outside of town near the railroad that bypassed the city, on what today is Elm Street, just south of Oregon Highway 47.

At the dawn of the Twentieth Century, the area around the railroad depot became known as "Carnation," and started to take shape as its own city. One of the first additions was the Carnation Hotel, as large and elegant as Forest Grove's prized Hotel Laughlin. Unfortunately for Carnation and Forest Grove, the Condensed Milk Bubble soon burst. The Carnation company overbuilt, the market was flooded with competitors including Borden, and then electric refrigerators became common. Forest Grove's Carnation plant, one of the first to open, became an early victim of the bursting bubble. Within a few years Edward Haines built his

84

electric trolley line from the station to downtown, and then the new-fangled automobiles came into vogue and railroad passenger traffic plummeted. The town of Carnation shriveled, and no longer needed a hotel.

One thing a college town always needs, however, is apartments, and the Carnation Hotel became long-term rentals for older students, a role the building served until about noon on April 15, 1969, when the ancient sawdust-burning boiler ignited into flames. Crews from Forest Grove were joined by an engine from Gaston, but the old wooden building kept burning. Fire Chief Justin George called a second alarm, then a third and then a fourth. Soon every department in Washington County had crews at the fire, but hours later as darkness fell, flames still were visible from a mile away. Fire crews spent most of their effort dousing fires started by falling embers in the Forest Grove Lumber Company yard, and somehow managed to prevent the damage from spreading. Ten hours later, Joe Vandervelden surveyed the rubble, comforted only by the fact that all of the tenants were accounted for, and all were uninjured. Ten years after the Hotel Laughlin was torched intentionally, Forest Grove's other once-grand hotel was a pile of ashes.

As the 1970s began, it looked as if political arson might return to Forest Grove, when on June 18, 1970, the old Lincoln Junior High School succumbed to flames. The school had been abandoned two years earlier and sold to Pacific University for a planned expansion. The spectacular fire that destroyed the building clearly was caused by arson, but investigators had no clear motive. The motive turned out to be boredom when a 15-year-old boy was arrested for the pointless crime.

Forest Grove firefighters spent the rest of the decade acclimating themselves to their new job of making medical housecalls, and things stayed mostly quiet on the fire front, except for 1975, when a rash of fires scarred downtown in a way not seen since 1919. On March 27 Pacific University's stately Marsh Hall went up in flames. On October 11 the Burlingham Seed and Feed warehouse on Ash Street succumbed, clearing land for the current Forest Grove fire station. Then on December 3, the Copeland Lumber Company, which had survived the 1919 fire, burned to the ground. Unlike the 1919 downtown fire, none of the 1975 infernos were suspicious; downtown Forest Grove simply had fallen victim to bad luck.

After the flurry of fires in 1975, Forest Grove again enjoyed a lull in major fires. On July 14, 1982, the *News-Times* ran a story about the city's new pumper and ladder truck, specifically designed to fight the large commercial fires that were becoming increasingly rare. The department scheduled training for the new equipment, hoping that it might not be needed for months or even years. Just after 6 that evening, an alarm sounded for a fire along Pacific Avenue. One of the downtown area's remaining wood-frame buildings, once a livery stable but now home to Floyd's Music Center, was ablaze. The new ladder truck was called into action. Soon it became apparent that more than a new truck would be needed for this fire, and at 6:54 a second alarm was sounded. The fire continued to spread to the adjoining Forest Grove Shoe Store and Ballad Town Café. By 7:17 flames were threatening City Hall, separated from the burning buildings by only a 10-foot-wide alley, and a third alarm was called. By now responding crews from throughout the county could see the dense smoke as they rolled out the bay doors of their distant stations. Meanwhile, the police called in reinforcements as well, and more than 30 county deputies, reserves and Explorer scouts responded to keep a crowd estimated at 1,500 people away from the scene. A natural gas company employee who lived nearby struggled to cut off gas to the buildings, but not before an explosion blew the front off of one of the stores, sending bricks flying into the street and at firefighters. At 7:54 a fourth building was involved and a fourth alarm was called. The crowd had never witnessed a fire of this magnitude, which City Manager Connie Fessler called "probably the worst fire the city's ever had in the downtown area."

When the smoke cleared it was obvious that her assessment was a bit overblown, at least compared with the 1919 downtown blaze. Nonetheless, the fire was a reminder to a new generation of the scars that fires can leave on a town. In the case of the 1982 fire, the most visible scar is a parking lot where an historic building once stood. Many Forest Grove residents are unaware of the many other scars around town, including empty industrial buildings where grand hotels once stood, even bare ground where once the fledgling town of Carnation thrived. An entire industry is gone; while economic issues bear much of the blame for the demise of the city's lumber mills, the sad fact is that the death knell for most was fire.

Forest Grove has survived many trials by fire over the years, each time emerging stronger than before. The fire department, which for most of its history was an all-volunteer force that responded only to fires, now is staffed round the clock by highly trained paid crews, including women on most shifts, who spend most of their time responding to medical calls, including many at one of Forest Grove's newest growth industries, retirement communities. They do not, however, have to empty parking meters or sweep City Hall.

Chapter

7

Trial by jury

Forest Grove's history is full of people walking to Forest Grove. Take, for example, Tabitha Brown, the town's first teacher, or Harvey Scott, Pacific University's first graduate. In fact, most of the good people who arrived in the 1840s walked for much of their journey.

On the other hand, the city's history of crime and intrigue is full of people who walked, or ran, or even bicycled away from Forest Grove. Most of the miscreants were chased down and caught, but some of the missing simply walked into oblivion, with their fates left to gossip and rumor.

Edward Austin thought he could victimize his own elderly mother and just stick around town. When his widowed mother decided in 1904 that she was too old to care for her farm anymore, she sold it for $4,000, a princely sum at a time when a dollar a day was considered good wages. She offered to split the proceeds with Edward, and asked him to walk into town and deposit the check into her account. He walked into town, but decided to keep all of the money for himself. Friends helped Edward's mother file a lawsuit against him, and when word leaked out about what he had done, he was not a very popular man about town. Instead of answering the suit, he just walked away. Newspapers printed urgent appeals for help tracking him down, but it seems that Edward Austin had unwittingly picked a good day to skip town without being followed, because as news of his disappearance was announced, the county was reeling from the most-sensational murder since newspaper presses came to town about 50 years earlier. In fact the dying victim had taken his case directly to the newspapers, stumbling into the offices of the Hillsboro *Argus* before expiring. That gave the *Argus* a scoop, but Forest Grove's *News* was all over the story as well, bumping its Edward Austin story to make room for this tale of sex, sisters, false identities and a bumbling escape from justice.

The story involved a man named Frank Bennett and another named Bert Oakman. The two men were roommates, who started dating a pair of sisters, Alta and Vesta Leadford. Bennett and the Leadford sisters were well-known and respected in Forest Grove and Hillsboro, but little was known about Oakman, who had ventured into town from Monmouth, Illinois, only a few months earlier. Things soon got serious between the men and their respective sweethearts, with talk of marriage. But then Bennett learned a little bit more about Oakman's past back in Monmouth, Illinois, including the fact that Oakman's wife and child were still living there. Bennett shared this tidbit with his half of the sister sweethearts, Vesta, who in turn told Alta and their father. When Oakman came a calling on the Leadford house that night he was politely asked to leave, although just how politely is left to the imagination. Being a Saturday night, Oakman knew just where to find Bennett. Forest Grove was a dry town, but Hillsboro was a wide-open saloon town, and Oakman and Bennett favored the one owned by Preston Southworth. Oakman went through the doors of Southworth's saloon and politely asked Bennett to step outside, although once again just how politely is left to the imagination. Bennett, the *News* reported, let Oakman cool his heels outside while he finished his beer with his brother and some local friends. When he finally stepped through the saloon's back door, Oakman swung twice. The knife he was holding severed Bennett's jugular vein, but Bennett had just enough strength to stagger next door to the *Argus*, where editors were still at work. "Oakman has stabbed me" were his last words. The ensuing search was called the largest to date in Washington County, which was rocked by the news of the brazen crime. The name Bert

Oakman was spread across papers from Forest Grove to Portland as the manhunt spread.

Oakman related his own story to the *News* the following week after he was found working for a dollar a day under an assumed name at a fish cannery on the Columbia River. He said that after he killed Bennett, he rode his bicycle to the edge of town, then slept on the hay of a stranger's barn. The next morning, the desperate killer hopped on his bicycle again and pedaled furiously toward Portland, where he hoped to plan his escape. About three miles outside of town he was flagged down by a Dr. Linklater. Oakman recognized the man because he had visited the doctor as a patient. Apparently the doctor didn't recognize the bicyclist, however, because he asked if Oakman had seen a fellow by the name of Bert Oakman. When Oakman asked why, the doctor replied "Murder. He killed young Bennett last night." "That staggered me," Oakman told the *News* reporter, "I did not dare show him I was the man and kept talking to him, perhaps 10 minutes." Oakman rode on, but as he pedaled he began to think that if the good doctor had recognized him, the police would be looking for a man on a bicycle, so "I threw my wheel into the brush and started to walk to Portland." Once there, he realized that "I did not have a cent. I crossed the Steel Bridge and walked on and on." He planned to follow the Columbia River home to Illinois in a perverse reverse journey on the Oregon Trail. But there's an adage of the Old West that says a wanted man won't get far on foot, and Oakman managed to make it only another 30 miles to the cannery, where he took a job for a dollar a day. After a few days, the cannery owner was impressed enough to offer him a raise to $1.05 a day, but then the owner saw a wanted poster and realized that the man he had just offered a raise bore a striking resemblance to the killer and notified police. Back on the Tualatin Plains, Frank Bennett was buried. His friends and family had carefully kept word of his death from his mother, who lay on her deathbed. The funeral proceeded without her, but when she finally heard about the murder she rallied and mustered the strength to testify against Bert Oakman two months later at his trial, where he was sent to prison for life. Meanwhile, amid all the hoopla over Oakman's trial, the *Forest Grove Press* reported that the Edward Austin case had a happier ending, when Austin quietly slipped back into town and deposited every cent of his mother's money into her bank account.

As Forest Grove entered the 1900s, murders still were a rarity, although some people argued that they were more common than the number of convictions would indicate. Sherlock Holmes was all the rage at the turn of the century, but the reality is that cracking some murder cases in the rural West still was anything but elementary; even fingerprints were not used in forensics as the 1900s began. The public and press often suspected foul play in cases that authorities chalked up to accident or suicide. In fact, a single issue of the *Forest Grove Times*, dated November 28, 1901, carried stories about two such cases, or more precisely, four such cases linked to two, and ultimately three, men. The first man was a farmer named John Lang, whose body was found in his home by a friend. Police called the county coroner, Forest Grove physician W.P. Via, and told him that the death was clearly from natural causes and that there was no need for him to come to the scene. About an hour later they called back and told the doctor that they had found evidence to suggest that Lang's death might not be what it seemed. First, when they turned over his body, they discovered that Lang's throat had been slashed, deeply enough to sever his windpipe. Second, a trail of blood had led them to a stable, where they found a bloody razor.

Via called fellow doctor Charles Large, who had preceded him as coroner, and together they set off to examine the scene. There they pieced together the sad case of 67-year-old John Lang. Lang rented the farm, but had become seriously ill and no longer could work it. His wife left him as he sank into depression at the imminent loss of the farm and his inevitable slide into poverty. He was not yet destitute. The doctors found $25 in his pants pocket. They also found letters indicating that he had another $300 in the bank. Still, he was sick and frail at 67 and with nobody left in the world to take care of him, $325 would not last long for a proud man like John Lang. The letters indicated that Lang had swallowed his pride and asked that he be allowed to live out his life at the county poor farm. He explained that while he wasn't technically poor, he would give the county his life's fortune, $325, in exchange for a roof over his head. The county had not yet accepted his request, and Lang feared he was about to be evicted. Doctors Via and Large surmised that Lang had gone out to the stable, perhaps to say goodbye to his horses, then sliced his own throat with a razor. He did not die instantly. He dropped the razor and had enough strength to stagger back to the house and collapse on the bed, where he died alone, with $25 in his pocket and a future too bleak to bear. His death clearly was not from natural causes as we know the term today, although suicide was not at all unnatural among the elderly in 1901. With no Medicare, Social Security or any safety net, people without family or a source of income often chose to simply kill themselves. Seeing no evidence of struggle, theft or other indication of murder, Doctors Via and Large added the name of John Lang to that list.

On the same page as the story about the unfortunate Mr. Lang was a story about a suspicious death that had been the talk of the town for many months and that was a significant reason Charles Large no longer was coroner. This particular story was of a minor court ruling that a woman's estate was not liable for the costs of performing an inquest into the cause of her death. So ended the saga of Anna Hatch, who was found dead in her Forest Grove home on Saturday morning, April 28, 1900. A dispatch in the next day's *Oregonian* explains how her story began, starting with her birth 48 years earlier in Germany. Anna moved to Oregon, where she met and married E.T. Hatch and settled south of McMinnville. Hatch went on to serve many terms in the Oregon Senate and became very powerful in state politics. In 1897, E.T. Hatch was awarded the lucrative job of Customs collector in Gold Rush-era Alaska. Anna moved to the frontier and hated it. The couple divorced. Their 15-year-old son stayed with his father in Alaska, while their 9-year-old son moved to Forest Grove with his mother. It was this now 12-year-old son who found his mother's body that fateful Saturday morning in April 1900. That was about all *The Oregonian* could print the day after her death, although the headline hinted that there might be more to come: "Coroner's Investigation Might Develop Sensational Facts." Ultimately, Dr. Large's investigation did indeed turn up sensational facts, but he ruled her death to have been from heart disease, with no foul play. Those sensational facts led to wild speculation. A sensational "suicide" a year later only made the speculation worse.

The first order of business in Anna's case was to determine the time of her death, which was set at Friday morning. Her son awoke that morning and went down for breakfast, but there was none on the table. He went to his mother's bedroom, but she was not there. He decided to spend the day playing with friends. Finally he went home for dinner, famished from having not eaten all day. Once again, the table was bare.

Frightened to spend the night alone in an empty house, he invited a neighbor boy to spend the night with him. When breakfast was not ready Saturday morning, the neighbor boy suggested that they search the house. Soon the son opened the door to a rarely used bedroom and saw the half-dressed body of his mother on the bed with a folded towel covering her head. Police wanted more information, and the boy obliged the best he could. He said that the last time he had seen his mother was about 9 p.m. Thursday when he went to bed, leaving her in the parlor playing games with a friend. With a little more prying, the identity of that friend became clear. He was W.H. Fletcher, a wealthy farmer from Anna Hatch's previous home in McCoy, an unincorporated community south of McMinnville. Police summoned Fletcher for a chat. At first he denied any romantic involvement with Anna and said that he had left the home not long after her son went to bed, but finally admitted that he had spent the night with her in the little-used bedroom so as not to be discovered by her son should he awaken during the night. And yes, he admitted, they had indeed had sex that night, though he still denied any long-term relationship. He awoke very early Friday morning, he said, and placed a damp, folded towel on his lover's forehead because she had been suffering from a headache the previous evening. Then he went downstairs, quietly started a fire in the stove, boarded the train and headed the 30 miles or so to his farm to tend to his crop of hops. Doctors told the coroner's jury that the towel and the autopsy both pointed to the possibility of death by chloroform, but they lacked a test to confirm that suspicion. Dr. Large ruled the death to have been from natural causes.

The revelation of sex between the divorcee and her wealthy lover sent tongues wagging around town, with *The Oregonian* reporting that speculation among gossips centered on three possibilities. One theory posited that she had succumbed to the "excitement" of the illicit sexual encounter, a theory that meshed with the strong puritanical culture of the town. Another theory held that she had killed herself out of shame or perhaps unrequited love. The third theory was that Fletcher had killed his lover.

When the older son from Alaska was cleaning out the house, he found letters in his mother's bedroom from Fletcher. They were torrid love letters that suggested the affair had lasted for some time, but the letters had ended suddenly in August 1899, about nine months before

Anna's death. There was nothing in the letters to suggest a break-up. The son also noticed that his mother's rings were missing. One ring she had worn for years; the other, which she had said came from "a friend," for just a few months. Finally, when he checked the stove there was no sign of a fire. The wood and kindling that his mother always loaded in the evening to have ready for breakfast was still there. The only sign of fire was some burnt paper, apparently letters. He also told a story people in Forest Grove had not heard before. It seems that his sister, then 19, had died under suspicious circumstances back in McCoy at about the time his parents had left town and divorced. His father's powerful friends had ruled his daughter's death a suicide and helped keep it out of the newspapers. Although some members of the coroner's jury still suspected foul play in Anna's death, Large remained steadfast in his ruling of natural causes. No charges ever were levied against Fletcher or anyone else. The daughter's case was not reopened down in McCoy, either.

Then about a year after Anna's case was closed, yet another young woman was found dead in the tiny hamlet of McCoy. Effie Emmett had grown up in the small town, where her father and Senator E.T. Hatch were great friends. In fact, the Senator was an elder at the church they attended and taught Sunday school for the town's smallest children, including Effie and the Hatch's own children. In 1897, the vibrant Effie was accepted to Stanford University, where her two brothers were students. Effie never graduated, however, and after a few years was working as a Customs clerk in Gold Rush era Alaska. Her boss was her father's friend, Customs collector E.T. Hatch. Her last name no longer was Emmett, however. It was Hatch, as in Mrs. E.T. Hatch, wife of the Customs collector. That had been her name, in fact, since just a few months after the suicide of her best friend, E.T. Hatch's daughter. After E.T.'s divorce from Anna was final, he traveled to Stanford, picked up Effie, took her to Reno for a quick wedding and returned to Alaska. As it turns out, Effie didn't like life in Alaska any more than Anna had, and soon moved back to McCoy to live with her parents. E.T. Hatch soon followed, and along the way bought a ranch along the Columbia River.

Hatch traveled to McCoy to pick up his young bride, promising her a new life on the ranch. Effie's mother had been caring for her daughter, whom she thought had contracted typhoid fever. E.T. Hatch said that Effie had recurring fears of going insane. After a day or two at the Emmett's home in McCoy he whisked away his bride to see her longtime doctor in nearby Amity. Contacted later, the doctor said he could find nothing wrong with Effie and sent her on her way. When they returned to the Emmett household, Hatch said his bride still was fearful of impending insanity, but Effie said she felt fine and they went to bed. At 5 the next morning, Hatch said, he awoke to an empty bed. He rallied the Emmetts to conduct a search. Hatch had a head start, having already discovered the footprints of a barefoot person in the dusty driveway. A story in the July 30, 1901, *Oregonian* picks up the hunt from there. "She evidently walked fast," a seemingly skeptical reporter wrote after visiting the scene, "for she stepped long." The search party followed Hatch as he traced what he presumed would have been the path of his bride's bare feet which *The Oregonian* reported must have "trampled over sharp rocks and through briars, climbing the rail fence and crossing the road where a path she had trod to school years ago formerly crossed. Then she climbed another rail fence topped with barbed wire, and hurried to the well, an old one used occasionally for watering stock. Her wedding ring was found on the top of a post beside the well; her body was found by her father at the bottom. Those who cared for Emma's body said there was still a little warmth in the corpse. The only visible injury was a slight abrasion on the forehead. The coroner's jury pronounced it a case of suicide while suffering from temporary mental aberration." The reporter then added this note: "No one is disposed to question the correctness of this verdict." Sarcasm aside, almost everyone seemed to question the verdict in all three cases, although no one had an easy answer. All anyone in Forest Grove knew for sure was that two wives of a prominent Oregon politician were dead, one death blamed on natural causes, the other on suicide. The politician's daughter, a childhood friend of his second deceased wife, also was dead from what was called an unexplained suicide. The politician and his long-time friend, a wealthy farmer who happened to have had sex with the politician's first wife the night she died of natural causes, both lived happily ever after.

As coroner, Charles Large was no stranger to controversy, and he responded vigorously to complaints about his role in some of these investigations. *The Oregonian* often printed his rebuttals to stories filed by its reporters from McMinnville, Hillsboro and elsewhere about his rulings concerning Forest Grove cases. The editors at the newspaper's offices in

Portland knew the doctor well, because among many other things, Charles Large was *The Oregonian*'s correspondent in Forest Grove. Those editors had chronicled his adventures well. For example, the Page 2 subhead of the December 30, 1890, edition of the paper read "Suspicious Death of Old Man Near Forest Grove." The banner, all-caps headline put it more succinctly: "LOOKS LIKE MURDER." The old man was Christopher Ibach, who had died mysteriously at the ripe old age of 50. Christopher's brother, Abraham, had discovered the body at the dairy farm they shared. He called the undertaker and said that the cause of death was obvious. Cattle, Abraham said, had killed his brother. A bull, to be more specific, had gored poor Christopher, killing him. No mystery, Abraham assured the funeral home; happens all the time. But Dr. Large was in charge of death investigations, and the undertaker turned over the case to him. When Large arrived, he talked to Abraham and to the brothers' hired helper, who lived with them. The hired helper had been sick in bed that day, but was awakened in the evening by Abraham, who told him that Christopher was in "a senseless condition" in the barn. The hired hand told Abraham to go back to the barn and "dash some cold water in his face." Abraham returned to his employee's sickbed to report that a dash of water had not cured his brother's ills. The sick hired hand got dressed, went to the barn, and discovered why: Christopher had a bloody hole right through his heart. That's when Abraham pieced together the evidence and pegged the bull as the killer. Dr. Large took the body for examination and organized a coroner's jury. The first hint that it wasn't a bull that killed Christopher Ibach came when Large discovered a hole in the man's back, even bigger than the hole in his chest. The bull's horn was not long enough to have inflicted such a wound. Doctors from Portland examined the body and said the wound was consistent with one created by a slug from a .44 caliber revolver. Other witnesses said that the Ibach brothers had been fighting for months over ownership of the farm. Large listened to the testimony and declared this a homicide committed by man, not bovine. His brilliant detective work was well-chronicled in *The Oregonian*, yet no one ever was convicted of the crime. Anton Pfanner, an eager Swiss immigrant with a banking background in his native country, was assigned to liquidate the Ibach estate, one of the largest in Forest Grove history.

Eighteen years later, the Forest Grove area again was rocked by news of killer cows. This story unfolded down Spring Hill Road, south of Forest Grove near Gaston, and was even stranger than the Ibach saga. Robert Wood was the victim this time. Robert lived with Harold and Mary Jennings and their son, Staff Jennings, who went on to become one of Portland's most prominent business leaders. Wood had been with Harold and Mary for years. They emigrated from England together, lived together as they crossed the continent to California and as they moved to Oregon, across Wapato Lake from Gaston. Robert Wood was living with the Jennings in 1905 when hired hand Harry McDonald took Mary Jennings hostage, proclaiming his love for the young mother and railing against the man who had captured her heart. That man, McDonald said, was not Harold Jennings, but rather Robert Wood. After a long standoff with a Sheriff's posse, Harry McDonald released Mary Jennings and blew off the top of his head with a shotgun. Life returned to normal, or what passed for normal, at the Jennings-Wood farm east of Gaston. In 1908, however, there was another suspicious death on the farm. Mary Jennings was sick in bed, and Robert Wood went out to milk the cows. A couple of hours later Harold Jennings found him dead in a field, with a hole through his heart. The cause, Harold told investigators, was obvious. Wood always carried a walking stick and used it to prod the cows into and out of the barn; clearly, one of the cows had bumped the walking stick, impaling his friend Wood. Terrible tragedy, Jennings said, and case closed. The investigators believed Jennings, although Wood's walking stick was nowhere to be found. But then new information emerged. It seems that Wood was more than a friend. He owned half of the Jennings farm and apparently was looking to cash out. A coroner's jury convened, but still concluded that Wood's death was accidental, caused, no doubt, by a miscreant cow. By now the Jennings were sick of Gaston and moved to Portland, where Robert Wood's brother, Owen, moved in with them. In 1918, Harold Jennings died on a lifeboat off the coast of Guam after a couple of weeks adrift. His body was cast overboard. Had he died a few days later, we learn in Lowell Thomas' *Wreck of the Dumaru*, his body would have been eaten along with those of later casualties by the survivors aboard the open life boat.

The Wood story caused a sensation in Gaston, but five miles north in Forest Grove the news was overshadowed by one of the most lurid murders those living in 1908 Forest Grove had ever witnessed. A 15-year-old boy was out gathering blackberries when he smelled an overpowering odor. Investigating, he saw a man's body in a shallow hole, covered with branches. He ran and summoned his father, who investigated further. Neither father nor son had ever seen this man before. He wasn't familiar to the sheriff either, or to the coroner. The only clue was a tin coin, stamped "E.E. Perdue, Spokane, Wash. 1907." The *Washington County News* of August 20, 1908, picks up the hunt. "It has been ascertained that Perdue, in company of a number of Swedes and J.J. Fisher, a bookstore man of Portland," had gone off into the Coast Range mountains in June to look for timber claims in anticipation of a proposed railroad from Hillsboro to Tillamook, which had touched off something of a Gold Rush frenzy among those looking to get rich honestly and those looking to get rich by preying on the honest folks. Elmer Perdue, J.J. Fisher and the company of Swedes were unfamiliar with the dense woods, so they hired a well-known local hunter, Walter Johnson, to be their guide. Johnson was the son of a wealthy Gaston hops farmer and son-in-law of Riler Thomas, an Oregon pioneer and one of the founders of the town of Nehalem. Despite his solid background, however, the 23-year-old Johnson "has been living a precarious existence in and around Portland for several years," the *News* reported. Fisher and the company of Swedes soon returned to Forest Grove, minus Elmer Perdue and their guide, Walter Johnson. When Johnson returned two months later, friends were suspicious because he was flashing large sums of money and paying off debts he owed around town. Police tracked down Fisher in Portland to learn more.

It turns out that most of the party had decided to return without staking a timber claim. Elmer Perdue, however, had enough money of his own, which he carried in gold, to buy his own claim, and he and Johnson had stayed behind in the woods for several weeks. That was enough for the sheriff, who went hunting for Walter Johnson, soon tracking him to East Portland. "Sheriff Stevens of Portland," the *News* reported, "took the prisoner in hand upon his arrival at jail and talked earnestly with him." It didn't take much earnest conversation before Walter Johnson told his story. "I killed Perdue," he said in a signed confession. "We slept together in the cabin and that morning we had some dispute about money matters. Words passed and I got my rifle and blew the top of his head off. After taking whatever of value he had in his pockets, I dragged the body away a short distance into the woods and placed it in a ditch where I covered it with leaves and brush. Then I went back to the cabin and cooked my breakfast." Tongues wagged about the case for months in Forest Grove, until Walter Johnson, the wayward son of a prominent family, was hanged. Supporters of Prohibition turned Johnson's case into a temperance lesson when the county sheriff reported that as he stood on the gallows waiting to hang, Johnson used his last words to preach a warning to boys on the dangers of alcohol.

By now, Forest Grove residents were starting to fear an epidemic of crimes committed by wayward sons, because the town still was reeling from a crime spree two years earlier involving a young man from a very prominent family. Carey Snyder's father owned one of the Midwest's largest banks, in Kansas City. Carey, it seems, was having trouble finding himself, so his father bought him a farm near Forest Grove and supported Carey and his family with regular checks until Carey found his calling. None of that was known on the evening of December 1, 1905, when two petty burglaries were committed. In the first, the blacksmith shop of Forest Grove Fire Chief Joe Lenneville was robbed of several punches and a sledge hammer. In the second, a pick ax and crowbar were stolen from the Southern Pacific Railroad depot in Dilley.

The next morning the reason behind the petty crimes became obvious, when Oscar Loomis opened the door to the Farmers and Merchants Bank, where he worked as a bookkeeper. The stench of dynamite hung heavy in the air inside the bank, and debris was blown everywhere. Police quickly determined that someone had used the railroad's crowbar to pry open the front door of the bank, then used the pick ax and sledge hammer to break through the brick wall of the bank's vault. Once inside the vault, they used Lenneville's punches and sledge to make holes in the safe, into which they inserted dynamite. Too much dynamite, it turns out, because the resulting blast blew the safe's contents all over the bank. Loomis collected what currency and silver he could find among the debris of paper and furniture strewn through the bank. When Loomis was done counting, he found that the robbers had left behind $88. That meant that they had managed to scoop up about $5,500, plus the bank's shotgun, making this one of the worst bank robberies in Oregon history. Police returned the tools to the fire chief and railroad, and set out to find the people responsible. Police suspected that the robbers had not gone far, because within days coins bent by the blast and paper money charred by the resulting fire started popping up around town.

On December 4, Carey Snyder told his wife Madge that he was going into Portland to conduct some business. When he arrived, he called her to say that he was catching a boat up the Columbia River to do some hunting, and would be back in a few days. He did not return, and his wife called police. By now the bank had hired the private Pinkerton company to investigate the robbery. "Pinkertons" were much feared by criminals, because they had a vast nationwide network of agents and operated without political restraints. When the Pinkertons assigned to the Forest Grove robbery heard about this missing man they had their colleagues in Missouri check into Snyder's past; soon they uncovered the rest of the story behind his move from Kansas City to Oregon some years earlier. It seems that Snyder had indeed found his calling in life, but it was not one that suited the son of one of the richest men in Kansas City. Back in Missouri, Snyder and his cousin, George Perry, along with a buddy, had formed a gang, and set about robbing people and stores. They were not very good at their trade, however, and soon were captured. Carey Snyder's father bought his son's way out of prison and sent him packing to Oregon. Perry and their friend were left to serve their time in the penitentiary; their sentences had ended only recently. As the Pinkertons canvassed Snyder's neighbors in Forest Grove, they showed them pictures of Perry. Yes, they said, he had been hanging around the Snyder farm for the past few weeks.

The trail went cold, and months passed with no sign of Snyder or Perry. Life around Forest Grove resumed its normal rhythms, and by May 1906 farmers were busy preparing their summer crops. A.P. Luther of Hillsboro was one such farmer, leading his horse-drawn plow along the edge of his field, watching closely to avoid plowing into the gravel right of way of the Southern Pacific Railroad tracks. There, along the tracks, partially buried and obscured by tall weeds, Luther saw a shotgun. When Sheriff John Connell arrived, he found that the shotgun was the one stolen from the Forest Grove bank. He also found a trove of other items, including burglary tools, a revolver, and a hodgepodge of ammunition, including cartridges from the same lot as those discovered at Carey

100

Snyder's home after his wife reported him missing. By now, however, Madge Snyder was of little use to investigators, having succumbed to "mental collapse" brought on by "hysteria." At first her hysteria was attributed to the strain of not knowing the whereabouts of her husband, but the Pinkertons were learning more. One of her friends told them that shortly before her "mental collapse," Madge said that on the night before the Forest Grove bank heist she, her husband, George Perry and another man rode their carriage to a barn north of Forest Grove to meet co-conspirators and plan the robbery. As it turns out, the co-conspirators were waiting at a different barn and missed their connection. The Snyder party drove home, this witness said, and dropped off Madge before disappearing into the night. This witness told the Pinkertons that Madge Snyder knew that her husband was to be murdered. She also knew the mystery man on the carriage that night, because he was in fact her brother. The Portland Pinkertons relayed this information to their colleagues in Kansas City, who dismissed it all as a ruse; Carey Snyder, they said, was back in Kansas City, but he kept evading capture. The trail went cold again.

By October, A.P. Luther had harvested the crops he was planting back in May when he stumbled upon the shotgun. Fall's favorite pastime in rural Oregon, hunting, had resumed. Harry Hanson was grouse hunting near what *The Oregonian* of October 2 described as a "jungle," but which today is suburban tract homes in Beaverton. Hanson shot a grouse, then tracked it through the thick brush, where he stumbled upon a man's body. Sheriff Connell was called, and he searched the clothing of the skeleton. In a pants pocket, he found a letter from Robert Snyder, one of the wealthiest men in Missouri, addressed to his son, Carey. The letter confirmed that the father had deposited money in the son's account and that he could have more whenever he needed it. The coroner arrived and decided on the spot that the skeleton was that of Carey Snyder, and that he had died from a bullet wound to the head. Police back in Missouri remained unconvinced, however, and asserted that Snyder had killed another man and staged the body to look like his. Snyder was, the Missouri detectives insisted, still alive. Madge Snyder was by now in a Kansas City mental hospital, her care paid for by her father-in-law.

She refused to testify, and her husband's death remained forever unresolved. Madge was described as petite and beautiful in the press of

101

the day, and an *Oregonian* story described her as "submissive" to her husband and father-in-law, describing in detail a day not long before Carey Snyder disappeared when Carey had administered a brutal beating upon her on the street in front of the Hillsboro Post Office, in full view of the public. When she was brought back to Forest Grove to help police investigate her husband's murder she begged to return to Missouri, where witnesses at the hospital said she had confided her fear of being cut off from the Snyder fortune if she told the truth about her husband. She refused to testify, and the death of Carey Snyder remains a mystery. A couple of months later, Robert Snyder lost his grip over Madge when he was killed in an automobile accident in Kansas City. He left his vast fortune to his wife, who almost immediately after his death moved to Boston. Madge Snyder sued the estate, revealing the existence of a son she and Carey had not long before his death. An out-of-court settlement divided the estate. A few months later, Madge Snyder married a wealthy man.

Five years later, the Forest Grove saga unfolded again, this time in a St. Louis courtroom, where the heirs of wealthy banker George Kimmel were suing an insurance company to collect on his policy. A good friend of fellow banker Robert Snyder, Kimmel had dropped out of sight about the time Carey Snyder moved to Oregon. The star witness, *The Oregonian* reported on February 22, 1912, was notorious train robber John Swinney, who testified that in 1898 he met Robert Snyder in Kansas City. Snyder, he said, told him of a cache of gold hidden near Coos Bay, Oregon. Snyder persuaded Kimmel to go retrieve the treasure, accompanied by his son Carey, Swinney and a man named Johnson. They found part of the fortune, Swinney testified, at which point Johnson pulled a gun and attempted to kill the other three. He succeeded in killing the wealthy banker Kimmel, Swinney testified, but he and Snyder managed to kill Johnson in self-defense. Kimmel's body was never found, and now every other person involved, save Swinney, had met a violent death. All but the elder Snyder had been murdered. No one ever went to jail for any of the deaths.

Long before the Snyder family caused such turmoil in Forest Grove, bankers had acquired a bad reputation in town. For the first 50 years of the city's existence, the town wasn't even sure it wanted a bank. The unregulated banks of the late 1800s were prone to collapse, often leaving depositors with little or nothing after accounts were settled. Most people in rural towns avoided banks at all costs, and from the pulpits of Forest Grove churches came cries of protest against the satanic institutions on Wall Street in New York and Lombard Street in San Francisco. Those who did use banks had to go into Portland or Oregon City for most of the century. For the most part, credit was extended either by merchants or by private individuals. Early newspapers often ran legal notices concerning these casual loans, either from lenders threatening to sue borrowers for non-payment or from wealthy farmers publicly demanding that merchants stop granting credit to people who said that the farmers had authorized them to borrow in their names. In 1891, however, more people were expressing interest in establishing a bank in Forest Grove, and a small item in the *Forest Grove Times*, printed next to legal notices concerning bad debts, introduced to readers a name that would become first famous and later infamous around town for decades to come: Anton Pfanner. "Mr. Pfanner's thorough business habits, coupled with strict integrity, recommend him as a most desirable trustee for agent for estates, investments and loans."

Pfanner had arrived in the area a few years earlier after emigrating from his native Switzerland in 1882. He lived in the small community of Greenville and had made a living for himself handling financial affairs for wealthy farmers. Having earned their trust, he now was making forays into Forest Grove, calling on wealthy merchants. Before long he had earned their trust as well, and was persuaded to buy the struggling Keep Bank in downtown Forest Grove. Within a year he had $85,000 in deposits, a sum rivaling some Portland banks. Most ordinary people still shunned banks, however, and rumors spread that Pfanner had fled Switzerland because he was wanted for bank fraud there. Nonetheless, within two years, the Pfanner Bank was booming. Then, just as suddenly, everything came to a crashing halt.

Thursday, June 10, 1897, started off as a routine business day at the Pfanner Bank, with trusted cashier Frank Kane running the bank that day. Around noon he got the mail, which included a registered letter from his boss, Anton Pfanner, postmarked from Portland. Kane was stunned by the letter's contents, which instructed him to close the bank immediately and turn over affairs to city pioneer Alanson Hinman. Don't worry, Pfanner said, there's plenty of money and no reason to panic, but close the doors immediately. At noon, Forest Grove once again was without a bank. The letter said that Pfanner no longer felt that he could stand the mental strain of business, and made vague references to venturing out to die among strangers. He said that he could not return to Forest Grove and face those who had trusted him, "an insane man," with their business. Fearing that Pfanner was about to commit suicide, his pastor and doctor took the first train into Portland to file a missing person report. The police chief summoned his officers and told them to keep a close eye out for the man believed to be the wealthiest person in Washington County. One officer had good news; he had talked to Pfanner at some length the night before on the sidewalk outside the Imperial Hotel on Broadway. He said that Pfanner seemed completely calm and collected as he stood arm in arm with the woman the patrolman presumed to be Mrs. Pfanner. That set at ease his friends' minds except for one thing. Pfanner was a lifelong bachelor and no one recalled having ever seen him in the company of a woman. At any rate, Pfanner had told the officer that he was leaving for The Dalles early the next morning, and the hunt was on. There was no trace of Pfanner in The Dalles, however, nor anywhere else.

A month went by, and then the Portland police chief received a letter from Leopold Huff, who was married to Pfanner's sister. Huff told the chief that as word of Pfanner's disappearance spread up and down the West Coast, an employee at a hospital in Victoria, British Columbia, recognized a patient as resembling Pfanner's description; the search had been hampered because there was no known photograph of Pfanner, who was notorious for going to great lengths to avoid having his image captured on film. Huff had rushed to Canada and confirmed the good news. Pfanner was being treated, he wrote, for "nervous prostration" and "mental imbalance," but was feeling much better and planned to return to Forest Grove soon to settle his bank's business. By this time, however, the Pfanner Bank business was anything but settled. Back in Forest Grove, Hinman had started to delve into the bank's books, confident that his friend Pfanner was an honest man. In his letter appointing Hinman to settle his affairs, Pfanner had included details of every aspect of the bank's business. When Hinman sat down with trusted cashier Frank Kane, however, he was in for a shock. None of Kane's numbers jibed with Pfanner's. The bank was insolvent.

104

About two months after he left Forest Grove, the *Washington County Hatchet* announced that Pfanner was back in town, or at least had been for one day. It seems that after arriving back in the Grove and spending the night at a friend's house, Pfanner decided that he had not yet recovered enough from his recent illness to discuss his bank's failure and hopped the morning freight train into Portland. *Hatchet* editor Austin Craig remained a Pfanner fan, however, and assured that the banker would return soon to settle his debts, "dollar for dollar." A hue and cry arose again in Forest Grove about the evils of banking, and townspeople vowed vengeance against Pfanner when he returned to town. Pfanner never did return to Forest Grove, however, so vengeance would have to wait. It took Hinman three years to settle the estate of Pfanner, eventually paying out about 32 cents on the dollar to most creditors. In the meantime, by 1900 Pfanner had disappeared without a trace. Prominent Forest Grove businessman and state Senator Edward W. Haines had bought the Pfanner Bank building and reopened it as the Haines Bank, leaving it in the capable hands of trusted cashier Frank Kane, who had operated it for Pfanner previously and since had been elected mayor of Forest Grove. Haines was an elder of the Congregational Church and a trustee at Pacific University. The town finally knew its bank was in good hands. Meanwhile, a warrant for Pfanner's arrest remained in effect, although police had all but given up hope of finding him. Soon, police and press picked up the story that Pfanner had been found in his native Switzerland, and that the rumors that had plagued him in Forest Grove were true; he was indeed wanted in Europe for bank fraud and had been captured and locked away in prison. Justice, it seems, had been served. On November 22, 1901, *The Oregonian* ran a story saying that it had confirmed that Pfanner was indeed in prison, and in 1905, word came that Pfanner had died in prison. Near the end of 1905, however, Forest Grove was rocked when John Thornburgh, one of the town of Greenville's best-known leaders, received a letter from a friend in San Francisco, telling him that the friend had run into Anton Pfanner on the streets and had since talked to him several more times. He said that Pfanner's hands were calloused like those of one engaged in manual labor. Ultimately the report was dismissed. In the minds of Forest Grove residents, Pfanner had died in Switzerland. In 1905, birth, death, Census and voter registration records were not online for anyone to review. In 2014 they are, and those records cast even more mystery around the life of camera-shy Anton Pfanner. For example, a man matching his name and vital statistics was declared dead in Switzerland in 1882, a few weeks before the seemingly same Anton Pfanner arrived in New York from the same town in Switzerland. Further, records indicate that the same man was alive and well in Forest Grove in 1890, and then alive and well in San Francisco in 1900, and again in 1910, listed as a laborer, and widower. On January 15, 1914, the *Forest Grove Press* reported that Anton Pfanner had died in Los Angeles, citing a friend of a friend, although no records are available to prove what really happened to one of Forest Grove's biggest mystery men.

The early 1900s were a turbulent time in Forest Grove as the area struggled to adapt to technological and societal changes of the Industrial Age and the Progressive Era as those changes slowly crept westward from the great cities of the East Coast. Electricity, telegraphs, and banks all were common east of the Mississippi River, but remained novelties in the rural West. Attitudes were changing as well, especially concerning the role of women and in the arena of crime and punishment. Those societal changes also were far more entrenched in the East than in the rural West, and helped fuel a small wave of westward migration among people who increasingly found themselves as outlaws. They hoped that they could outrun progress by fleeing to the Wild West. Many, such as Carey Snyder, found that eventually those changes would overtake them, even at the very edge of the continent. A strange concurrence of such events would make August 1903 one of the strangest months in the annals of Forest Grove crime.

The bizarre string of events began in Hillsboro, when a grifter named Daniel "D.J." Tromley arrived in town from Michigan. Tromley rented a home near the county Courthouse and began telling anyone who would listen that he was a private investigator. Exactly what Tromley was investigating remained private, because all locals ever saw him do was to get drunk and chase members of the opposite sex, then threaten to kill anyone who tried to interfere with his pursuits. His drunken escapades landed him in the Washington County Jail several times, never for long enough to deter his wanton behavior but long enough for him to analyze the security at the lockup, which was primitive compared to many he had seen back East. Eventually that lack of security first would haunt him, and then propel him into infamy. On the evening of Monday, August 17,

1903, D.J. Tromley was in his by now familiar cell at the jail, arrested for a drunken melee involving an unwed Hillsboro woman, whose loud parties with Tromley at his house were a growing source of irritation for his neighbors. The neighbors most annoyed by these shenanigans were the young men of town, some who fancied the affections of the young woman for themselves and some who wanted to defend the honor of all Hillsboro lasses. After the jailers left for the evening, about 25 of these young men broke down the door of the jail, released the lever that operated all of the cell doors, tied a noose around D.J. Tromley's neck and led him into the streets and to the brickyard at the east end of town. Along the way, the men told Tromley that he would be hanged, but that was not to be his fate this hot August night.

When the mob brought him to his knees in the deserted brickyard, Tromley, in the words of a *Forest Grove Times* story, "begged for his life like a pig for swill." The vigilantes spared Tromley's life, but not before they stripped him naked, covered his body with hot tar, and coated him in a thick layer of chicken feathers. They then released him into the night, where he found aid and comfort at the nearby home of Charley Stewart, who gave him some coal oil with which he removed most of the tar. D.J. Tromley then managed to find his way in the darkness to Portland. Whether he was clothed by the time he reached the city is unclear, but what is known is that his destination was the home of the widowed Mrs. Gelahweiler, whom, it turns out, he recently had wed before landing in Hillsboro. Tromley, the *Times* reported in its story mocking him for the episode, was demanding that the folks who tarred and feathered him be prosecuted. While the news story made light of the tarring and feathering of a philanderer, the editorial page took a different tone. The editorial urged local residents to cast aside their old Wild West vigilantism, which the writer attributed to the "Southern" influence of many of the area's settlers. Tromley was returned to the Washington County Jail to await modern American justice.

The Tromley saga had transfixed the community, but by the following week it was eclipsed by a new and brazen crime involving Forest Grove's remaining bank and two of its most prominent citizens, Frank Kane and Edward W. Haines. On August 26, 1903, a young man entered the bank owned by Haines, Forest Grove's most prosperous businessman, and managed by Frank Kane, who also happened to be

Forest Grove's mayor at the time. The earnest young man presented a bank draft endorsed by a wealthy but reclusive local farmer named Walter Bernards. The polite young man said that he wanted to collect the $300 on behalf of his friend, Mr. Bernards. In 1903, $300 was not a trifling sum; in fact, it was about the average annual wage of a hardworking laborer. Frank Kane was suspicious, but everything about the draft seemed to be authentic. The endorsement signatures of Bernards and the earnest young man, J.H. Burke, were distinctly different and created with different pens using different colored ink; for bankers in the rural West of 1903, those clues were good enough to deem a transaction as honest and legitimate. But Kane knew Bernards and worried that something wasn't right about the transaction. He asked J.H. Burke if he could wait until the next day to collect the $300. Burke agreed, and left the bank. Kane jumped on his horse and rode out to talk to Walter Bernards at his farm outside town. Bernards looked at his supposed signature on the draft and confirmed that it certainly looked authentic, but assured Kane that he had not signed such a draft for anyone named J.H. Burke. Kane suspected a forgery, and returned to Forest Grove to inform his boss, E.W. Haines.

Kane and Haines decided that they weren't going to let Burke get away with this one. They kept their appointment to meet with him on August 27. Apparently, however, Kane and Haines had not taken to heart the previous week's *Times* admonition against vigilantism, because they did not contact Forest Grove's appointed town marshal. Instead, Kane greeted Burke at the door as the bank opened and led him inside. As Kane examined the draft at the counter, Burke's eye was drawn to the door, where bank owner E.W. Haines was standing. When Burke glanced back at Kane, he found himself staring down the barrel of the cashier's revolver. Turning to make his getaway, he walked right into the barrel of another revolver, this one in the hand of Edward Haines. Just like that, Burke was captured and on his way to the Washington County Jail to join D.J. Tromley, another grifter from the East who thought that he could con the good folks of the Tualatin Plains. Their stories of crime were not over, however. In fact, the saga of Danny Tromley and J.H. "Slippery" Burke had hardly begun. When Forest Grove's bankers, Kane and Haines, drew their revolvers to capture a forger, they did not know that they had ended a cross-country crime spree. The mystery continued to grow, however, because as word of his many other crimes started to trickle in, the true identity of "J.H Burke" just got murkier.

Within a week, the bankers had moved on with their lives and were in the news for other reasons. E.W. Haines was reporting that he had 20 or so men hard at work constructing the most modern of dams on the Tualatin River to supply Forest Grove with electricity, and dashing young Mayor Frank Kane, bank cashier who foiled both Anton Pfanner's fraud and J.H. Burke's forgery, was being married in the wedding of the year to socialite Florence Contris. Crime news had shifted to the bizarre case of a home burglary, in which a teen-age girl interrupted an attack on a woman visiting the family from California. The screams of the girl, Minnie Warren, awoke her father, who grabbed a rock and confronted the masked suspect, who had climbed into the sleeping woman's bedroom with a ladder. The intruder then pulled out a gun and ordered the man, his daughter Minnie, and the visitor from California to line up against the wall, but not before Minnie pulled the mask off of his face. The burglar robbed the family of jewelry and cash, and then fled into the night. The attacker was, the family said with certainty, their neighbor, Richard H. Kennedy, who happened to be a Forest Grove resident and until recently minister of the Hillsboro Congregational Church. The sensational crime stunned residents of both cities, who swore that the minister was incapable of committing such a heinous act. Besides, he had what seemed like an airtight alibi: he had taken the train to Portland earlier and there had been no return train in time for him to have committed the crime. The police case rested on a theory involving the suspect's means of transportation, one that still was relatively rare in the area, a bicycle. Kennedy, they said, had ridden a bicycle from Portland to the Warren home, where he had visited with the family earlier in the week, getting to know the woman visiting from California. The Reverend Mr. Kennedy was lodged in the Washington County Jail along with D.J. Tromley and J.H. "Slippery" Burke. The judge ordered what was in 1903 a huge bail of $1,000, which the Reverend was unable to post. Unlike his jailmates Tromley and Burke, however, Kennedy had some very wealthy friends, including Dr. Charles Large; former newspaper owner and Forest Grove Mayor Walter Hoge; and the man who had captured Burke, bank owner and state Senate President E.W. Haines. With friends like that, the

Reverend Kennedy was sprung from jail easily and legally. Tromley and Burke would have to find other means of escape.

On the morning of September 9, four days after Kennedy's release, jailers arrived to find "Slippery" Burke and another county hooligan, notorious burglar John Tom "Bricktop" McNamara, missing from their cells. They had two clues to what had happened: Two holes in the brick wall of the jail, and one prisoner who had not escaped, grifter D.J. Tromley. Tromley told the jailers that the two hardened criminals had threatened to beat him to death if he told authorities how they had escaped, but he spilled the beans quickly. All of the cell doors in the primitive jail were controlled by one lever. During the day when the lever was up, releasing the doors, Burke and McNamara had jimmied the latches on the cell doors to prevent the latches from catching when the lever was pulled to lock them in for the night. After the jailers left, the inmates opened their cell doors, but still were locked in by a main set of iron gates. Those gates, however, were no obstacle to Burke and McNamara, who used steel rods that had been smuggled in for them to hastily chip away at the brick wall, creating the first of the two holes deputies found. Unfortunately for the scofflaws, the wall they cut through turned out to be reinforced with iron bars. Not to be deterred, they attacked another wall, which led them from the jail to the sheriff's office. From there, they unlocked the sheriff's door and escaped into the night. Now three of Washington County's four most notorious inmates were loose. D.J. Tromley was behind bars, and by now his wife had joined him. It seems that the day before the daring escape, the Hillsboro fire department had been called to a fire raging in a house near the jail, which just happened to be the house that Tromley had rented before his arrest. His new bride was outside the house when firefighters arrived, and afterward showed them where an expensive grand piano that belonged to the home's owner had burned in the blaze. Firefighters were suspicious, however, because there was no trace of a piano; no charred strings or pedals. Nothing. Nothing, that is, except the strong smell of gasoline. The new Mrs. Tromley was arrested, and led police to where the piano really was, untouched, at the home of Charley Stewart, the man who had aided Tromley after his tar and feathering. The Reverend Kennedy was accounted for, free on bail at his home, and Burke and McNamara were on the lam, but the Washington County Jail was still near capacity in this wacky month of August 1903.

Local marshals remained busy, too, with now three fugitives to hunt for, because a couple of days before the daring jail escape, another brutal criminal had eluded capture. John McPherson was new to Forest Grove, arriving with his wife and teenage daughter from somewhere "back East." The nature of the demons he was fleeing remains unknown, but the *Times* reported that he already was known in the area for his "beastly and vicious character," which manifested itself, among other ways, in severe beatings of his child. By 1903, child abuse was widely viewed in East Coast cities as a crime; not to the degree that it is today, but still as a crime. On the other hand, many in the rural West still believed in the old adage "spare the rod, spoil the child." Oregon still was debating a notorious case a few years earlier near Albany in which a son had killed his abusive father; the sides in that case formed largely along urban-rural lines, with the rural side defending a parent's right to mete out violence to a child. But this time McPherson went too far, even by rural standards. The savage beating he administered to his daughter sent his wife fleeing for help, and police responded. Unfortunately, McPherson was able to leave the constables flat-footed escaping into the night on his bicycle. The *Times* urged time in the penitentiary for McPherson if he ever was caught.

Burke and McNamara, meanwhile, also were on the loose, with few clues to their whereabouts other than reports that they were travelling together, possibly headed east. Two weeks after the escape, a sheriff in The Dalles, Oregon, more than 100 miles east of Forest Grove, got a tip that the fugitives were in his town. That tip led to the quick capture of "Bricktop" McNamara, but "Slippery" Burke again avoided justice. Undaunted, word spread to other sheriffs along the Columbia River in Oregon and Washington to be on the lookout for Burke, and the eagle-eye sheriff of Skamania County, Washington, spotted him in the town of Carson. Burke surrendered without a fight. The jail was several miles west of Carson, however, in the county seat of Stevenson, and the sheriff was alone on horseback. Holding Burke at gunpoint, the lawman ordered the fugitive to walk to Stevenson as he followed on his horse. The sheriff's plan worked for a couple of miles until "Slippery" Burke suddenly dived into a thicket of blackberry brambles and into the forest. The sheriff fired several times into the brambles, but once again Burke avoided justice. For two days, every lawman in the Columbia River Gorge pursued the Forest Grove Forger, and on Monday morning, September 21, a deputy spotted him back on the Oregon side of the river near the town of Cascade Locks. Instead of continuing his journey east, Burke had backtracked toward Forest Grove. Faced with the barrel of the deputy's gun, the docile Burke threw up his hands and surrendered. The deputy did not have a horse, so he ordered Burke to walk ahead of him the few miles to the jail in Cascade Locks. The deputy's plan went smoothly for a while, until Burke suddenly turned and sucker-punched him, wrestling him to the ground and stealing both of his revolvers before leaving the deputy, whom the *Times* described as "crestfallen," to make the rest of the walk into town alone, without his quarry.

In 1903, communication between law enforcement officers was slow and unorganized, especially across state lines, and even more so across national borders. But while Burke was on the lam, police back in Forest Grove were piecing together the brazen criminal's past. As teletypes spread around the country, police in other towns reported that the slippery Mr. Burke had worked his way west scamming small-town banks out of $100 or so at a time. When "J.H. Burke" reached the town of Martinez, California, just north of San Francisco, he hit a major score, cashing in on $300 drafts at two banks in the same town. Then he headed north, hitting banks in small towns in northern California and southern Oregon, until he encountered Frank Kane, suspicious bank cashier and mayor of Forest Grove, Oregon. So now police knew that they were on the trail of a major criminal who had learned that he could scam small-town bankers across the rural West, many of whom were still learning about such things as bank drafts. But even retracing his crime spree, police kept coming up against dead-ends. No one, it seemed, knew exactly who J.H. Burke was or where he came from, making the search for him very difficult.

Eventually, however, the teletypes made it across the border into Canada, where the Royal Canadian Mounted Police knew a secret about J.H. Burke. The Mounties knew that J.H. Burke was really J.H. Hamlin, a Canadian citizen, and they had been hunting him for months. This clue seemed to explain why J.H. "Slippery" Hamlin had headed east up the Columbia River, because it made sense that he planned to follow it back

112

up into Canada. This new clue, however, did not explain why he had backtracked after twice eluding capture, at least until the Mounties found another clue. "Slippery" Hamlin had a brother, who they believed was living in a cabin near Vancouver, Washington, directly north of Portland.

When this tip reached Vancouver, law enforcement officers convened to investigate. Clark County Sheriff Elbert S. Beisecker quickly learned that Hamlin's brother had a remote cabin outside of town, and he took a deputy to investigate. Sneaking up to the cabin in the dead of night, Beisecker reported later, he overheard two men, one of whom was bragging about his exploits while a fugitive from justice. That was all the sheriff needed. Smashing the window, he leveled his gun at J.H. Hamlin, a.k.a. "Slippery" Burke, and yelled "Throw up your hands or I'll kill you!" "Hamlin uttered a curse," the *Times* reported, "and made a dash for the door. The sheriff fired twice and the man staggered but kept on. By the time he got the door open the sheriff was around the corner of the cabin ... and shoving his revolver in Hamlin's face told him if he did not stop he was a dead man. Hamlin then submitted." The sheriff threw Hamlin into his buggy and galloped off toward Vancouver. Wounded in the arm and leg, this time "Slippery" Hamlin would not elude capture. After he recovered he was sent back to jail in Hillsboro, where he rejoined his buddies D.J. Tromley and his wife, and "Bricktop" McNamara. This time the jailers had fixed the lever on the cell doors to prevent an escape like the one the desperados had made a few weeks earlier. It appeared that Hamlin was in for a long stint behind bars.

The whole time his fellow prisoners were on the run, con man D.J. Tromley had been biding his time in jail, probably happy to be safe from the people who would tar and feather him again if they got a chance. To pass the time, he had been busy working on a project. The crafty Mr. Tromley had acquired a file and a saw blade from visitors, implements that jailers frown upon, precisely because of projects such as the one Tromley had embarked on. It seems that he had memorized what the jailers' keys looked like for the locks they had installed after the escape. Working from memory at night after the jailers went home, he had crafted three keys from the saw blade, perfect replicas of the one for his own cell and for the cells that held his pals "Bricktop" and "Slippery." He was nearly done with one that would have opened the door to the entire cellblock when jailers caught him in the act. The sheriff decided that his three desperados would not be allowed any more visitors until they could be tried.

Tromley and McNamara were sentenced to terms befitting the relatively petty nature of their crimes, but by the time J.H. Hamlin went on trial for his crime spree of forgeries, assaults and escapes, he had garnered widespread infamy, and observers expected a long stint for him at the penitentiary in Salem. Hamlin decided to plead guilty, however, and threw himself on the mercy of the court. He provided papers that proved that he had served valiantly as a soldier in the Philippines, a war in which many Forest Grove residents had fought. He had come back from the war broke, he told the judge, and sought his fortune from unsophisticated bankers, figuring that he could do so without a weapon or violence. The judge took pity on him and sentenced him to just six years in prison. Courtroom observers were stunned.

The greatest courtroom drama for Forest Grove residents, however, was yet to come, with the eagerly awaited trial of Congregationalist Reverend Richard Kennedy for the brazen home invasion assault and robbery. Several hundred spectators showed up at the Courthouse, where both the prosecution and the defense had assembled some of the most powerful lawyers in the state. Kennedy's wealthy supporters even landed the services of a judge from Albany to help free the minister. The state laid out its case, relying heavily on the unwavering certainty of the victims that the attacker was Kennedy, a neighbor who was well-known to them. Prosecutors also found a receipt for a bicycle that Kennedy had rented in Portland the day of the crime and which he failed to return until the following day, providing ample opportunity for a roundtrip to and from the crime scene. In his defense, Reverend Kennedy relied on his alibi that he was 20 miles away when the crime occurred. He admitted that he had rented the bicycle, but said that he had ridden it from Portland north to St. Johns, which now is part of Portland but which then was an independent city. That journey north had carried him far away from the scene of the crime, more than 20 miles west. His business in St. Johns, he said, took longer than he planned, so he rented a room for the night instead of pedaling back to Portland in the dark. The defense called the owner of the St. Johns rooming house, who said that she had rented a room to Kennedy, and while she hadn't seen him that night, she noticed a light on in his room not long before the time of the crime. As the jury retired to consider a verdict, many observers thought that things did not look good for the minister.

The Reverend Kennedy came into the trial with a distinguished background, but a very troubled recent past. Educated at Harvard, he had come West to preach, landing at the Congregational Church in Hillsboro. In Forest Grove he established himself as a writer of national renown and was known to have what the *Times* called one of the most impressive private libraries in the state. He quickly acquired many very influential friends in the university community of Forest Grove, including local newspaper editors who would go on to stand by him through his trial for the home invasion attack. A few months before the home invasion, however, the congregation had decided, for reasons not disclosed, to sever connections with Kennedy, leaving him unemployed and far away from friends and extended family on the East Coast. Then things got even worse for Kennedy and his family, when their house burned to the ground, destroying everything they owned, including his famous library, and leaving him destitute. Still, his friends refused to believe that he was capable of committing the acts for which he stood accused. Dismissing the eyewitness accounts of the victims, the *Times* focused on the fact that two of the three were women. At a time when the pages of newspapers were full of ads for tonics that promised to cure the nervous and hysterical properties that most women were thought to possess, editors urged readers to "take the charitable view that the ladies, in their intense excitement, were simply mistaken," a sentiment echoed at the trial by the defense.

Times editor Austin Craig, another staunch Kennedy supporter, directed his venom at the Reverend Cephas Clapp, an Oregon pioneer and head of the powerful Congregational Church in the state. After Kennedy's arrest, the Reverend Clapp visited him in jail as his "spiritual adviser." Clapp reportedly told other church officials that Kennedy had confessed his crime during that jail cell visit, and while Clapp could not testify against Kennedy because of clergy confidentiality, church officials refused to intervene in any way on Kennedy's behalf, including helping his supporters raise money for his steep bail. Craig raged against what he saw as a betrayal by the church of a completely innocent and honorable man. Much to the surprise of most legal observers, the jurors in Kennedy's trial came to see the Reverend in the same light, acquitting him of all charges after an all-night deliberation. Whatever the truth, Kennedy was a free man with very powerful friends, but was not welcome back to the Congregational Church. With both his religious and literary careers in ruin, he was forced to find a new line of work, which ended up being a travelling salesman for an insurance company in Saginaw, Michigan.

The early years of the Twentieth Century were bringing tremendous change to Forest Grove. Railroads were allowing people to move around the country more freely than ever before, changing the nature of western towns. Forest Grove no longer was home only to settlers, most of whom came to town and quite literally settled for the rest of their lives. Now strangers and transients became more common, and some of them were fleeing the restrictions of modern American society, hoping to find remnants of the Wild West on the dirt streets of Forest Grove. What they found instead was a strange amalgam of the Old West and Progressive Era, of rifles and refinement. They found that a man could no longer treat his family like slaves or livestock. They found that when it came to gender, Oregon was decidedly progressive, with Forest Grove granting women a limited right to vote in its 1891 city charter. At the same time, rural society still was ruled by men, with women still considered too emotionally unstable for positions of authority.

One changing aspect of society was especially slow to reach rural Oregon, however. While the state slowly was relaxing laws that excluded blacks, Oregon still was overwhelmingly white, and all too often openly hostile to people of color. The Native Americans had been relegated to reservations, and while hundreds of Chinese workers had been shipped in to build the railroads, most were literally run out of town after the tracks were laid. Still, as the new century dawned, many small towns had one or two Chinese immigrants who were tolerated, if not always fully embraced. Forest Grove had Quong Lee.

Forest Grove had survived for the first 50 years of its existence with a ragtag history of law enforcement, often relying on untrained "marshals" or deputized representatives of the county sheriff, and even loosely organized vigilantes. Fire protection had been equally haphazard, with well-intentioned but often bumbling volunteers left to their own devices to fight blazes. By 1900, however, rural Oregon towns were recognizing the importance of a skilled fire department, with Forest Grove being among the leaders in that regard when veteran firefighter Joe

Lenneville landed in town just when he was needed most. Now city fathers wanted to bring the same sense of professionalism and stability to law enforcement, and in 1907 they turned to the same man to provide it, naming Joe Lenneville town marshal.

Lenneville was a blacksmith by trade and as tough as any man in the rural West, but he also was known for his compassion, his analytical mind, and his embrace of change. He would need all of those qualities as marshal, as he learned almost immediately. Within a week he made his first arrests, of several young men accused of hurling rocks at a laundry owned by Quong Lee. Lee was in the papers often, more often than not for editors to mock his appearance and accent. Sometimes he was referred to simply as "the Mongolian," "the Oriental," or "the Celestial," or "our genial heathen Chinee." A story in the July 26, 1906, *News* was typical. It seems that Quong Lee had been injured in a construction accident some years before, knocking out three front teeth. Unable to continue in construction, he moved to Forest Grove and bought a laundry in what was described as a shack, and in which he also lived. Quong Lee worked tirelessly and finally saved enough money to have three gold teeth cemented into his jaw. "Alle samee heap good job," the *News* quoted him as saying. "Fifteen dolla me spendee." The reporter expressed hope that the new teeth might improve Quong Lee's diction, to which Quong Lee is alleged to have said that within days he would be able to speak English as well as any "'melican." The mockery in the newspapers was tame compared to what Quong Lee had to endure from others, however.

Almost exactly a year after Quong Lee got his new teeth, July 25, 1907, he was back on Page 1 of the *News*, in a story about the first arrests of Joe Lenneville's law-enforcement career. A gang of young men had gathered outside of Quong Lee's home and laundry, hurling threats at him and hurling large rocks at the wooden shutters that covered the windows of his rustic home. The rocks were big enough to smash through the shutters and the glass, allowing the miscreants to terrorize Quong Lee and steal his chickens. Quong Lee only recently had built the shutters because he was tired of having to constantly replace windows broken by hooligans. Lenneville was not going to stand for this sort of behavior and swore out arrest warrants for those involved. More specifically, he swore out warrants for those who lived within city limits, because he lacked authority to go after those who lived across the line. Despite the harassment, Quong Lee had many friends in Forest Grove, some of whom had witnessed the attack and agreed to testify against the suspects in court. They were convicted of misdemeanors. Yet while Lenneville took the case seriously, the *Washington County News* still used the opportunity to make fun of Quong Lee. "When seen in his shack," the *News* reported, "Quong Lee's teeth were chattering like he was haveing (sic) a chill and holding up his five digits to indicate the number of lads that had made him a call the first of the week, he began to mutter, 'Alle same fi boy, blakee door, wake me up. I no sabe. I no want to make trouble. Maybe they killee me. I no know.' And the old pensive Chink went back to his tub with this thought on his mind."

Quong Lee went back to his tub, cleaning the laundry of Forest Grove, and local gangs went back to terrorizing him. Although newspapers mocked him for his fear that "maybe they killee me," another high-profile case in Washington County suggested that his fears were not without merit. A few years earlier in the unincorporated hamlet of Raleigh in the eastern part of the county, a man of Chinese ancestry had been shot and killed. His name varied from news account to account, and as often as not he was referred to simply as "the Chinaman." In reality, his name didn't matter, because he was killed simply for being Chinese. It seems that a man of Chinese descent had been seen in a Portland bar with a fat wad of cash. A group of thugs had followed him to an enclave of Chinese immigrants in Raleigh, where they lost his track. Undeterred, the thugs barged in on two men and beat them violently, demanding that they identify the man with the cash. One of the two Chinese men broke free and ran, until the thugs caught up to him. The bullet that killed him came from about head level, and exited from his lower back. Coroner Charles Large testified that the most logical explanation for the trajectory of the bullet was that "the Chinaman" had been on his knees begging for mercy when he was murdered.

After another year of harassment and still harboring the thought that "maybe they killee me," Quong Lee was awakened by a noise in the middle of the night. What happened next propelled him to publicity he never imagined. The headline in the May 31, 1908, *Oregonian* proclaimed "Wounded by Chinaman." The basis of the story was fairly simple. A young Forest Grove man, Clyde Wilson, got drunk with a friend late one night and kicked in the door of Quong Lee's home. By now Quong Lee

118

had acquired a gun, and he used it to shoot at the intruder. "Wilson," *The Oregonian* noted, "is 30 years old, lives with his widowed mother, his father dying but recently." Clyde Wilson was hit in the neck but survived to tell his story to police. He said that he kicked in the door of Quong Lee's home shortly before midnight, and "with some bottles of beer went to the laundry to drink and have some lunch." Clyde Wilson was expected to survive, but a couple of days later he died from his wounds. Quong Lee, the Mongolian, the Celestial, the Oriental, the Chink of Forest Grove, was arrested for the murder of Clyde Wilson, who wanted nothing more than to kick down Quong Lee's door shortly before midnight to drink beer and "have some lunch." The county Prosecutor didn't see how the shooting constituted a crime, however, and Quong Lee returned to Forest Grove. The harassment didn't end, however, and in 1912 Quong Lee closed his laundry for good. When the *News* asked him what he planned to do, the dejected Quong said simply that he didn't know.

While Forest Grove had not decided what it wanted to do about racial diversity, by 1908 the city had for the most part moved on from the Pfanner scandal and accepted that banks were around to stay. Edward W. Haines had resurrected the ghost of Pfanner Bank and the new institution was rolling along, easily surviving several bank panics and bank holidays, as well as the notorious conman J.H. "Slippery" Hamlin. E.W. Haines himself was still a state Senator, and was now Senate President. Pfanner's trusted cashier, Frank Kane, had been serving in the same role for Haines, running the bank while Haines ran his other businesses or served in Salem.

In February 1908, Haines returned from Salem for a meeting at his bank. He learned that his books did not match those kept by Frank Kane. The Haines Bank was insolvent. When this scenario played out 10 years earlier, it was Kane's word against a man who had declared himself insane and apparently fled the country. Under those circumstances, Anton Pfanner's protestations of innocence carried little weight, and he was believed to be the swindler. The tables had turned by 1908, however, because now Kane's accuser was one of the most powerful politicians in Oregon. Kane went to prison for embezzlement. Haines picked up the pieces and started yet another bank in 1913. Stung by Kane's embezzlement, Haines wanted a cashier of even greater integrity, and he turned to young Earl Buxton, the son of a prominent family and now

119

assistant postmaster. Buxton was hesitant to leave such a prestigious and secure job, but did so after being offered part ownership in the new bank. With two of the town's most trusted men in charge, deposits flowed into the new bank. For four years the bank flourished, and Earl Buxton became clerk for the school district on top of his other responsibilities. Talk of satanic influences at work in the banking business all but died. In late 1916, a month after being elected school clerk, Buxton's life became even richer when he married the beautiful and well-to-do Miss Rita Macrum.

Three months later, Earl Buxton disappeared without a trace. Fearing the worst, the bank called police and hired private investigators to examine the books and find Buxton. Early newspaper reports only inflamed these fears, reporting that at least $2,000 was missing from the bank. Investigators quickly discovered that the $2,000 was Buxton's own money; he had withdrawn it, leaving $400 in his account. Every penny of everyone else's money was accounted for without any trace of impropriety. All police had to go on was his young newlywed bride's testimony that he had gone into Portland or Oregon City to conduct business. He had asked her several times to go with him, but Rita had declined. She said she knew nothing of the $2,000 and did not know how much money he had because they never discussed business. Fears of kidnapping, robbery, or even worse spread around town. When a reporter from *The Oregonian* interviewed her, Rita told him "I have no idea what happened to him, unless he met with foul play or is suffering from some mental derangement." Mental derangement? Yes, his beautiful newlywed said, "he was subject to frequent fits of despondency and worried over trivial matters a great deal." Whether the reporter or police were concerned about her discussing Earl Buxton in the past tense so soon after his disappearance is unclear, but the search for the popular young man ramped up. Rita Buxton continued to insist that she had no inkling of her new husband's whereabouts.

Then three months after his disappearance, Rita Buxton told the newspapers that her husband had written to her from Columbus, Ohio. He had decided that prospects for advancement in Forest Grove were dim, so he packed up and headed for a town with booming business potential, Columbus. He's fine, Rita Buxton assured everyone in Forest Grove, and she headed off to join him. For the next several decades the

120

News-Times mentioned the officially unsolved mystery of Earl Buxton, including a story in the Forest Grove Centennial edition on October 5, 1972, speculating that the Buxtons did reunite, but in Florida, not Ohio. In those decades, Census and death records were not readily available online. Today they are, and Census records pick up a Rita Buxton, married to an Earle Buxton, living in Orlando, Florida, for many years. Earle Buxton died in September 1960, in Winter Park, Florida. Despite the *News-Times* story in 1972, it turns out that Buxton had been hiding in plain sight. Nearly hidden in the October 13, 1960, edition of the *News-Times* itself was a brief, four-sentence obituary for him, with no reference to his disappearance more than 40 years earlier.

The turbulent first decade of the 1900s had brought to Forest Grove a level of crime and intrigue the likes of which the town had never seen. The decade was capped off with a couple of incidents that stunned the area. On January 21, 1909, William Heltzel, one of the best known men in Banks, came into Forest Grove to conduct some business. For reasons unknown, back in Banks a man named Monroe Huber lay in wait to ambush Heltzel on his return from the city. Huber, the *Forest Grove Times* reported on January 28, was well-known in Banks himself, but mostly for being "at times insane." Heltzel managed to pass through Banks without Huber seeing him, so the angry ambusher stalked him to his farm outside of town. There Huber confronted Heltzel and his hired hand as they left the barn. Inside the house, Mrs. Heltzel heard what she thought was a gunshot and raced outside, only to hear her husband plead "Monroe, don't shoot me any more!" Huber did shoot again but missed and ran off into the evening. Mrs. Heltzel placed a frantic call for help to the operator in Forest Grove, who dispatched doctors Charles Large and Guy Via, but by the time they arrived, William Heltzel was dead. The only connection the sheriff could find between Heltzel and Huber was that Huber once had worked for Heltzel on his farm, which elicited concern for another well-known farmer for whom Huber had worked, William Thornburgh. The sheriff immediately called the Thornburgh residence to alert them to the potential danger.

Thornburgh and his family were in their house when the phone rang, but chose not to answer it because Monroe Huber also was there, pointing a gun at the family and warning that he would shoot them if they tried to pick up the receiver. The sheriff called back several more times

121

throughout the night, but with the gun still pointed at them, the family just let the phone ring. The next morning the sheriff gathered some more men and went to the Thornburgh farm to investigate. Monroe Huber, who had spent the night pacing back and forth menacing the family, saw the horses arriving and bolted from the house. The sheriff and his men entered the house and were relieved to find the family shaken but safe. As the posse organized to search the nearby woods for Huber they heard a muffled gunshot. A short time later they found Huber, slumped against a tree with a self-inflicted gunshot through his heart. No motive ever was determined for the crime spree. "As he has passed to a higher tribunal than ours it is not for us to judge or condemn," the *Times* opined, quickly adding that "his act was the act of a maniac."

In a strange twist of fate just four months later, the Thornburgh family and the small town of Banks would find themselves in the middle of another bizarre murder case, one that said a lot about the changing culture of the rural West. On Saturday morning, May 15, 1909, John Roselair sat down for breakfast at his cabin just north of Banks in the community of Buxton, near the cabin in which Elmer Perdue was murdered a year earlier. Before breakfast was finished, Roselair had killed Lizetta, his wife of just a few months. Lizetta was at least Roselair's second wife, and perhaps third, according to some accounts. The fact that he killed Lizetta came as no surprise to some of Roselair's neighbors around Banks.

John Roselair was well known in Forest Grove, Banks, and Hillsboro. Among those who knew him well were the folks charged with protecting abused children, the employees of the Girl's and Boy's Aid Society. The leaders of that group met Roselair in 1896 after he savagely beat his eldest daughter, Marie, with an iron rod in what the Aid Society's superintendent called one of the worst cases of abuse she had ever investigated. Roselair made no apologies for his treatment of Marie, nor for how he treated Johanna, Marie's mother and his wife at the time. Roselair was known for preaching the Bible at great length to anyone who would listen, and found verses to justify literally yoking his wife Johanna to pull a plow and for never sparing the rod when it came to his children. A judge ordered that Marie be taken from the Roselair home to live with a foster family. Roselair preached the Bible in a manner that an *Oregonian* reporter described as "(reasoning) well along religious lines, not like a fanatic, but like a man who is sure of his ground." In his interpretation of Scripture, women were meant to be slaves to men, and he wanted his daughter back under his roof. He persuaded more than 70 of his friends and fellow church members to sign a petition demanding Marie's return. The Aid Society objected vehemently, but when Marie stood mute in court, she was returned to live with Roselair.

Not all who knew Roselair deemed him a fit parent, however, and for years the Aid Society fielded complaints about the way he treated his family. In 1902, complaints about how he treated Marie reached a fever pitch, but the complainants all wished to remain anonymous and the Roselair children refused to testify against him, so no action was taken. The Progressive Movement was rapidly changing how society viewed the rights of children, however, and by 1906 officials had seen enough. A former employee of the Aid Society who had dealt with Roselair in the past was now chief officer of the juvenile court in neighboring Multnomah County, and intervened to remove Johanna and her four children from the home. There would have been five children, the official told the court, except that one child had died under mysterious circumstances. Finally free from Roselair's grip, in 1907 Johanna, Marie, and the other children fled to live with Johanna's sister in Michigan.

Society had not changed enough to put John Roselair behind bars for his cruelty, however, and he immediately set out to find a new woman to be his slave. He placed ads in Portland newspapers seeking a wife. Several women later told investigators that they had responded to his ad but opted out of marrying him. Roselair persisted in his hunt and met Lizetta, who made her living telling fortunes on a Portland street. John and Lizetta married in the fall of 1908 after she promised to give up the occult and adhere to his strict religious rules. They moved to his cabin near Banks, where they were living in January as Monroe Huber went on his murderous rampage and took William Thornburgh hostage nearby. After Roselair killed Lizetta in May, a grand jury was impaneled to investigate the second shocking murder of the year in the remote area. The foreman of the jury just happened to be William Thornburgh's brother, John, who listened as neighbors testified that Roselair's marriage to Lizetta had been tempestuous from the start and that he had hinted that he might kill her for being disobedient. Yet Roselair denied any criminal motivation in her death, which he described as a tragic accident.

That Saturday morning in May, Roselair said, started like any other, with him sitting down for breakfast. He ordered Lizetta to bring him some milk. She complied, but used a spoon to skim off the cream on top. Roselair demanded that she give him the cream, and she again complied, by throwing it in his face. At this point, Roselair told the sheriff, he grabbed a knife and a hatchet and slashed angrily at the pan to defend himself from Lizetta dumping milk on his head. It was only when his wife dropped the pan and threw her hands in the air that Roselair realized that instead of hitting the pan, he had instead struck his wife in the arms and neck, about 15 times, to be exact. Quickly determining that she could not survive these accidental wounds, Roselair said, he decided to slash and beat her with the hatchet several more times to ensure that she would not suffer. He told his story in a matter-of-fact way at the county jail, citing Biblical justifications for his actions. This time, however, the community did not rally to his support, and instead a lynch mob of at least 150 people formed outside the jail, demanding frontier justice. An *Oregonian* reporter wrote that the sheriff did little to dissuade the mob and refused to bring in extra protection, but eventually cooler heads prevailed and Roselair lived to testify before Thornburgh's grand jury, where he again calmly told of his wife's demise. The grand jurors did not believe his story and bound him over to stand trial. The wheels of justice moved much more quickly in 1909 than they do today. Within months, John Roselair was on trial for murder, and had a new defense: Insanity. The jury did not believe that story, either, and sentenced him to death. He appealed all the way to the state Supreme Court, but on September 8, 1910, he was hanged in Salem, although not before a 15-minute speech from the gallows, delivering a sermon on the lesson to be learned from his situation. That lesson, he repeated several times, was that "a woman should never attack a man. It is all wrong, and this woman is the cause of her own accidental death."

In the decades since, unfortunately, many criminals have proved themselves to be as dense as John Roselair. Instead of walking away from confrontation, they escalate it, and in far too many cases the crimes still involve women and children. People still rob banks, set fires, commit hate crimes and steal from family members. Some of those crimes still go unsolved, but Forest Grove's police, prosecutors and medical examiners have been much better students than their criminal counterparts, learning important lessons from the mistakes of their predecessors.

Chapter

8

Water, water everywhere and not a drop to drink

It rains a lot in Forest Grove. Not as much as many Californians think, but still plenty enough to grow huge trees, produce bumper crops for farmers and keep rivers and streams flowing briskly. It rains enough that early residents of the city could harness the water to create cheap electricity, although it didn't always rain enough to provide consistent drinking water or to wash all of the raw sewage from the streets. Rain is one of Forest Grove's most abundant, and totally free, resources. Still, almost from the day the first settlers arrived, there have been fights over water.

These fights often were over life and death matters, as outlined in an editorial in the June 20, 1895, *Washington County Hatchet*, after the town's flour mill burned to the ground. "When some time ago impure water sacrificed its sixth victim of this winter among our young people, attention was called to for what so often has been urged: the imperative need of a pure and abundant water supply. With those six human lives in mind it seems insignificant to suggest that the $8,000 lost to the fire and the wiping out of a leading industry should be a warning to provide water."

Early settlers dug wells. Shallow, productive wells. No problem, until your neighbor digs a well too close for your comfort. As Pacific University grew and the town started to grow around it, all the new wells were starting to strain the shallow aquifer. As downtown grew denser, it no longer was practical to dig a well for each building. Then in the 1890s a fire brigade formed and its members believed strongly that having a source of water might help it fight fires. About the same time that the fire brigade was forming, excitement was spreading through town about the advent of electricity. Creating power required large supplies of water, either to turn turbines or to boil water to create steam. By the 1890s, there were so many demands for water that a hodgepodge of individual wells no longer was the answer.

Forest Grove did not have a major river, as Astoria, Portland, Oregon City and Salem did. The Tualatin flowed close to the city, but there was a problem: Gravity. The city was built on high ground to avoid floods, but the elevation meant that to tap the Tualatin, the city would have to pump the water uphill for a couple of miles. In 1895, that would have been a major engineering feat. What Forest Grove did have was Gales Creek; not a river but enough of a creek, it seemed, to provide the small town with all the water and electricity it needed in 1895. And just southwest of town on B Street, right where it crosses Gales Creek, Forest Grove city fathers saw a solution.

George Naylor was an early, entrepreneurial Forest Grove pioneer, and owned the land upon which sat a powerhouse, built to provide power for a cannery. The powerhouse produced far more power than the cannery used, so a plan was hatched. The city would buy a fully functioning, steam-driven powerplant for $10,500, including a pipe from Gales Creek for the plant's boiler with enough left over to fill a city water tower. Forest Grove had solved two of its most vexing problems and at the same time had planted itself at the forefront of a public electricity revolution, bringing power to its people.

Soon, however, Edward W. Haines entered the picture. E.W. Haines was a dashing figure around town, tall, slender, and sporting jet black hair and a full mustache that curled upward in the handlebar style of the day. Haines arrived in Forest Grove in 1882, drawn west from his native Hardin County, Iowa. Haines was drawn by the same influence that had drawn so many to the city over the years, namely education. Soon he had a degree from Pacific University, and gathered the capital to open a flour mill of his own, just northwest of town along the banks of Gales Creek. He diverted water from the creek, which he turned into steam, which he used to create electricity to grind wheat into flour. Soon his mill was processing 65 bushels of wheat per day, and he added a second shift to keep up with demand. Soon after that he was running three shifts, creating electricity 24-hours a day. He created so much electricity, in fact, that he figured he had enough to sell to Forest Grove to keep lights operating all night. He went to the City Council and offered to supply the city's electricity and water, all for a whopping $300 a year less than the current private contract cost the city. While a $300 annual savings might not sound like much today, it represented more than 10 percent of the town's water and electricity budget. On top of all that, he promised to provide all-night lights for homes and to power street lamps until midnight. The City Council jumped at his offer and signed a tentative agreement. Soon Forest Grove's lights would shine all day, or at least from sunrise until midnight. Just as important was the other part of his plan, which was to build an electric rail line from the depot a mile from town into the city's center.

Some folks disapproved, however, because they favored public ownership of utilities. Prominent among this group was Alanson Hinman, one of the town's leading citizens and a member of the City Council. A handful of others disapproved because they, too, had tapped Gales Creek for power and were selling small amounts to the city. Together, they demanded proof that Haines could make good on his lofty promises. Undaunted, on April 19, 1901, Haines invited civic leaders and reporters to come to his powerhouse and see that he could deliver far more than he promised. His audience was won over, with the next day's *Oregonian* proclaiming in a headline "Plenty of power for lights." By summer, Haines had the contract to illuminate Forest Grove. By late summer, however, Gales Creek was not as full of water as it was on April 19, the typical peak of its flow from the melting snow in the Coast Range and the steady rain of late winter. By the end of another hot, dry summer, the streamflow was so low that the promise of street lights until midnight seemed like an impossibility.

Forest Grove quickly was becoming something of a laughing stock when it came to electricity. A newspaper columnist in Gales City, a tiny hamlet a few miles up Gales Creek from town, taunted his big city neighbors in the January 15, 1903, *Times*. "People who do not live at Gales City must be very careful when they come to this place that they don't get bewildered and take it for Portland as we have electric lights here." The correspondent especially taunted downtown businesses, because tired of waiting for electric street lamps, they had purchased "Rockefeller Oil Lamps" for the streets. The lamps were fueled by coal oil supplied by the Standard Oil Company, which had a virtual monopoly on petroleum products in the United States, allowing it to control fuel prices. As an example, soon after the Forest Grove lamps were installed, Standard Oil doubled the price of the oil to light them.

In the meantime, Alanson Hinman went to court to void the contract between Haines and the city, citing among other factors that Haines had promised electricity at least as plentiful and reliable as when the city produced it, and was falling short. There also was the matter of the $300 annual savings. That figure, which Haines, his City Council supporters and the *Forest Grove Times* had touted as the city's cost of power plant maintenance actually represented Forest Grove's entire maintenance budget for streets, sidewalks, etc. Haines and Mayor Walter Hoge fought the lawsuit, and the *Times* rallied public support for Haines with editorials. Although those editorials were unsigned, it was no secret that Mayor Hoge owned the paper. Haines was a very powerful man, having taken over the town's bank when previous owner Anton Pfanner left it insolvent. Haines had powerful friends in the state Capitol as well, because he was a state senator who chaired the committee on banking. A Washington County judge dismissed the lawsuit with hardly a hearing, and it appeared that public power was a thing of the past in Forest Grove.

E.W. Haines wanted to capture all of the contracts for electricity in Western Washington County before his rivals from the Portland area could move in, but Gales Creek clearly couldn't support the cities of Cornelius, Banks, Gaston and beyond, because it couldn't even support Forest Grove in the summer. Haines established a powerhouse along a much more robust water source, the headwaters of the Tualatin River. Running normally, he bragged, the dam and powerhouse would supply four to five times the power that Forest Grove would use, and production could be increased easily if needed. On February 1, 1904, Forest Grove was plunged into darkness for four days as Haines moved generators from Gales Creek to the Tualatin. By now, a growing chorus of critics doubted that Haines could complete the move in such a short time, or that his new dam would perform as promised when it did go on line. He still had his primary cheerleader on board, however, and Mayor Walter Hoge used the pages of the *Forest Grove Times* to lavish praise on his friend, gloating in the February 11 edition that Haines met his four-day deadline, although he acknowledged that corners had to be cut in order to do so. It seems that the gauge that measured how much power was flowing out of the generator broke during the move, and it took several days for a new one to arrive from San Francisco. To meet the deadline, Haines had his men at the remote dam guess at how much electricity might be needed in a town they could not see nor communicate with. Hoge admitted that lights waxed and waned a bit, but never went out entirely. Better yet, the engineers never sent enough power to blow up all the lights and set the town on fire. That threat was very real, Hoge said, because output from the dam far exceeded even what Haines had predicted. Hoge taunted Haines' detractors, assuring them that electricity would be unlimited from now on.

Oregon's small rivers long have confounded those who live along them. In the winter and spring they can quickly bury a town in floodwater, yet by late summer they can slow to a comparative trickle. The Tualatin's headwaters were no exception. The summer of 1904 was brutally hot and dry. By August, lights in Forest Grove went dark because there wasn't nearly enough water in the Tualatin to power the generators. Within a few days, Haines had moved an old steam generator to the powerhouse, and Hoge assured his reading public that this would solve the problem permanently. It did not, and Forest Grove suffered through the end of summer and early fall with flickering lights and frequent blackouts. By Thanksgiving enough rain had fallen to get the dam back to full strength.

Even full strength, however, proved to be problematical. The flimsy power lines that creeped up and over the densely wooded hill from his Patton Valley dam into and across Scoggins Valley and on into Forest Grove frequently snapped when winter storms dropped branches on them. Even under good conditions, the poorly insulated lines lost much of their power on the way into town. Haines had labor problems with the workers at the remote dam, leading to a threatened strike over working conditions, including a shortage of promised chewing tobacco. In July 1906, Haines' voltage regulator at the town's telephone system failed. The phone system's outgoing fuses worked, preventing the surge from spreading through the wires and starting fires all over town. The only fire was in the telephone switching room, as the excess power burst wires and set the walls ablaze. This time Forest Grove kept its power but lost its phones. The *Washington County News* covered the fiasco with a small story, under a glowing profile of "the enterprise and business foresight of one of our prominent citizens," namely E.W. Haines.

In the fall of 1906, Haines encountered the opposite problem that plagued his dam's first year; this year the river went from trickle to torrent in a few short weeks and blew out part of the dam. With the Tualatin now the source of Forest Grove's power, the city went completely dark again for weeks while repairs were completed. Through it all, E.W. Haines kept his powerful friends happy, and kept his contract to supply the town with power. The Council even gave him a vote of confidence at a special meeting called to discuss the issue that drew a large crowd to the Council chambers, which were lit by candles because the power was out.

Although the *Forest Grove Times* loved Haines, the folks over at the competing *Washington County News* were less enamored of him, culminating in a long story cataloging the many complaints against him harbored by the editors. E.W. responded with a long letter to the editor, which the *News* published at the top of Page 1 on October 17, 1907, under a headline dripping with sarcasm: "FAULT LIES WITH CITY: Communication to *The News* So Places the Blame, but Offers a Remedy." Technically, Haines pointed out, his contract with the city called for him to deliver current only to the city limits; what happened to it after that, he asserted, was the city's problem. His crews did the best they could to maintain the system within Forest Grove, but nothing that happened could be blamed on him once the electricity crossed city limits. He acknowledged that much of the savings he had promised citizens had been eaten up by the city hiring maintenance people to work on the lines, but he said the shoddy work the city did only added to the woes. "Nothing has ever happened to cause any trouble to the lights in any part of the city that a large number of people have not felt that the fault was with us," Haines wrote. "Sometimes it was, but many times we had nothing whatever to do with it." He complained that the city didn't even own a portable volt meter, so could not prove when the problem lay with his system. He went on to offer his remedy for these problems: The citizens of Forest Grove should pay him more money so that he could hire a full-time maintenance man and replace the wiring within city limits.

Haines did not get his wish, and in December 1907 he had bigger worries. The nation's boom and bust economy since the start of the Industrial Age had caused another panic, and all banks were ordered closed to prevent a run on deposits. When the "bank holiday" was lifted, E.W. Haines joined the owners of the other two local banks in proclaiming themselves safe, solid and secure. Even the editor of the *News* agreed that Forest Grove residents had nothing to fear about their reopened local banks.

About a month later the banks were still open and the lights were still on, at least most of the time, but things were not looking so bright for E.W. Haines. On a trip home from Salem, where he now served as Senate President, Haines discovered that his bank was insolvent. He accused cashier and former mayor Frank Kane of embezzling $20,000 worth of deposits, money belonging to Haines' powerful supporters. To add to his woes, the much-larger Oregon Electric Railway rolled into town to compete with Haines' electric railway, which he opened in 1906. After his bank failed and some of his supporters abandoned him, his opponents were getting the upper hand. Among other things, the city still didn't have the street lights Haines had promised for years, and the Council decided things had to change. The city still owned and operated its small powerhouse on B Street and used it for municipal purposes, but in the 13 years since the city bought it, Forest Grove's electricity needs had multiplied, and there was no way the small generator could produce enough to light the entire town. One faction wanted to upgrade the B Street plant and go back into the public power business. The pro-private power forces had another idea, and had the votes to pass it. The city would accept bids to sell its generating plant on B Street in return for a private company's promise to upgrade it.

Wounded but not without some remaining powerful supporters, Haines was not about to give up. He made an offer to become exclusive supplier of power to the town. By now, however, the majority of the City

Council had abandoned hope that he could ever deliver on his promises, and rejected his bid. Instead, the Council offered a 25-year contract to A. Welch, an Albany businessman, to take over the city plant to generate electricity as of December 1, 1909. Haines agreed to supply power until that date. But while no one in Forest Grove seemed sorry to see Haines replaced as supplier of electricity, many were outraged at the deal with Welch. For starters, merchants tired of waiting for street lights had taken it upon themselves to purchase "Rockefeller lamps," and did not want to lose their investment, and the deal with Welch required electric streetlights. More critical was price; accustomed to paying about three cents a kilowatt from Haines, residents suffered sticker shock at the five-and-a-half-cent tab in the proposed contract.

Welch and the city renegotiated the contract, including lower rates and a shorter term. The weary citizens of Forest Grove waited for work to begin on the B Street powerhouse and what they hoped finally would be a stable electricity supply. They grew nervous as December 1, 1909, approached because nothing seemed to be happening on B Street. Welch assured the town that while he was running behind schedule, he would supply power from other sources until the powerhouse could be upgraded. Behind the scenes, Welch was engaged in frantic talks with E.W. Haines. It seems that Welch did not have an alternative source for power and wanted desperately for Haines to sell him his dam and plant. Haines was not about to do so, because he still had contracts with other towns and other customers outside the Forest Grove city limits. Welch pleaded with Haines, and when the City Council learned the truth they pleaded with Haines as well. Haines was having none of it, and threatened to turn off the lights on December 1. Further, he wrote an open letter to citizens that he wouldn't sell them any more power even if they offered him a new contract. Haines made good on his threat, and on December 1, 1909, instead of reliable electricity, the city of Forest Grove was plunged into darkness yet again.

The bitter battle played an integral part in the mayor and most of the City Council being swept from office in December 1909, and one of the first acts of the new leaders was to scrap the proposed sale of the power plant. Instead, they committed the city to public ownership of its electricity. They hastily authorized the purchase of a larger boiler for the B Street plant and 200 cords of wood with which to power it. They also ordered city crews to immediately start trimming trees that were snapping power lines and sapping power from them. Finally the Council decided to not purchase electric streetlights, leaving the downtown merchants with their Rockefeller Lamps and the residential areas still in the dark, a situation that would persist until 1914, when the city finally got 24-hour lights. Forest Grove's public utility would create its own power until 1939, when it started buying power from the federal Bonneville Power Administration's new Bonneville Dam on the Columbia River.

The new Council was not rid of E.W. Haines, however. Not by a long shot. At their second meeting in 1910, the new Council granted Haines a permit to install private power poles through the city to move his electricity through Forest Grove and on to his customers in the nearby cities of Cornelius and Banks, all in exchange for a $10 per year lease. With that order of business out of the way, the Council placed a large order of wooden pipes to help solve another of the city's water woes, specifically the sorry state of the town's drinking water from Gales Creek. The wooden pipes would carry water from a new 12-mile-long pipeline that would bring fresh water from Clear Creek in the Coast Range foothills. The pipeline had been pledged years ago but delayed by legal wrangling involving the city and the man from whom it bought its water: E.W. Haines.

Haines had lost his bank, lost his electrical franchise with the city and was struggling to save his railroad. He still had several things going for him, however. He was a powerhouse in the state Republican Party, and was on the boards of the town's two most powerful institutions, Pacific University and the Congregational Church. He also still held the contract to supply the city with drinking water, which was worth as much as the power contract had been to him in annual revenue. Both his electricity and water systems had been rickety and plagued by problems. In giving up his fight for the power franchise, Haines as much as admitted that he didn't have the wherewithal to bring his electrical utility up to modern standards. He also was threatened by a new electricity colossus forming in Portland. This company, which later became Portland General Electric had a source of power, Willamette Falls, that dwarfed anything Haines could muster, and a contract to supply power to Portland that gave its owners resources that Haines could only dream about. But at the same time that his hopes were dimming for electricity, his water utility looked like it was here to stay, with a new $70,000 infrastructure. How Haines came to have $70,000 to invest in a water system but lacked the resources to upgrade his electric utility is a long and controversial story, but then so is every aspect of his relationship with the city of Forest Grove.

Gales Creek had failed as an adequate supply of water to create electricity, and by 1910 the City Council agreed that it also had failed as a source of drinking water. Residents complained about the taste and of getting sick. Haines produced a report from a biologist that the water from the creek was safe to drink, but he knew there wasn't enough of it regardless. Haines came up with a plan to supply Forest Grove with water to last for decades. All he needed was a new dam and pipeline from the headwaters of a much purer source, Clear Creek. Well, he needed that and $70,000 from bonds that the city would sell and that taxpayers would repay. Once the dam and pipeline were in place, he could sell the taxpayers all the water they could drink for the next 25 years. The city would pay Haines for the water, then charge its citizens extra to pay for interest on the bonds and to install and maintain pipes from the main pipeline to distribute the water door-to-door. Once again there was an outcry from many in the community, and the company that had agreed to sell the bonds for the city objected as more details of the deal emerged. Haines again filed suit and took it all the way to the state Supreme Court to have the bond issue declared valid. However, Haines could not sue the bond company directly, because the deal was between the city and bond company and he was not a party, so he did the next best thing. He sued Forest Grove. The City Council still supported the bond issue, however, and hired attorneys to side with Haines. The convoluted suit caused headaches for judges, who just passed it up the chain for the Supreme Court to figure out. The bond issue was upheld, and work began immediately. Haines would get his pipeline. City taxpayers would get good drinking water, but were faced with a new problem. Forest Grove desperately needed a new City Hall and had hired Harry Nauffts to build it. When talk arose of the pipeline job, worth many times more than the City Hall project, the Council awarded that contract to Nauffts as well. He didn't have the resources to build both, so he put the eagerly awaited City Hall on the back burner for many months. As 1909 ended, Haines had lost his power contract with the city but in its place he still had a long-term agreement to sell water to Forest Grove. As 1910 began, Haines sold his powerhouse on the Tualatin for $60,000 and exited the electricity business. E.W. Haines invested $45,000 of that windfall and built a new building for another bank he had just purchased. E.W. Haines was back in the utility business, back in the banking business and back on top.

Problems continued to plague the water system that city taxpayers built for Haines, but it was a dramatic improvement over the previous version. Even after the city took control again when Haines left town, the water supply was sufficient for about the next 40 years. By the 1950s, however, first farmers and then cities were running out of water in the summers, although they still found themselves with far too much water when the winter floods came. At the urging of Oregon's Congressional delegation, the Army Corps of Engineers came up with a plan to solve both problems with one huge project along the Tualatin River.

The river's headwaters are in the Coast Range mountains, and its first few miles feature spectacular waterfalls and rapids. But after the last of the waterfalls, the river enters Patton Valley and hits farmland, flattened by glaciers, floods of biblical proportions and even an ancient inland sea that once sustained sharks. The distance as the crow flies from the top of its headlands to where it empties into the Willamette River is less than 50 miles, but once it hits the flatlands, the Tualatin begins to meander, curving north, east, south, east, north, thus taking about 80 miles to complete its journey. The Tualatin just is in no hurry to get to where it's going, especially when it's swollen with floodwater. The Corps of Engineers proposed a huge dam in Patton Valley, to create a reservoir that would hold back the floods in the winter and store the excess water for summer when the river ran shallow. From the dam to the Willamette, the Corps would dig channels across the river's S curves, cutting 20 miles off of its length. Downstream farmers and sportsmen objected to the plan, favoring instead a project that would clear vegetation from the banks and then encase the river in concrete to keep its water moving swiftly. Upstream, close to Forest Grove, the concerns were more personal, and involved the death of an entire community, Cherry Grove.

Cherry Grove was no stranger to dams. It owed its very existence to a dam built in 1913 by the Lovegren family, which created Cherry Grove as a utopian community. Because of the dam, Cherry Grove was one of the first rural communities in the West with electric lights. When the dam burst four months later, the Lovegrens' lumber mill, and the jobs and power it created, were gone. E.W. Haines had a hydro dam there before Cherry Grove even existed, but he sent his electricity into Gaston and Forest Grove. Cherry Grove went dark for more than 20 years, ultimately becoming one of the last remote towns to get lights from the Rural Electrification Administration. The people of Cherry Grove knew about dams, and they didn't like them. They especially didn't like this 1950s version, because it would have submerged their homes and farms under water. Oregon's Congressional delegation warned the people of the Tualatin Valley that they better agree on a plan fast, or the rest of Congress would spend the money elsewhere. Congress ended up spending the money elsewhere, and Forest Grove's thirst for water only increased.

By early 1953 Forest Grove still was drawing enough water from its primary pumping station at Clear Creek and its backup at Gales Creek to meet its needs, but only with the aid of reservoirs during the dry summer months. But in the fall of 1953 heavy snow started falling across the Coast Range and Forest Grove and just wouldn't stop. In January 1954 the snows melted and the rain set in. A torrent of water washed down Clear Creek, so strong that it gouged out a new channel in many places, including near where Forest Grove extracted its water supply. Worse yet, the channel it carved undercut the city's pipeline, which collapsed. This time, Forest Grove was in danger of losing water because of too much water. The city assured its residents that it could meet their needs, if necessary, by using all of its rights to water from Gales Creek, but doing so would cut off water to all the farmers downstream.

Bickering continued until Congress did indeed yank its support for a dam, and Forest Grove's boom and bust, love-hate relationship with water only got worse. Finally Washington County cities got together to share the cost of water from the Tualatin and elsewhere, and then joined with farmers. With everyone working together, Scoggins Dam was built, damming Scoggins, Sain and Tanner creeks to create Hagg Lake in the mid 1970s. The region's water problems were solved ... until the early 1980s when it became apparent that the region needed still more water. Once again, all eyes turned to the Tualatin, and plans began anew for a dam that would submerge Cherry Grove. This time opposition was fierce, led in part by 93-year-old Levi Lovegren, engineer on the ill-fated dam in

1913. The idea died. There is water everywhere in Forest Grove, but clearly there never will be enough.

One of the most pressing needs for water in the 1950s was for a cause few people consider, and which almost no one wants to think about: treating sewage. No one but the sanitation department needs to worry about sewage when things are going right, but when they're not, sewage quickly gets everyone's attention. In Forest Grove's early years, few things got people's attention more than sewage.

For about the first 60 years of the city's life, homeowners were allowed to dispose of their sewage as they saw fit. Until the advent of indoor plumbing, the usual means of doing so was to dig a hole in the ground and put an outhouse over it. As toilets moved indoors, people wrestled with the best way to drain them out of the house. Some people ran a pipe out to the pit their outhouse once had guarded and created a cesspool. Some people installed drain fields designed to let the sewage dissipate and decompose in the ground. A surprising number just replicated the outhouse model and had the toilet dump straight into a hole beneath their house. Others ran a pipe and discharged their raw waste into the nearest drainage ditch or waterway; the waste often finding its way into Council Creek, which flowed conveniently through town and into Gales Creek, just south of the city. Still others just emptied things into the street. The town's ditches were designed to drain rainwater into Gales Creek, but now those ditches carried not only stormwater but also the city's raw sewage into the local waterways. In the rainy winters, there was ample water to rush whatever sewage was dumped into the ditches out into Gales Creek and then the Tualatin, where it became a problem for other towns downstream. In the dry summers, however, the sewage tended to just sit there, baking in the sun. By 1890, this had become enough of a problem that the city's first water system was designed for three primary purposes: to provide water for fire protection, to provide water to create steam to power an electrical generator, and to provide enough water to keep the drainage ditches flowing in the summer. As an unintended consequence, the water dumped into the ditches in the summer also provided the town's children a cool place to play.

By 1900, doctors were getting tired of treating children for intestinal ailments, sometimes fatal, caused by playing in raw sewage. City fathers were tired of fielding complaints about how neighbors were befouling the neighborhoods. The city passed an ordinance mandating that homeowners dispose of their sewage in a way that was not offensive, but did not mandate how it must be done or even what constituted "offensive." Neighbors often decided such matters for themselves. For example, in one neighborhood people complained about a neighbor who emptied his sewage into the street. When he rerouted his pipe to dump the sewage into a ditch instead, the neighbors were satisfied and the case was closed. In 1912, the ordinance was amended to create a committee to determine what constituted an offense, but the city's doctors and others were fed up and demanded a sewer system. The powerful Woman's Club entered the fray as well. Fed up with the flies that were making life miserable in Forest Grove, the women passed a resolution asking townspeople to shun stores that left raw meat uncovered in their sidewalk displays, and for schoolchildren to be instructed on the dangers of flies and the raw sewage that attracted them. Finally, in August 1912 citizens packed City Council chambers to demand that something be done about the open sewers. After a more pressing debate about whether W.C. Kahle should be allowed to open his pool hall on Sunday (he was not), the Council listened to the citizens' concerns. The Council had been elected on a platform of paving the streets in the downtown business district and solving the sewer issue, and had made good on its paving promise, but had failed to act on the sewer issue.

Plans were drawn up for a system to simply install pipes in the existing ditches, allow everyone to hook up if they were lucky enough to live close to one, then run the pipe out to Gales Creek, which would then whisk it away into the Tualatin. Plans were scrapped when an engineer pointed out that when Gales Creek floods, as it does on a regular basis, the sewage would have nowhere to go and would back up in the pipes and eventually into the houses. That plan obviously wouldn't work, so they devised a plan to extend the pipe all the way to the Tualatin. One problem was solved, although not for the folks living downstream on the river. But now the city had a new problem on its hands; townspeople did not want to pay to dispose of their waste, something that always had been free. After three years of wrangling, work was begun on the sewer system. Before it was completed, Council members had quit in protest, the city engineer engaged in public yelling matches with the mayor, and the city was faced with sticker shock when the final bill was presented.

The city's engineer estimated that the sewer would cost $86,000, so the city jumped at an offer from Elliott Construction of Portland to do the job for $58,000. Elliott went to work, laying the pipe and covering it quickly; too quickly, in the opinion of the city engineer, whose job it was to inspect the project. As he uncovered the pipes to inspect them, he found what he considered to be unacceptably shoddy work and ordered many repairs. The contractor complained to the Council and persuaded the majority to take his side on the matter. Work continued apace and the city engineer continued to complain to little avail. Fed up Council members resigned. The company was given authority to do most of the inspection itself, and soon finished the project and presented its bill to the city. The $58,000 project, the company said, had turned out to cost $73,000, and the owners wanted their money. The company and city engineer bickered back and forth until the city hired a consultant to inspect the system. The consultant reported the next week that it was impossible to test the system because it was plugged by mud and many of the pipes were full of concrete from shoddy construction. Within weeks the contractor sued the city, and now said that after reviewing bills, he was owed not $58,000, not $73,000, but $88,000. The trial began in 1916, but a recess was called when the contractor's attorney became ill. By the time he recovered, World War I had erupted and many of the key witnesses were fighting in France. The trial would not resume until the war ended two years later, and when the suit finally resumed, the contractor had raised his bill to $125,000, more than twice his original bid, and Forest Grove still did not have a functioning sewer.

The city won its case, but with appeals and other wrangling, in 1922 the Council still was paying off its attorney, E.B. Tongue of Hillsboro. Six years after the trial began and 10 years after deciding it needed a sewer, Forest Grove finally felt confident enough to timidly approach the subject of building one that worked. The city proceeded a little too timidly, because a year later nothing had been done and the state of Oregon stepped in. Forest Grove residents were still getting sick from sewage and towns and landowners downriver were getting sick of the raw waste that floated through their communities. One of those landowners was the city's attorney, E.B. Tongue. The state told Forest Grove that it was preparing to file suit against the city if it didn't act immediately. More than a year later the state had not sued, but neither had the city come up

140

with a plan. Fed up, the Rotary Club took matters into its own hands and worked with engineers to provide suggestions. Most agreed that the city should start from scratch, ripping out the non-functioning system and beginning anew. The bank that held title to the old system since the contractor's loss in court had a different plan. It wanted the city to buy the system and rebuild it so it would work. Either plan was going to be expensive, however, because by 1924 the state had laws requiring that sewage be treated before being dumped into Oregon's rivers.

The city opted to follow the bank's plan, and moved onto other business. At the same meeting the Council discussed a new demand from the state, this one to arrange for garbage service. That discussion led to a solution to yet another urgent problem facing the city. Once again, flood-swollen Clear Creek had overflowed its banks and undermined the city's water pipeline near its intake. By now the city had a reservoir with enough water to meet its needs for a few months, but once again Forest Grove was on the verge of losing drinking water unless it could build a dike and save the pipeline. The Council agreed to a plan to fix two problems at once. It would hire a company to pick up the town's trash and haul it up to Clear Creek, where it would be dumped to create the needed dike to protect the intake and pipeline.

A few months passed, the pipeline wasn't repaired and the reservoir was nearly empty. Forest Grove did not lose its water entirely, but emergency ordinances placed dramatic restrictions on water use, and the fire department feared it wouldn't have enough water to battle a large blaze. Except for monitoring such things as watering lawns and washing cars, however, the city had no way of knowing who was using too much water, because it was the only town in Washington County that did not have water meters. Citizens at the Council meeting were not happy that they would be charged to have meters installed, but that concern took a backseat to one that had brought them to the meeting in the first place. With not enough water left to fill the drainage ditches that flowed into Council Creek and keep the creek itself flowing during the dry summer, the creek had gone stagnant and was now more human waste than water. The stench was choking the city. The Council members listened to the complaints and decided that now might be a good time to think about installing a working sewer.

The next year the city had not acted and the Rotary Club again stepped in, negotiating with the bank that owned the old sewer and settling on a price of $33,000 for the city to regain ownership of the lines. Council members thanked the club for its efforts but said that it would have to hire an engineer to assess the cost of rebuilding it before it could act on the proposal. While the city decided what to do, a man named John Wegner, who lived next to Council Creek, came to address the Council. His entire family had become ill because of the sewage, he said. He and his children recovered, but his wife died from her illness, and he wanted $15,000 in compensation for negligence on the part of the city. As with many other problems, Council members ignored Wegner's problem, hoping that it would just go away.

More months passed without action and now the Chamber of Commerce stepped in, passing a resolution demanding that the city build a sewer. First, however, they wanted the city to get out of the electricity business and turn over its plant to Puget Sound Light and Power Company to operate. Council members were unanimous in their opposition to getting out of the power business, but agreed to listen to a proposal from the Seattle company.

The Chamber's broadside on both issues was the product of a turbulent time in Oregon's history, a time in which public debate raged about social class, taxes and socialism. Forest Grove found itself at the epicenter of those debates in Oregon, so while it had been many years since public ownership of the electrical utility had been a major issue locally, by 1925 public ownership of utilities had become a major issue throughout the West. The sewer issue was just as contentious, despite the fact that by 1925 every important institution in town was demanding that one be built; now the debate was not so much about sanitation as it was about how to pay for it under Oregon's chaotic tax system.

The Tualatin Plains had since its settling been agrarian and egalitarian in nature. The earliest settlers in the 1840s and 1850s had been given hundreds of acres each by the federal government. The settlers used their free land primarily for personal use. They hunted deer, ducks, bears and other animals for food. They cleared the forest for wood to build their homes and barns, and to cook and heat their homes with. They used the cleared land to graze small herds of cattle and engage in relatively small-scale agriculture. Large-scale farming was impractical with teams of horses or oxen, and there was little market for their produce because most of their neighbors grew their own and they had no means of shipping it to faraway cities. That left most of the early pioneers land-rich and cash-poor, but that didn't matter because there was not much to buy when food, housing, water and heat were all free.

The land wasn't worth much either, really. There are numerous stories of 320-acre donation land claims being traded for a single horse or enough money to flee back to the relative comfort of the Midwest and East Coast. One pioneer who profited from cheap prices was John Walker, who traded a horse for a land claim east of Gaston. He then passed on the land to his son and grandson. By 1904, that grandson, Raleigh Walker, still had no use for hundreds of acres, so he donated a large chunk of it to the Seventh-day Adventist Church to build the Laurelwood Academy boarding school. Similar donations from Harvey Clarke, Elkanah Walker and others were used as the grounds for Pacific University. To raise money to build the campus and pay staff, Pacific University then sold off pieces of the land for working capital. Those sales allowed shopkeepers to build downtown Forest Grove and for families to buy small plots, just big enough for a house, a few chickens, a dairy cow and a garden. The land was cheap, but because it had not cost the University anything, the school still made a substantial amount of money.

All this cheap, abundant land was both literally and figuratively the foundation of Forest Grove's economy until about the time of the First World War. Nearly all services and goods were local. Even the handful of industrial operations, such as sawmills, canneries and milk condensers, were small-scale, with owners and managers who didn't make much more than the people they employed. People had no insurance and little money for health care, so doctors couldn't charge very much for housecalls and office visits, which meant that many of them, too, had lifestyles more middle-class than aristocratic.

"There was seldom much variation in political ideas between economic and social classes in Oregon in 1916," Thomas Jon Rykowski wrote in *Preserving the Garden: Progressivism in Oregon*, a 1981 doctoral dissertation at the University of Oklahoma, and "the tendency toward social and political conformity was strengthened by the First World War." But after the war, the Industrial Age finally began to creep into Oregon in a major way. In addition, the cheap land was becoming scarce, at least within easy reach of the city in the days before the widespread use of automobiles and construction of good rural roads. Tension mounted between those who owned land and those who didn't. The introduction of steam and gasoline powered agricultural implements allowed those who had held on to large tracts of land to farm at a commercial scale, and trains and trucks expanded markets for what they grew. To meet the demands, some farmers hired low-paid laborers to work the land, while others rented their farms to others to work. A fair number of those tenant farmers in the Forest Grove area were Japanese immigrants. Meanwhile, improved railroads and shipping created national and international markets for timber, so sawmills hired low-wage laborers and the docks in Portland and Astoria hired low-wage longshoremen, again often turning to immigrants.

"If conformity characterized the period preceding the war, the postwar years, at least in the minds of many, seemed to be years of diversity," Rykowski continues in his dissertation. "Oregon showed visible signs of unrest following the war. … The old society and its traditions seemed to be disintegrating. But into the breach stepped the churches, fraternal organizations and other traditionalist influences."

None of that seems to have anything to do with electricity and sewers in Forest Grove, Oregon, or with why the Rotary and Chamber were demanding the city launch a public sewer utility while simultaneously closing its public electric utility. None of those social changes seem, on the surface, to explain why it was taking the city so long to build the sewer that everyone wanted, either. But think of it this way: While the old guard in Forest Grove clung to the traditional way of life, the Progressive Movement was gaining a foothold in urban centers and in academia, demanding improved civic services, including sanitation. In other words, there were fissures developing between the two bedrocks of Forest Grove, agriculture and academia. It's no wonder that many of the city's merchant class felt conflicted.

On the one hand, people were concerned about the recent Russian Revolution and about the growing unrest among laborers in America. Business owners suddenly were in a panic about the still poorly defined movement known as socialism. "The state bureaucracy was attacked," Rykowski writes, and more ominously, "Public utilities were suspect." Public power became a huge issue in Oregon for more than a decade as its popularity grew. When the Roosevelt Administration offered money for public works programs, Oregon Congressman Charles Martin fought hard for Bonneville Dam. Yet when Martin, a supporter of the Ku Klux Klan and Adolf Hitler, was elected Governor, he fought hard against the formation of the mammoth public utility created to sell its electricity, the Bonneville Power Administration, which he considered "Bolshevik" in nature.

In 1925, the Klan was considered in Oregon to be a fraternal organization, and Forest Grove was a stronghold of the Klan, supported both by members of the rural poor and city business leaders. The Klan often cooperated with the Chamber, Protestant churches and other organizations to support the traditional way of life on the Tualatin Plains. When it came to the flashpoint issue of privatizing public utilities, each constituency found something to like. Wealthy business leaders saw big money to be made and wanted to keep it in their hands, not the government's. Meanwhile, the rural poor resented what they feared would become entitlements for the urban working class when many rural Americans still lacked such basic utilities. They found much to agree about when it came to water and electricity, as well. Sewers, however, were a different matter. If people chose to not pay for water and electricity, it just meant that their homes would be dark and dry. On the other hand, if people didn't pay their sewer bill, everyone would pay the price. Sewers, the businessmen agreed, should be the responsibility of taxpayers.

But in 1925, the Oregon tax system was a mess. Since 1844, some form of property tax had been in effect in first the territory and then the state of Oregon. That worked fairly well for the first 80 years, but by the 1920s, state and local governments needed more money for things such as streets, highways, police and fire departments, and of course, sewers. Property owners bristled at the thought of paying for services that in some cases they didn't use, and also bristled at the thought of those who didn't own property being allowed to vote on services for which they did not directly pay taxes. Since the turn of the century, Oregonians had argued over whether to implement an income tax. Some people wanted local income taxes, while some wanted a state tax. Some people wanted to tax only the relatively wealthy, others only the relatively poor. Some wanted a flat tax, while others wanted a progressive tax system. Still others feared that any additional revenue would allow the government to grow in power and influence, and objected to any change in the tax code to stem the rise of the nebulous "socialism." The debate reached its zenith in the 1920s, with Oregon's first income tax taking effect in 1929. In 1925, however, there was no clear means of financing a sewer system.

At that, we return to the Forest Grove City Council meeting of Tuesday, March 10, 1925. The mayor vowed "to get down to brass tacks" on the sewer issue, and took swift and dramatic action; he formed a committee to discuss it. In the discussion about whether to privatize the electric utility, Puget Sound Power and Light reported that it could not make a determination of the electrical system's value because the city powerhouse had meters to measure how much electricity was flowing from the plant at any given moment, but did not have meters to record the total output of the plant over time. The mayor vowed to get right on that problem as well.

The committee formed to discuss the sewer issue made rapid headway, and within a few weeks heard an engineer's report on how much it would cost to fix the Council Creek sewage problem. His proposal was to encase the creek in concrete from 200 feet before it entered the city to 200 feet after it exited on the other side, to protect citizens from the waste. Total cost would be $42,000. The Council decided that if it was going to cost that much to fix Council Creek, this would be a good time to come up with a permanent solution to the city's overall sewage problem, by creating a system to treat the sewage instead of dumping it into the Tualatin River. In the meantime, the Council voted to assess a levy against property owners along Council Creek to pay for the creek to be encased. The property owners immediately hired an attorney and the city backed down, deciding instead to assess all property owners in the city to pay the cost. The other property owners promptly hired an attorney and threatened to sue. The city hired an attorney, who told the Council that they lacked authority to tax anyone outside the watershed. Perplexed, the Council postponed a decision on that matter but finally voted to buy the old sewer system for $33,000 and allocate $30,000 for repairs. Within days consulting engineers told the city its estimate was far too low, but the city decided to press on anyway.

Meanwhile, the city was faced with a more imminent emergency. The town's reservoir was nearly empty again, with only enough water for a few days. By now the intake had been fixed, so the city decided that the problem lay in its citizens using far more water than was being pulled from Clear Creek and ordered drastic reductions. The reductions worked and the reservoir began to slowly refill. Too slowly, one city employee thought, so he measured how much water was flowing into the pipeline at Clear Creek and how much was coming out at the reservoir. He found that the pipeline was delivering only half the water to the reservoir. Closer inspection revealed that the aging dam and intake on Clear Creek was so battered that they had to be replaced immediately. Work began on a new dam, and Forest Grove faced the very real prospect of running out of water before it could be built. Fortunately, the dam was finished in the nick of time.

Contracts for the project to encase Council Creek in concrete and to rebuild the sanitary sewer were in limbo, however, in large part because the Portland Rose Festival parade fell on the day that bids on the projects were due. The City Council gathered in Forest Grove to open bids at the 2 p.m. deadline. The deadline passed, but the city engineer was not in attendance to review the bids, so the Council waited for him to arrive. Finally an hour later he burst into the room. It seems that he had been in East Portland picking up a bid from a contractor. As he tried to race across the Willamette River with the bid, he was stopped as police blocked traffic for the parade. By the time the parade passed, he had waited more than an hour. The Council was split on whether to accept this bid. Some said that because it was in the hands of a city employee before the deadline it should be considered, while others argued that it should not. The argument spread to the audience, which included many of the bidders and their families. The *News-Times* reported that chaos ensued. "Into the scheme of things," the paper reported, "entered a group of 10 contractors battling for their individual bids (and) a pretty Syrian woman who leveled her scornful finger at the puzzled heads of councilmen and demanded that they award $25,600 to her husband." After threats of lawsuits the Council decided to reject all of the bids and start from scratch. The sewer would have to wait. But then a ruckus arose over bonds. Council Creek watershed property owners howled in protest when it was learned that they would be expected to bear the cost of encasing the creek alone, while the cost of the overall sanitary sewer would be borne by every taxpayer in the city, whether they would be connected to the sewer or not. After a chaotic meeting full of yelling and threats of lawsuits, both projects were put on hold. Finally, in July 1925, contracts were awarded for both projects and Forest Grove was about to get its sewer, albeit 13 years after it had been approved originally.

Construction started at a dramatic pace, and by just before Christmas 1925, both projects were completed or nearing completion. After 13 years of delays, the Council Creek project, the sewer repairs, and construction of a filtering plant in the Fern Hill wetlands were about to be completed in less than a year. But then the *News-Times* reported that "charges and counter-charges … brought a meeting of the City Council on Tuesday evening to the point of open warfare." The city already had paid the Council Creek contractor after an inspection found that he had done excellent work. In fact the city overpaid him when a bookkeeping error led to a check 10 percent larger than was due. When the city realized its error, it asked the contractor to come to the meeting and return the overage. Instead, the contractor sent his son to the meeting without a check. Yes, the son explained, he and his father realized that they had been overpaid, but they considered that to be the city's fault, so they cashed the check and had no intention of issuing a refund. Soon the contractor for the sanitary sewer project joined the fray, demanding more money because when he bid on the project he hadn't realized that the Fern Hill wetlands were, well, so wet. Digging through the muck was straining his equipment and taking much longer than he anticipated. The paper reported that fisticuffs were threatened at least a dozen times before the meeting was adjourned amid loud threats of lawsuits. Christmas 1925 would not be a merry one for many people in Forest Grove.

Just before Easter 1926, all the combatants were back at it, joined by angry taxpayers. Problems had been found in connecting the Council Creek storm sewer into the main sewer system. Contractors pointed fingers at each other and at the city, threatening to sue just about everyone in the room. The property owners along Council Creek had retained attorneys for a possible legal battle anyway, and now they were enraged that they might have to pay for the overpayment to the contractor if the city couldn't recover its money. Now they, too, were ready to sue just about everyone in the room. The meeting adjourned as the threats continued. Easter 1926 would not be a happy one for many people in Forest Grove.

Meanwhile, the city had not responded to John Wegner's demand for $15,000 for the death of his wife. He sued the city, now demanding $27,000. The sewer still was not in operation. Work on the Clear Creek water supply system had found problems much worse than anticipated, and managers told the city that the whole system had to be replaced. Managers of the city's electric department were saying the same for their powerhouse. Forest Grove was carrying $300,000 in debt, a huge amount for a city its size, and was facing the need to take on much more. The city was on the brink of bankruptcy. The Rotary, the Chamber, the *News-Times* and just about every other institution in town were sick of the often bumbling City Councils of the past 25 years and demanded change. Among other things, they demanded that the city revise its charter to adopt the city manager form of government, in which affairs of the city are run by a professional, full-time administrator, rather than elected officials trying to run things while operating their own businesses. In addition, even business leaders were demanding the once unthinkable: higher taxes to avoid taking on more crippling debt.

The City Council flatly rejected the call for a city manager, but agreed to put it to a vote of the people. On Wednesday, April 20, 1927, voters spoke, although not many. In a city of almost 2,000, only 275 went to the polls. When the ballots were tallied, the count was 137 for, 137 against, with one completely blank ballot. A September revote resulted in the city manager idea failing, but voters approved an additional $56,000 to rebuild the Clear Creek water system, work that was completed on time, on budget and without a lawsuit. The next year, John Wegner lost his wrongful death suit against the city, but the Council Creek neighbors took their case to court and won, although the city appealed it all the way to the Supreme Court. Portland General Electric stretched powerlines into Forest Grove in a direct challenge to the city's utility, so the city sued and lost. Fed up with losing lawsuits, the Council called for the city attorney to be fired, but the Charter said terminations must be signed by the mayor, and the mayor refused.

By 1933, the eight-year-old sewer was declared wholly inadequate and in need of repairs that would cost more than the system had cost to build. Now devastated by the Great Depression, voters rejected new bonds to pay for the project, but city fathers thought that the Depression might work in their favor and applied for money from New Deal agencies. One after another, the requests were denied until in 1938 the Works Progress Administration stepped up and agreed to write a check. After a year of red tape, the project again was in jeopardy. The WPA said that the grant amount was not sufficient and that the city would have to sell bonds to pay for the extra amount. The city finally agreed and the work was done. Less than a year later, the state found the sewer plant to be inadequate and ordered a new one built. Now in 1940, 27 years since the city had authorized a sewer system, it still was not complete.

For the next decade the city struggled for ways to finance a new plant, and along the way welcomed two new large canneries. The canneries pumped tons of sewage into the already strained system, and one refused to pay its bill, resulting in yet another lawsuit. In the summer of 1949, both canneries were at full production, and the Tualatin River was running low. Suddenly thousands of dead fish started lining the banks of the river. When the state investigated, it discovered dead fish from the mouth of the river all the way to Forest Grove's sewage outflow pipe. Beyond the pipe upriver, the fish were fine. The city was forced to finally act and bought up farmland around its Fern Hill sewage plant to create filter ponds. The system worked, but before long the city was in court defending itself against lawsuits from neighboring farmers complaining about the stench from the Fern Hill wetland ponds. The city worked to clean up the wetlands, including spraying herbicide on toxic and foul-smelling weeds. The cropduster chose a windy day, and the herbicide blew onto a neighboring farm, destroying a year's worth of hops. The farmer sued. Mercifully, in 1970 Washington County voters created a sewer district to cover the county's wastewater treatment. Forest Grove was out of the sewage-treatment business after spending more than half of the city's first 111 years battling over the smell, the illness, the death and the litigation caused by human waste.

Forest Grove endured equally tough battles over water and electricity, but decided to stay in those businesses, with generally good results. The battle over water continues in other ways, however, and every winter townsfolk are faced with flooded streets and crawlspaces and fight a never-ending war against moss and mildew caused by the rain for which the region is famous. Perhaps as citizens shake their fists at the dreary clouds and complain about too much rain, they should pause and reflect on what life once was like in Forest Grove in the not-so distant past.

Today the lights stay on 24 hours a day with very little downtime. Today citizens take it for granted that water will come from the tap for their morning coffee. Today, when the rains finally stop and the sun bakes the city, children have a municipal swimming pool to cool off in, so today we don't count the annual toll of pediatric deaths caused by the disease-ridden ditches full of stagnant sewage. Still, while wondering if the rain will ever stop, it's fair to ask a corollary question: Will Forest Grove ever truly have enough water?

Chapter

9

Wine and whiskey everywhere and not a drop to drink

One should never doubt the resolve of a 66-year-old woman who walked much of the way from Missouri to Oregon, and there is no doubt that Tabitha Brown and the rugged 1840s missionaries intended to keep their adopted hometown dry. When Rutherford B. Hayes walked to Forest Grove in 1880 it was in no small part because his First Lady, Lucy, wanted to see a town without a saloon. When the Cleveland Browns, Chicago Cardinals, Dallas Cowboys and Pittsburgh Steelers trained in Forest Grove in the 1950s and 1960s, they came because more than 100 years after it was founded, Forest Grove still was dry.

The idea of a "dry" Forest Grove seems somewhat absurd today in light of one of its biggest early crops, hops for beer, or its current major crop, grapes for wine. The idea always has been absurd, because whiskey and other alcohol was readily available from doctors and pharmacists, as long as there was a "medicinal" need for it, such as feeling irritated, anxious or depressed. For a time, Forest Grove residents even could buy Heroin, a brand name for a morphine-based cough syrup, as long as a doctor or pharmacist approved. Yet for about the first 130 years of the history of the settlement that became Forest Grove, there were non-stop legal battles and even violence surrounding taverns and liquor stores, and Prohibition was all but etched in stone.

The prohibition against sales of alcohol was etched in the deed to the land that Pacific University sold for the townsite, or at least people were pretty sure that it was; for decades, buildings were bought and sold under the assumption that such a deed existed. Whatever the reality, it was clear that the missionaries intended to enforce sobriety, at one point even creating a private police force to apprehend anyone caught in the liquor trade. On August 11, 1901, *The Oregonian* praised the motives of Pacific's founders. "The sincere desire to protect the young men of future generations from the temptation of the open saloon, during the character-building years, is conspicuous in this interdiction." Yet even as efforts were underway to impose Prohibition across the land, *The Oregonian* predicted that such efforts were doomed to eventual failure, "since all experience teaches that prohibition in a matter of this kind does not prohibit." It's unlikely that the anonymous editorial writer lived long enough to see his prediction come true in a legal sense, at least in Forest Grove.

The founders of Pacific University decreed in spirit, and purportedly in legal deed, that more than just spirits would be eternally banished from downtown Forest Grove. When the Tualatin Academy and Pacific University granted land for the town, the deed said that the university reserved, in perpetuity, its right to reclaim the property from anyone who allowed gambling or served "ardent spirits as a beverage." By 1890, however, most of those pioneers were dead, and Forest Grove residents started testing the water to see if it was safe to go wet. It was not. In January 1891, the city authorized the private "Law and Order League" to hire undercover agents to arrest and prosecute people within the city limits of Forest Grove who sold alcohol without a prescription.

According to a story in the July 26, 1891, edition of *The Oregonian*, finding people to arrest was not difficult. Almost immediately, three prominent Forest Grove residents were arrested and charged with selling the agent alcohol. The most-notable name among those arrested was Charles Large, the county coroner and Forest Grove's most prominent doctor. The three were convicted, and Dr. Large received the worst punishment, a fine of $400, a staggering sum in 1891. His fellow convicts were fined $150 and $70 for their roles in the dastardly plot. Large objected, and his fine was reduced from $400 to 50 cents. Still not satisfied, the trio hired perhaps the area's most famous attorney to appeal the ruling, based in no small part on the fact that the judge who issued the ruling was a prominent member of the Law and Order League and played a role in hiring the undercover agent. The appeals court ruled that the criminal charges, filed on behalf of "the people of the town," were invalid because they should have been filed by "the Town of Forest Grove." All charges were dropped, and all fines, including Dr. Charles Large's 50 cents, were returned. The case was covered in great detail by *The Oregonian*'s Forest Grove correspondent, Dr. Charles Large.

In the 1890s, Forest Grove saw sobriety as something more than a moral imperative; they saw it as an economic boom as well, mainly in the form of the Keeley Institute. The "Keeley Cure" came out of a small town in Illinois and steamrolled across America, claiming to permanently cure more than 99 percent of all addictions not just to alcohol, but also to morphine, opium and tobacco, among other substances. The "cure" was revolutionary for its time, treating addiction as a physical disease instead of a moral deficiency. It consisted of injecting "Chloride of Gold" into the veins of patients several times a day for about a month. Politicians and business leaders across the country clamored for the Keeley Institute to locate a center in their city, and Forest Grove hit the jackpot, landing the first one in the Northwest. Patients came from throughout the West to Forest Grove for the treatment. In the March 6, 1892, edition of *The Oregonian*, a Portland journalist ventured to Forest Grove for the first time to investigate the Keeley Institute. The results of what the paper called "a definite and exhaustive" investigation filled nearly an entire page of the paper.

About the first quarter of the story was of the long train trip out to the city and about the awe-inspiring beauty the reporter encountered on his journey. His first observation was a familiar one by now; he was amazed at how far outside town the train station was. Although horse-drawn taxis were available to carry visitors the mile and a half or so through the countryside into town, the reporter decided that the day of his visit was perfect for walking to Forest Grove instead. As you approach town on foot, he told his readers, "you at once see it is a beautiful place, reveling in nature's most lavish gifts of scenery, while the hand of man,

154

inspired by nature's munificence, has been industrious in adding to the charms." Walking through the residential area he was astonished by the beauty of the homes and gardens, stopping in front of the house of Portland banker I.A. Macrum. Marveling at its beauty, the reporter tells us that it is rumored to have cost $15,000 to build. Then, acknowledging that this glowing travelogue "is a digression," he gets to the point of his story. First, he lavishes praise for the bona fides of the men who own and operate the Keeley Institute, including the man in charge, Dr. F.L. Taylor, and the facility's manager, Frank Davey. Davey is singled out for praise in part because he was a retired newspaper reporter and "one of the best-educated men, one of the best-read men, one of the strongest minded men and one of the ablest men generally in the whole state of Oregon." He also, we are told, is a perfect example of someone cured of his demons by the Keeley Cure. Davey did not want readers to take his word for it, however, and willingly threw open the private files of patients for the reporter to review. After this "definite and exhaustive" investigation, *The Oregonian* assured its readers that "the Cure is genuine, complete, and permanent." Curiously, this endorsement came only a week after an editorial in *The Oregonian* scoffed at suggestions that the Keeley Cure could cure anything. The *Forest Grove Times* attacked *The Oregonian* and demanded that they take the train to Forest Grove and examine the personal files of Keeley "graduates." The Keeley Institute, already one of the *Times*' largest advertisers, now launched an ad campaign in the pages of *The Oregonian*. Forest Grove, it seemed, was poised to become an anti-booze boom town. The man in charge of *The Oregonian*'s editorials, however, remained unconvinced and had a very personal interest in the doings of Forest Grove. That man, Harvey Scott, had walked to Forest Grove himself many years earlier, and he believed that the town was succumbing to charlatans. Harvey Scott and the editors of the *Times* engaged in a lively editorial debate for several years.

The *Times* ran stories about desperate people coming to Forest Grove as a last resort to cure their addictions and save their lives. These stories ran next to the largest advertisement in the paper, which was one for the Keeley Institute. Invariably the *Times* assured its readers that those desperate people would find redemption in Forest Grove, although follow-up stories, if there were any at all, didn't get such play. The Keeley ad budget was relatively small potatoes at *The Oregonian*, however, and soon Harvey Scott was running stories of people who had spent their life savings at sobriety clinics looking for a cure, only to commit suicide or end up in the penitentiary instead. By the mid-1890s, Forest Grove had become enough of a sobriety tourist destination that other copycat clinics had sprung up, and Keeley fought back, demanding that *The Oregonian* retract allegations that any of the "suicides or jailbirds" were Keeley graduates, because "the unfortunates who come to us are cured and restored to lives of usefulness." The Keeley people also demanded that *The Oregonian* report that the only certain cure was to be found in Forest Grove, and that no facility in Portland could deliver results.

Through the early 1890s, many in Forest Grove saw the Keeley Institute as one of the town's major industries, and hoped to ride a wave of prosperity as a wave of prohibition swept across the land. There were dark clouds over the Institute elsewhere, but not in Forest Grove. Nowhere were the clouds darker than in New York, where officials were concerned about a disturbing trend of people dropping dead after repeated Chloride of Gold injections. Keeley fought back with advertisements and letters to the editor insisting that any deaths must be the result of imitators using "Bi-Chloride of Gold," rather than Keeley's "double Chloride of Gold." Still, Keeley was by now ready to adjust its claims of success-to-failure ratio from 99-to-1 to perhaps 20-to-1. People kept flocking to Forest Grove, and the *Forest Grove Times* trumpeted the Institute's virtues in almost every edition. By 1894, business was booming. Suddenly, however, Forest Grove faced a threat to its prosperity; it was on the verge of losing the Keeley Institute. The reason was one that cities of all sizes would come to recognize: Dr. Taylor, owner of the Oregon franchise, wanted taxpayer subsidies for his business. "The company asks no great encouragement," the *Salem Statesman* reported after company officials visited the state Capital. "These terms are easy. Salem must meet them and add yet one more to the growing list of enterprises and institutions."

For folks back in Forest Grove, these were fighting words. City leaders still were bitter about the last institution it had lost to Salem, the Indian School. It seems that after the school moved on the promise that Salem could finance the school, the city had instead secured money from the state, something the Legislature had refused to do for Pacific University and Forest Grove. The *Times* and city fathers were not about to lose another major institution to Salem and rallied support from the public for keeping the Keeley Institute in Forest Grove. They agreed that what Taylor was asking for was quite reasonable. The *Statesman* article had laid out his request: All the Keeley people wanted was for taxpayers to build offices and a hotel for its exclusive use, with a promise that Keeley could use the facilities rent free for at least five years. Oh, and they also wanted $3,000 cash, which was larger than Forest Grove's entire annual budget. In return, the city would get 30 non-voting shares of company stock. Newspaper editors in Salem and Forest Grove both demanded that their city fathers meet the demands. On August 9, 1894, sensing that Forest Grove was destined to lose the Institute to Salem, given that city's offer of the abandoned "blind asylum" as a home base, the *Times* editors offered a sarcastic money-saving tip, suggesting that there was no need to replace the signs, which read "Oregon Institute for the Blind." The *Times* pointed out that the signs could be amended simply by painting one word at the front of the name and one at the back: "Keeley Oregon Institute for the Blind Drunk." The *Yamhill County Reporter* chimed in when the move was official: "To get plenty of business," the paper opined, "an institution to unmake drunkards should be located in a drunkard-making town." Leslie Keeley died in 1900. The company he founded nearly disappeared overnight, losing more than half of its patients in the first year. His "cure" evolved somewhat, but the last few holdout practitioners finally gave up in the 1950s.

By the close of the 1800s, many residents of Forest Grove still were not willing to give up whiskey and cigars, and others were not willing to give up the fight against vice (or the profits that fight earned them). Forest Grove had turned over its law enforcement authority to the Law and Order League, which collected "subscriptions" from residents and hired private investigators and prosecutors. The town's "wets" were growing weary of both the prohibition and of the heavy-handed ways in which it was enforced. Forces were gathering for a fight. On the one side you had the voters of Forest Grove, tired of being one of the few dry cities around. On the other side you had members of the Women's Christian Temperance Union, intent on making the entire nation dry. Dr. Large's arrest in 1891 was just a precursor to a series of arrests that saw prominent doctors and pharmacists handcuffed on charges of selling liquor to people who lacked a prescription for the "medicine."

The most high-profile case involved an investigation by the Law and Order League into liquor sales by prominent Forest Grove pharmacist Charles Miller. Miller was no stranger to the Prohibition wars. On April 6, 1897, for example, his pharmacy had been torched by an arsonist, although no arrest was made. Now, just recently back in business, he was the primary target of the Law and Order League after defying University President Thomas McClelland and his crusade against alcohol. Documents from the Pacific University Archives reveal that the investigation was directed personally by McClelland, who sometimes had the undercover agent come to his home late at night to deliver updates on the case. The undercover agent's reports, written on letterhead from the University's attorney, paint a picture of drugstores very different from today. The undercover operative, identified in papers as "Agent #1," writes of the stores being largely deserted during the day on Saturday, September 16, 1899, only to come to life "after supper." By about 6:30, the clerk would retire from the front of the store to a back room with a bar. Agent #1 said that the drugstores were well-known as speakeasies, not only to Forest Grove residents but also to residents of surrounding towns in which saloons were perfectly legal. Forest Grove druggists had several advantages over legal saloons, including that they could serve alcohol on Sunday, unlike licensed taverns that were subject to regular inspections. Also, as one clerk told the informant, druggists could afford to sell beer and whiskey more cheaply than in other towns because "even if they were convicted and fined it would be a nominal sum which they could afford to pay and would not amount to what a license would (cost) in other towns." University President McClelland, however, assured the agent that residents of Forest Grove were adamant about eradicating drinking, and that Thomas Tongue, a member of Congress and perhaps Oregon's most prominent attorney, would prosecute the case on behalf of the city.

The agent told of many people from neighboring cities making the trek to Forest Grove, as well as a steady stream of "drummers," or travelling salesmen, including one for the *San Francisco Examiner* and another representing a "Portland pickle company." A hotel owner from Tillamook frequented Miller's drugstore, the agent wrote, and many out-of-towners easily found their way to the drugstore to pop a cork on a bottle of beer, including a man visiting to enroll his daughter at Pacific University.

But among the out-of-towners, the agent told McClelland, there always were Forest Grove residents bellying up to the bar. Some clearly were not regulars, such as the young man so befuddled by the workings of a corkscrew that he had to solicit help to uncork his beer. Others were regulars, however, who gathered nearly every night to drink. Their presence at the drugstores was so common that wives, friends, and bosses knew to come knocking when the men were needed back at home or work. Furthermore, Agent #1 told McClelland, those regulars included some of the town's most-prominent citizens. One of the most regular regulars, the agent wrote, was Fred Kane, brother of local banker and Mayor Frank Kane. Kane and the other regulars, the agent said, routinely broke both of the University's strongest covenants by gambling to see who would pay for the group's illegal booze. Another prominent drinker's name was obscured in the reports to protect his identity, although Agent #1 dropped some tantalizing clues about the mystery man. We know, for example, that "he was 54 years old, five feet eleven inches, 180 lbs., chin whiskers gray, and was a G.A.R. man," or Civil War veteran and member of the Grand Army of the Republic. That description narrowed down the possible identity of the mystery man somewhat, but then Agent #1 helpfully added that he was a county judge who would be presiding over a lawsuit against the city of Forest Grove the following day.

Still, McClelland assured Agent #1 that despite the powerful townfolk imbibing, the Law and Order League would prevail in court because of the skill of Thomas Tongue, the man McClelland had hand-picked to prosecute the case. Unfortunately, however, McClelland had neglected to ask Tongue if he was interested in being prosecutor. Agent #1's last notation in his reports was the startling news that when Tongue finally was informed of the investigation he announced that he instead would take the case as druggist Charles Miller's defense attorney.

By now, however, the University and other members of the Law and Order League had invested a lot of time and money into the investigation. Agent #1 had written earlier that McClelland had acknowledged that other pharmacists also were operating speakeasies, but that Miller was his target. So while other pharmacists were fined for their crimes, McClelland ordered agents to arrest Miller. He did not order the arrest of any of Miller's prominent customers, however, believing that they could be compelled to testify against his nemesis.

A story in the November 16, 1899, *Forest Grove Times*, tells the tale of Miller's trial. The Law and Order League had charged Miller with allowing his clerk, Bert Bowlby, to sell a bottle of whiskey to one Scott Parker, who in turn gave it to Willie Jones, who "got drunk thereon." The otherwise innocuous case drew such a crowd that court had to be adjourned and the Law and Order League rented a dance hall to accommodate spectators, adding further to the costs of the case. Hugh Via, proprietor of one of the town's competing drugstores, testified on Miller's behalf, saying that Parker had approached him on the day of Miller's arrest, seeking to buy whiskey. Via said that when he refused and asked if Parker had tried Miller, Parker said he had and had been refused, confiding that he had simply walked across the city limits to the saloons outside of town to purchase his whiskey. For reasons never publicly addressed, the Law and Order League did not call any of the other people identified in the report, including the county judge, the mayor's brother, or frequent patron Theodore Wirtz, who happened to be the brother of the city recorder, the man responsible for filing, and trying, the case in the city court. The League relied instead on the testimony of Parker and Jones, each of whom proved to be unreliable witnesses. Congressman Tongue managed an acquittal on two counts, but the city recorder found Miller guilty on the most serious charge. Tongue and Miller prepared to appeal.

Meanwhile, pressure mounted to overturn the town charter, which had been amended in 1891 to officially ban alcohol. In the election of December 1899, a slate of candidates pledged to bring booze to Forest Grove, and captured every seat on the City Council, including Mayor. The city had been riveted to the Miller trial, and while feelings were mixed about the verdict, the real fireworks erupted when the leaders of the Law and Order League, McClelland and a prominent minister, came to the last meeting of the "dry" City Council and presented a bill for the cost of the Miller trial. After a long and what the *Times* described as "lively" debate, the City Council was deadlocked. The outgoing mayor cast the deciding vote to pay the tab. The Law and Order League's move angered many of its supporters and caused outrage among its detractors, including the incoming Mayor and Council. At their first meeting, those Council members were stunned when the Law and Order League came back and demanded even more taxpayer money, including a bill for renting the dance hall in which to hold the trial. This Council refused and said that it would not pay to continue the case in appeals court. The bizarre chapter in jurisprudence was not over yet, however. The Law and Order League insisted that the city had authorized it to enforce vice laws, and refused to drop the case. Tongue and Miller proceeded with their appeal.

The raucous proceedings at the appeal trial ended the awkward relationship between the League and the city. Scott Parker, who claimed to have bought the liquor from Miller, recanted his testimony and said that he had bought it out of town and had allowed Willie Jones, a minor, to drink it. He said that members of the Law and Order League discovered this and threatened to send him to jail unless he testified that he had bought it from Miller. He also testified that McClelland had personally offered him free tuition to Pacific University if he would testify at the trial, a charge that the March 28, 1900, *Oregonian* labeled as "ridiculous." Jurors were not convinced that the testimony was ridiculous, however, and eight of the 12 stood firm in their verdict to acquit Miller. The judge sent orders to keep voting, but eventually declared the jury deadlocked and called for a new trial. With threats of lawsuits now flying against everyone involved, the Law and Order League meekly agreed to pay the court costs and drop its case. After all the legal documents were signed exonerating the pharmacist, the main witness, Scott Parker, wrote to *The Oregonian* recanting his recantation of his testimony and denying that the Pacific University president had offered him free tuition.

Despite Parker's confession and confusion, things were not about to get better for the thirsty denizens of Forest Grove. Thomas McClelland left to become President of Knox College in Illinois, but not until the trustees of Pacific University lowered the boom, sending registered letters to nearly every business owner in the town, reminding them of the original deeds barring gambling and sales of alcohol. The deeds stated that if any business owner "shall sell, exchange or give away such ardent spirit to be used as a beverage, or allow any gaming upon such premises, then these presents shall be null and void, and the said president and trustees shall have good right and full authority to return upon said premises and to have, hold, use, occupy and enjoy the same just as if this deed had never been executed." In other words, the officials of Pacific University said that business owners could forget about nominal fines and futile arrests; now they were prepared to evict every business and repossess every building in town if necessary to keep Forest Grove dry. The threat caused an uproar that lasted for months. Tempers flared the next year when the Congregational Church, the spiritual force behind the university, burned to the ground. The church fire was an obvious case of arson, and allegations spread through town that the church had fallen victim to the fight over prohibition.

Meanwhile, Pacific University started making good on its threats of lawsuits against property owners to take back the city's buildings. The university invoked feudal claims under old common law statutes, targeting pharmacist Charles Miller, among others. When Miller, who was renting the space for his store, agreed to relocate, the university's legal case fell apart. The college lost its case, the property owner lost her tenant, and Charles Miller moved his business. The university struggled to enforce its deeds, but met with problem after problem. Sometimes the original deed had been lost. Other times the property had changed hands several times with the Prohibition clause missing. Finally in August 1901, the college scored a major victory, and its deed was upheld by a Washington County court. The victory was muted, however, because the judge ruled that only "ardent spirits," were covered. Under traditional use, that phrase referred to spirits with enough alcohol content to easily ignite. Beer, most wine, hard cider and other popular drinks were not covered, the judge ruled.

In 1904, a new City Council was elected, evenly split between "Drys" and "Wets." The first order of business was an ordinance to reinforce the prohibition of alcohol. The debate over alcohol had dominated Forest Grove politics in 1903, as several saloons defiantly opened, with their owners claiming that cities did not have a right to regulate the sale of alcohol. The city cited an 1892 edition of *Black's Law Dictionary* to assert that the sale of alcohol was presumed to be illegal unless a city specifically authorized it. Nonetheless, the City Council voted, and the result was a tie. Still, the *Forest Grove Times* reported the vote as a resounding victory for the "Drys." New Mayor Walter Hoge cast the tie-breaking vote, and then reported the story in the town's newspaper, which he owned and edited. The saloons soon closed.

While prohibitionists argued that those wanting a drink could simply walk across the city limits to a tavern, some city leaders saw a larger issue: the loss of revenue. In the days before an income tax, cities made most of their revenue from licenses. Joseph Gaston, namesake of the town six miles south of Forest Grove, was an outspoken prohibitionist, but in *Portland, Oregon, Its History and Builders,* Gaston pointed out a powerful reason prohibition was politically unpopular. In 1901, he wrote, the city of Portland generated a total of $234,422.20 for its general fund, and $169,730.96 of that sum came from fees on alcohol. "History would be of little account," Gaston wrote, "if it preserved no record of the frivolities, vices and profligacy of mankind."

Things stayed ugly, and the *Times* and *Oregonian* got into another war of words when the Portland newspaper reported that farmers outside of Forest Grove were protesting the town's dry policies. *The Oregonian* cited Frederick William David as the leader of this revolt. Forest Grove leaders were furious, and accused *The Oregonian* of bias, because its local correspondent was Dr. Charles Large, who was a frequent target of the *Times* and the city leaders of Forest Grove. Local leaders adamantly assured the public that Fredrick William David would never under any circumstances support sales of alcohol in town.

Frederick William David's role in the debate is as murky as his overall role in Forest Grove history, but more than a century later his legacy once again would play a key role in another kerfuffle involving alcohol. The confusion about David begins with the imposing geological feature that bears his name. Unlike many of the area's early settlers, David did not walk westward over the Plains to Forest Grove. Instead, he made a long *eastward* journey to his adopted home. Born in a wine-making region of Germany, David sought adventure in rugged Australia for a few years before emigrating to the United States, settling on a farm just a few miles northwest of Forest Grove, on what today is known as David Hill. Some references to geographic names suggest that David Hill is an allusion to one of the earliest settlers on the Tualatin Plains, David Hill, for whom the city of Hillsboro is named. In reality, the names are purely coincidental, because David Hill is named for Frederick William David. The fact that David selected a hill for his farmsite, however, is not at all a coincidence. From his early days in Germany, Frederick William David knew that south-facing slopes are ideal for growing wine grapes. By 1892, David Hill, the imposing edifice that on clear winter afternoons literally casts its shadow over notoriously dry Forest Grove, was home to one of

Oregon's largest wineries, owned and operated by Frederick William David. By 1904, both sides were using David as a pawn in the Prohibition debate, although the best the Dry side could come up with was that David was fine with the ban on sales of alcohol inside the city limits, knowing that townsfolk could take a ride or stroll a mile or two to his winery if they got thirsty.

Perhaps even more ironic than Frederick William David's role in the 1904 debate, however, was the role the winery he founded played more than a century later, when the once proudly dry city of Forest Grove launched a major tourism advertising campaign, calling itself the "Birthplace of Oregon Pinot Noir," based on the claim that in 1965 Charles Coury, then owner of the David Hill vineyard, planted the first release of what would become Oregon's signature wine. A howl of protest arose among vintners of neighboring Yamhill County, who argued that Eyrie Vineyards had preceded Coury's planting by eight months. Soon it was revealed that Hillcrest Winery in Southern Oregon's Umpqua Valley had beaten both by four years. Yet while Forest Grove might not be the Pinot pioneer it thought it was, there's no question that one of the town's pioneers grew Black Hamberger, Sweet Water and Red Top Mound grapes and produced hundreds of gallons of German-style sweet wines every year.

Promoting the wine industry was the furthest thing from the minds of Pacific University leaders in the early 1900s, however, even as city leaders softened their stance on alcohol and the revenue licensed saloons could bring to the city. The City Council, acting on the provision of the town's charter that allowed it to "regulate" the sale of alcohol, granted a liquor license in February 1905 to Albert Watson to open a saloon. Pacific University sued to overturn the license, pursuing the case all the way to the Oregon Supreme Court, eventually prevailing on a technicality. On February 20, 1906, the justices ruled that the charter allowed the city the right to "regulate" sales of alcohol, but not the right to grant licenses. With the question of liquor once again up in the air, voters took another run at the charter on January 14, 1907, this time clarifying the city's right to license or prohibit saloons. The same election ushered in a Wet mayor and Council majority, but by the summer of 1907 it was clear that this administration was firmly united with the Drys. Decades of legal maneuvers had not shut off the spigots entirely, as several "blind pigs," or unlicensed saloons, had been able to flourish under the guise of medicinal facilities. The best known blind pig was "The Iron House," operated by obstetrician, *Oregonian* correspondent and former coroner, Dr. Charles Large. The new City Council and their Dry backers pursued prosecution against Large, and in a packed courtroom on July 31, 1907, Judge Walter Hoge, the former crusading newspaper editor, found Large guilty, fining him $100. Large closed The Iron House. While the closure marked a turning point, the litany of litigation continued for several more years, until national events eventually overtook Forest Grove's parochial prohibition efforts.

In Oregon, Forest Grove has been in the forefront of nearly every trend involving alcohol. In 1843, the Tualatin Plains was home to the heart and soul of the Oregon provisional government in Champoeg, including Joseph Meek, Joseph Gale, Harvey Clarke, William Doughty, John Griffin, David Hill and Alvin Smith. One of the first provisions they included in 1844 was a ban on sales of alcohol. In 1845 that ban was overturned, and for the next half century spirits flowed freely throughout most of the state, except for Forest Grove and a few other towns. All the while the Forest Grove region was the center of hops farming and the nascent Oregon wine industry. But by the early 1900s, the cause of Prohibition was stirring in the state. Not surprisingly, Pacific University participated in and hosted many debates on the subject. In 1915, Oregon became one of the first states to go dry, although the law had little tangible effect on alcohol sales in much of the state. The Women's Christian Temperance Union and others continued to press for the Eighteenth Amendment to ban the sale of alcohol nationwide. World War I pushed the amendment over the top in early 1919, in part because of the patriotic fervor against Germany and its reputation for brewing.

Beer was big business in Oregon, and many Oregon cities turned a blind eye to the liquor trade, as did many cities across the nation. Joseph Gaston, in his history of Portland, acknowledged that Portland breweries annually produced "about a barrel of beer to every man, woman and child in this city." But the devout prohibitionist assured readers that his beloved Oregon preferred to be dry and that much of the bountiful beer production actually was destined for "Siberia, China, Japan and the Philippine Islands." Regardless, the Volstead Act, enacted later in 1919, gave the federal government enforcement power over Prohibition, and its enforcement effectively shut down most large commercial operations, including Portland's German-born operators such as Henry Weinhard. None of this enforcement sat well with the large and already alienated German population in and around Forest Grove, tired of being targeted by wartime propaganda and anger. That, coupled with the region's remote and rugged hills and valleys and the abundant crops of barley, hops, wheat and grapes, made the area a haven for bootleggers. Suddenly, instead of repelling drinkers, the Forest Grove area was becoming a magnet, led by flamboyant Portland businessman Fred Dundee, a famous driver of a steam-powered race car named "Whistling Billy" and a major player in the Portland trucking industry. Dundee liked loud, alcohol-fueled parties, and was not about to let the police in Portland shut down his entertainment. He built a lodge near the crest of the hill between Patton and Scoggins valleys and created a legendary party palace that in 1985 landed his property on the National Register of Historic Places. Legends of stills in Patton Valley, Scoggins Valley, Gales Creek and other remote areas flourished. Prohibition didn't curtail the liquor business within the city limits much either, because alcohol remained legal for medicinal purposes. As a proudly dry bastion of a now dry country, Forest Grove somehow managed to remain very wet. Having now at least superficially achieved its founders' original goal of legally enforced sobriety, Forest Grove turned its attention back to other issues, such as its continued lack of a functioning sewer system.

The town avoided the worst of Prohibition's problems; there's no evidence that organized crime ever made substantial headway in the city. That does not mean, however, that there weren't scandals and crimes involving liquor. For example, on April 25, 1918, a Page 1 *News-Times* story reported on a case that had "created a sensation unparalleled in the history of Washington County." Since statewide Prohibition began in 1915, poor Oregonians had relied on speakeasies and moonshiners to quench their thirst. The wealthy had better options, including liquor shipped in from states where it still was legal. The practice was not uncommon and the law rarely resulted in arrests. One shipment from San Francisco in April 1918 was different. Someone in California tipped off federal marshals about five large crates that left the Bay Area aboard a freight train headed north to Oregon. The crates were stenciled with the words "Crockery" and "Handle With Care," and addressed to "John W.

Hart." But the real recipient was not John W. Hart, the informant told marshals, and if the crates really did contain crockery it was filled to the brim with wine, whiskey and gin. It was a major haul, to be sure, but the size of the shipment was less an issue than were the names of the men suspected of awaiting the shipment in Oregon.

Federal marshals had plenty of time to alert their colleagues in Portland, because even by 1918 train routes between San Francisco and Portland were slow and prone to weather delays and track damage. The train roughly followed the route up the California valleys and over the Siskiyou Mountains, which had been plotted by Jesse Applegate and his brother in 1843; the same route that stranded the Donner Party and nearly caused the death of Tabitha Brown. In the intervening decades conditions had improved, but the route remained rugged. Marshals in Oregon patiently awaited the train's journey up the Applegate Trail and planned an arrest. Two of the men expecting packages were among the county's best-known businessmen, Charles B. Buchanan and banker John W. Bailey. They would face serious charges. The third man, however, was the prime target, and he faced very serious consequences. His name was Jesse Applegate, although not the Jesse Applegate who carved the path from California to Oregon.

Jesse C. Applegate, the target of the probe, was a grandson of the trail's namesake. Born in the Southern Oregon town of Drain, he settled in the Tualatin Plains, near where Tabitha Brown landed. By 1918, Applegate had become one of Oregon's top law enforcement officials, and as Washington County Sheriff he was charged with enforcing Oregon Prohibition, not for finding ways to circumvent the law. Yet at 3 o'clock on Thursday morning, April 25, 1918, Sheriff Applegate, John Bailey and Charles Buchanan found themselves waiting in the darkness for the Oregon Electric Railway car as it rolled through the night to its terminus in Forest Grove. When the train stopped at a tiny, out-of-the-way depot south of Hillsboro, John Bailey presented the bill of shipping to take possession of the crates for the fictitious John W. Hart. At that point marshals emerged, threw handcuffs on the men and hauled them to Portland. By mid-morning that same day, all three were in court and entered guilty pleas. The judge released them on their own recognizance until sentencing on Monday so they could settle up business affairs. One of the affairs Jesse Applegate settled was submitting his resignation as

Sheriff of Washington County. When the trio returned to court, Bailey and Buchanan were fined $400 each. Applegate's fine was just $250, but he was immediately taken to jail to serve 10 days in conditions inhospitable to lawmen responsible for their fellow inmates' presence in the cellblock. The *Forest Grove Express* reported that fellow inmates immediately subjected Applegate to a kangaroo court, charged with "breaking into a jail where he was not wanted." He reportedly bought his safety for the remainder of his sentence by handing over to his fellow inmates the six dollars he had on his person. Despite howls of protests from Prohibitionists demanding that Applegate face federal charges as well, he lived out the rest of his life as a government employee, including working for the Oregon House of Representatives until his death in 1936.

Applegate was not the only local resident with ties to the liquor trade who went on to spend a career in government. Perhaps the strangest such example was Charles Miller, the pharmacist who had tangled for so many years with city and university leaders in the 1890s and early 1900s. Miller had persevered after his pharmacy was burned, endured an arrest and spectacular trial, and rebuilt after being evicted in a battle over Pacific University's deed enforcement. By 1912, however, Miller had had enough, and went to work for the Bureau of Internal Revenue (later the Internal Revenue Service). As a pharmacist, he became active in the battle of the "Revenuers" against illegal sales of alcohol and narcotics. After passage of the Volstead Act in 1919, Detroit, Michigan, became ground zero in the battle. The narrow Detroit River, which formed the international border between Detroit and Windsor, Ontario, was a superhighway for bootleggers and drug runners from Canada, and the Bureau of Internal Revenue, which was then in charge of the fight, wanted to assign its top agent to the Detroit bureau. They found their man in Oregon, and assigned Charles Miller to the role.

Jesse Applegate's successors as sheriff had pledged to enforce Prohibition laws, but relatively little was done over the next few years. By 1923, however, the federal government was measuring success in new ways, and Washington County rose to the top. Instead of simply counting the number of arrests and convictions, Oregon's director of prohibition, Dr. J.A. Linville, started gauging enforcement efforts based on the amount of money raised from enforcing dry laws. Washington County judges became known for penalizing drinkers with enormous fines.

Some Prohibition crimes were more serious, or at least seemingly so. On May 14, 1928, Forest Grove was rocked by a strange, at least somewhat organized crime involving a bootlegger. Shortly after midnight Oscar Duley and A.F. Schendel, both Forest Grove police officers recently deputized by the county, pulled over a car driven by suspected bootleggers in front of the Masonic Home, which today is a hotel and, ironically, a large brew pub. What happened next is not entirely clear to anyone involved. The two officers thought that they had disarmed the three suspected bootleggers, but suddenly one of the men pulled a second concealed revolver and got the two officers to surrender. By the time help arrived, the patrol car was found with its headlights and spotlight blasted out, but the officers were nowhere to be found. A massive search for Duley and Schendel ensued. Hours later, the two were found a few miles away in Hillsboro. They told their superiors that they had been kidnapped by the bootleggers and driven into Portland where, at the corner of Sixth and Sheridan streets, the kidnappers suddenly released them and returned their service revolvers. Now stuck in Portland, 30 miles from their patrol car, the officers decided to call friends in Hillsboro to come pick them up. After arriving in Hillsboro, they called their supervisors to say that they were fine. Forest Grove's most notorious organized crime story would go unsolved, and two months later Officer Duley took a better job as a railroad policeman.

On December 29, 1931, police thought they had another crime mystery on their hands, but this one did not go unsolved for long. A little after 4:30 on an otherwise peaceful Tuesday morning, Forest Grove night watchman Lawrence Williams saw a bright orange glow in the hazy pre-dawn darkness south of town. He awoke Fire Chief Walter Vandenvelden, and the two rushed to the scene. A Page 1 story in the December 31 *News-Times* explains what the perplexed officers found when they arrived at a farm south of the village of Dilley. A large barn lay in ruins, already consumed by fire. So far, there was nothing mysterious about the scene; old wooden barns full of dry hay, gasoline and other flammables can and too often do burn to a pile of ashes within a few minutes. The farmhouse looked serene, with smoke wafting from its chimney; again, nothing unusual there, because farmers rise early and cook breakfast and coffee to start their day. However, there was no sign of any early rising farmers on this cold morning. Officers checked the house and could see a fire burning in the fireplace, but no one answered their knock on the door. Entering the house, they found that the interior had been stripped bare of furniture, pots and pans and people. Yet the fire in the fireplace indicated there had been people there within the past couple of hours. After the barn fire had burned itself out and the sun shed some light on the situation, Vandervelden started his investigation. The barn, too, was nearly empty, except for the charred, twisted remains of a very large still. He then found 6,000 gallons of highly flammable mash, the concentrated starter for making whiskey. Some of that mash had been splashed throughout the barn as an accelerant. This was no small operation. Clearly there were many people in the area who had been able to find whiskey at the height of Prohibition. Neighbors told the officers that the farm was owned by a very nice couple who had moved to Idaho a few months earlier, and that a young man had been renting it. Soon the Oregon State Police, unaware of the fire, arrived at the farm to serve a search warrant on the barn, which, under the circumstances no longer was needed. It seems that state officers had seen a truck full of sugar a couple of nights earlier in nearby McMinnville, which aroused suspicion that it was to be used for moonshine. The officers even arrested the driver, but had to release him after 24 hours when he refused to talk and they could find no evidence of wrongdoing. They traced the man to this farm south of Dilley, which he had been renting from the nice couple who moved to Idaho. They went back to the judge and had the warrant changed from one authorizing a search to one authorizing an arrest. Meanwhile, the sheriff at McMinnville, the county seat of neighboring Yamhill County, got into the act. It seems that at the same time the state police were arresting the driver of the sugar truck, he was arresting the driver of a truck that housed a large, portable still. No connection between the cases could be found, however, suggesting that Yamhill residents had their own steady supply of whiskey.

In 1933, Prohibition was overturned nationally, and in most states booze flowed freely; much more freely, in fact, than most people today can imagine. Oregon was one of a relatively few states to balk at complete freedom, and established the Oregon Liquor Control Commission, citing the opportunity to help control alcohol abuse, and of course raise tax revenue in the process. The Prohibition wars were over in Oregon, as well, except in Forest Grove and a handful of other communities, which steadfastly enforced their dry laws. In the first city election after Prohibition ended nationally in 1933, Forest Grove voters said "no" to allowing sales of 3.2 percent alcohol beer by the whopping margin of three votes, 286 to 283. The battle would be bitter. In 1934, one Forest Grove grocer decided that state laws superseded local ordinances; he asked for and received permission from the OLCC to sell beer. The *News-Times* reports that the grocer enjoyed very brisk business, at least for the two days it took city attorneys to persuade the OLCC to suspend the license until a new election could be held on the issue.

But then, just when it looked as if voters might change their minds, Pacific University re-entered the fray with a bombshell: It finally had discovered the long-lost deed to the business district of Forest Grove, forbidding alcohol no matter what voters said. The deed, signed on July 13, 1852, looked solid, except for one detail: Oregon was not yet a state in 1852, and the deed had never been registered after statehood was granted in 1859. Everyone involved hunkered down for yet another round of lawsuits and countersuits over the issue, but then the deed went missing again. A search of University archives in 2013 did not turn up the 1852 deed, or even an official record of such a document, but several other handwritten deeds from land sales in 1854 and later clearly include the Prohibitionist language. Those deeds are for primarily residential neighborhoods, however, which didn't help forbid saloons; the documents address only the sale, not possession or consumption of spirits, ardent or otherwise.

By today's standards it's easy to view these remaining prohibitionists as a group of stubborn, obstinate dead-enders. Viewed in the context of the times, however, a different picture emerges. Even in Oregon, with its relatively strict laws about the wholesale trade of alcohol, there still were few statewide laws regulating private establishments. In 1939, the Legislature finally passed laws allowing the state to regulate restaurants, hotels, clubs and other places where alcohol is served. Liquor industry lobbyists flooded Salem to have the law overturned and succeeded in having the measure referred to voters for approval; Oregon voters said "yes," and the measure was law. As those laws established age limits, hours of operation, sales to obviously intoxicated patrons and other restrictions, most dry communities were satisfied and lifted their prohibitions. By about 1950, the wets were victorious ... although still not in Forest Grove, where the battle would rage on for decades to come.

Licenses were granted, then quickly withdrawn. Election after election reaffirmed, at least narrowly, the town's prohibition. Most citizens were not overly concerned, because there were plenty of bars, liquor stores and groceries just outside city limits to serve their desires. Inside the city limits, however, merchants were seething, watching their customers desert them for competitors with beer and wine on the shelves of stores and on the tables of diners. Social clubs were losing members as well, and in 1947, a group of citizens organized and demanded a liquor license for their private club. This group was a hard one to say "no" to, because they were all veterans of World Wars I and II. The American Legion's veterans were tired of watching their brethren across the country gathering over a glass of beer to share old war stories while they had to settle for a glass of Coca-Cola instead. We fought and in many cases were wounded in defense of this country, they argued. The least you can do is let us have a drink now that we're home. The request was denied, but the city's prohibition law was starting to spring leaks.

The issue got even murkier in the early 1950s. Forest Grove was watching nervously as neighboring cities started to gobble up land for expansion. City fathers wanted to get in on this annexation craze as well to build its tax base, but they faced a problem. The areas adjacent to the existing city limits were where taverns and stores that carried liquor had established themselves to serve those wanting an easy walk to Forest Grove after imbibing. So when the city annexed a swath of homes and businesses on its east side, a swath that included the Circle Inn tavern and a grocery store that sold beer and wine, it allowed those businesses to continue sales, but outlawed any new licenses. Even this compromise was troublesome, however, with constant bickering between the city and the owner of the Circle Inn over hours of operation, noise, litter and other issues. Over time more taverns and stores that sold beer and wine were annexed and allowed to continue service. In the 1960s the city even annexed an area containing the Pine Inn, which sold hard liquor by the glass.

While city businesses fretted, Forest Grove sports fans found a reason to cheer for prohibition. In August 1955, Forest Grove residents got to see real live National Football League action, or at least activity,

172

when the Pittsburgh Steelers held their training camp at Pacific University. Portland had been selected as the site of the 1955 season's first exhibition game, pitting the Steelers against the Los Angeles Rams. The Steelers started their training in upstate New York, but the coach decided to move to a facility close to Portland but away from the temptations of the city, including alcohol. Forest Grove was the logical place. The city rolled out the red carpet for the team, meeting the players at the airport and forming a caravan to their temporary home in a Pacific dormitory. On a day off, Chamber of Commerce members picked up the players in their personal automobiles and another caravan carried the team to the Tillamook Cheese Factory, where the *News-Times* reported that some of the players attempted to lift a 500-pound block of cheddar.

In 1957, Forest Grove got another shot of football, as the Chicago Cardinals came to town for a short training camp in Forest Grove before an exhibition game in Portland, similar to what the Steelers did in 1955. In the spring of 1960, the Cleveland Browns announced plans to do the same. The town bustled with anticipation, and then got news it could hardly believe. In 1960, a new football team had been created in Dallas, Texas. Its coach was Tom Landry. Although Landry would go on to become one of the NFL's greatest coaches, most fans had never heard of him in 1960. Forest Grove fans would become some of the first to hear his story, and they loved what they heard. Landry considered Texas in July to be too hot for the marathon training sessions he planned. He thought that what he believed would be a cool maritime climate in Oregon would be ideal. Landry also was a devout Methodist Sunday School teacher who disdained alcohol and wanted his players as far removed from it as possible. When he discovered that Forest Grove was dry, he opted to conduct the team's entire first ever training camp there, with the possibility of making it an annual event. All this meant that the summer of 1960 would be a frenetic one for local sports fans, with two NFL teams training in town.

If Landry was expecting a moist climate, he got what he expected. Forest Grove typically has hot, dry Julys and Augusts. Not Texas hot, but still hot, and dry. This year it rained hard and frequently, causing Landry to cut short a number of training sessions. If Landry expected an entirely dry town in terms of alcohol, he didn't get exactly what he expected, as his camp was wet in that regard as well. Not as wet as the weather perhaps,

173

but wet enough. Longtime Forest Grove businessman Tim Schauermann, a teenager at the time, recalls: "The players flew into Portland, were bused to Forest Grove, which had no taxi service, and were stuck. But they were inventive. They started offering any teenager with access to a car to take them to Portland for a $10 bill." After about a month, Forest Grove bid fond farewell to the Cowboys, and rolled out the welcome mat for the Browns. Forest Grove was Football City. Both teams suggested that they might return.

In the spring of 1961, Forest Grove eagerly waited to hear which, and how many, NFL teams would train in the city. Finally on June 15, the *News-Times* broke the town's heart with a Page 1 headline: "Cowboys, Browns Absent." The Cowboys had received a better offer from Saint Olaf College in Northfield, Minnesota. The college and town were similar to Pacific and Forest Grove, but about twice as far from a major city, making liquor runs more difficult. To add insult to injury, the New York Giants did decide to train in Oregon that year, but were lured away by Willamette University in Salem. Hope faded for the city's football fans, but then in 1963, the Cowboys had a change of heart; quarterback Don Meredith and the rest of the team were coming. More good news followed in 1964, when the Cowboys returned once again. They did not return in 1965, however, nor did they or any other team hold another training camp in Forest Grove. Being dry no longer was enough to land the city a training camp.

By the time the Cowboys left for good, Forest Grove was dry only in the most technical sense of the word. Because of annexations, loopholes and compromises, beer and wine were readily available, although often only by jumping through hoops. For example, in the city's core, the City Council had decided to grant beer permits to two "pool halls." That did not mean, however, that people could sip on a drink while playing billiards. The permits prohibited patrons from drinking the beer inside the pool hall. "The patrons not only had to drink off premise they also could not open the bottle on premise," Schauermann recalls. "So local taverns sold beer and the patrons went into back alleys to drink a bottle, then came back in to play pool or shuffleboard. One such 'alley' was a three foot wide opening in the middle of the block bounded by (Council Street), 19th, Main and Pacific Avenue. I used to work in the garbage business and we used that walkway to get to the back of a

174

restaurant fronting Pacific, a tavern fronting Main Street and the *News Times* newspaper next to the tavern. The alley was covered in beer bottle caps about two feet deep. Hugh McGilvra, the editor and publisher of the *News Times* told me he often got phone calls from unhappy wives instructing him to go next door and send their husbands home."

In September 1965, two establishments applied for liquor licenses. City Council members denied the Tip Top restaurant's request because they deemed it to be too close to Pacific University, but stunned the city by granting a request from the owner of a Hillsboro restaurant called the Copperstone. The Copperstone's owner planned to open a second restaurant at Pacific Avenue and Hawthorne Street, and won historic approval to sell liquor by the glass. The Forest Grove chapter of the Women's Christian Temperance Union immediately circulated a petition to stop the license, but managed to gather only 35 signatures. It appeared that more than 100 years since the founding of Pacific University, Forest Grove residents would be able to legally buy a cocktail within city limits. Anticipation built, but in November the Copperstone's owner was sentenced to four months in jail for tax evasion. The City Council withdrew its support for his liquor license, and Forest Grove once again was denied legal cocktails.

As the 1960s drew to a close, just about everyone was fed up with the confusion and mess that the patchwork quilt of laws had created. In 1967, the city's "Gay Nineties Festival" committee asked the city for a permit to have a beer garden in one of downtown's vacant buildings to help raise money for community organizations. The Gay Nineties folks included many of the town's movers and shakers, and this request was for a good cause, but the Council shot it down on a unanimous vote, with one Councilmember helpfully suggesting an ice-cream parlor instead. In April 1969, the Elks wanted to build a lodge and requested a liquor license like just about every other lodge in the country had. The City Council again said no. The Lodge president, Richard Heisler, would not back down. "There won't be a lodge if we can't have a bar," the *News-Times* reported the head Elk as saying. Council member Bill Gardner objected to "this inroads into a dry city," at which point someone asked City Manager Dan Potter if Forest Grove really was dry. After some thought, Potter replied that perhaps the city was better described as "damp." This time the community would not back down, either, and demanded that the city reconsider. Two weeks later it did, and the Elks got their liquor license. Things in "damp" Forest Grove would never be the same.

A year later, the head of the Gay Nineties committee was back in front of the City Council, asking for a full liquor license. Young Aldie Howard was not there in his role with the Gay Nineties festival, however, nor in his role as president of the town's Booster Club, but rather as a prospective restaurateur. Howard had been granted a license to serve beer and wine, but wanted more. He said that businesspeople visiting town were unhappy with the lack of a restaurant at which they could enjoy fine food and cocktails in a family friendly atmosphere. The Council gave him all of the usual objections about children and of course the welfare of Pacific University students. Aldie Howard had ready answers for every objection. He was the father of a small child himself. He was former student body president at Pacific University and loved the school. Oh, and his wife was the dean of women at the college. Still, the Council wouldn't budge and postponed a vote until it could hold a hearing in the Forest Grove High School Auditorium to accommodate the many citizens the Council anticipated would want to speak out against the idea of a restaurant that served cocktails. In the meantime, the *News-Times* ran a number of stories about Howard's plans. Perhaps publisher Hugh McGilvra was just tired of shooing wayward husbands home from the alley behind his paper, because the stories cast Howard's plans in a favorable light.

The restaurant, on Main Street between Pacific and 19th avenues, was to be called the Coffee Grinder, built around an antique grinder that had been on display at the neighboring First National Bank for years. It would be open from 8:30 in the morning to 1:30 in the morning, offering everything from muffins to martinis, with an emphasis on steaks. "We want to cater to all," Aldie Howard told the *News-Times*, "and there are some people who want a drink with meals." His pleas fell on deaf ears, and he was denied a liquor license, despite the fact that the anticipated community opposition failed to appear. Howard did not give up, however, and ran for City Council himself. The older members of the Council filed for re-election and took steps to make themselves more attractive to younger voters, even eliminating the last of the city's "blue laws," designed to regulate business on Sunday. The last law to be stricken was one prohibiting "bowling, skating, movies and card playing" until 2

176

p.m. on Sundays. Those strides toward modernization were not enough for the old guard to hang on, however, and Aldie Howard and his supporters gained control of City Council. One of the first pieces of business the new Council considered was a liquor license for the Coffee Grinder. Opponents demanded that Howard not vote on the issue, and he happily obliged; the vote was four to one in his favor, so it didn't matter. Forest Grove was officially, once and for all, wet.

Aldie Howard's triumph didn't settle every issue, of course, not after more than 100 years of battles over imbibing. It would be another decade, in 1980, that the city finally got a liquor store, and only then after a public vote on the issue. In the mid-1990s some entrepreneurs announced plans for a topless bar downtown. The proverbial assortment of strange bedfellows, from churches to feminists, joined to fight the effort and used liquor licensing as their weapon of choice. The topless club took a hike out of Forest Grove.

Today on the surface Forest Grove looks like many small towns in America; churches, a college, grocery stores, pool halls, restaurants, taverns and a liquor store. It has other attractions most small towns lack, including a large destination hotel and brew pub, a sake brewery and too many wineries to count. It does not have an NFL training facility, but then how many small towns do?

Beneath the surface, however, Forest Grove has a history that has been shaped, more than in most any other Oregon town, by beer, wine, booze … and the statutory but illusory prohibition against all of the above.

Chapter

10

Newspapers at war

Harvey Scott walked to Forest Grove in 1857, legend tells us. His stroll was much shorter than Tabitha Brown's 14 years earlier, however, measuring a mere 200 miles from near Tacoma, Washington. Although he didn't know it at the time, he was walking straight into what would become a brutal newspaper war that pitted him against many of the state's most powerful men and, ultimately, against one of the state's most powerful women, who just happened to be his own sister.

While Harvey Scott fought his battles in Portland, the town he walked to in 1857 also became home to some of the most colorful newspaper wars in the Northwest, which continue to the current day, long after most dueling newspapers had given up the battle. Perhaps ironically, while newspapers often are called the first draft of history, they do a very poor job of writing their own history. The strange twists and turns of Forest Grove's journalism history often have been reported selectively by the papers, ignored by those to whom they happen or exploited by competitors. Still, there's no question that few forces have had an influence on Forest Grove as profound as the printing press and the people who own one.

Forest Grove's newspaper history begins in 1847, the year Tabitha Brown arrived, and before the town was known by its current name. The Oregon Territory's first newspaper, *The Spectator,* launched in Oregon City in 1846, and every other town in the state wanted a newspaper of its own. Unfortunately, printing presses were all but impossible to come by in the Oregon Territory, and in 1902 George Himes of the Oregon Historical Society recounted the often harrowing early days of Oregon journalism. The only known press in the region besides *The Spectator*'s was near what today is Walla Walla, Washington, in the hands of missionary Marcus Whitman, who used it to print religious pamphlets. Whitman acquired the press in 1839, but by then it already was well-used and equally well-traveled. Whitman got the rickety old press from missionary friends in Honolulu, who had acquired it 20 years earlier from missionaries in Boston. Even after Whitman acquired the press, it kept on travelling, being hauled by mules up and down the Columbia and Snake rivers for use by smaller missions. Himes related that on one such journey, the mule carrying the press along a steep cliff fell to its death, and conditions were so treacherous that the printing press spent the winter at the river's edge before being retrieved the following spring. It still worked, and still was coveted.

No one coveted that press more than business and political leaders in the territorial capital, Salem. Those leaders asked one of Marcus Whitman's best friends, teacher and businessman Alanson Hinman, to cajole Whitman into letting them rent the press to start Oregon's second newspaper. Whitman agreed, and in 1847 Hinman headed west toward Salem with the printing press in tow. Hinman made it to The Dalles, Oregon, and sent word to the folks in Salem that he had accomplished his mission, and now needed only to plan the treacherous journey through the Columbia River Gorge without losing mules or the press. Oh, and by the way, he told the folks in Salem, the deeply pious Whitman had attached a long list of restrictions against what could be printed with the press. When the politicians in Salem saw the restrictions, they told Hinman not to bother with the rest of the trip, and the press was left in The Dalles.

The Dalles, however, was not destined to become the second town in the Oregon Territory to have a newspaper. Before the printing press could be returned to Marcus Whitman back in Walla Walla,

Whitman and his family were killed by Indians in what became known as the Whitman Massacre. Hinman and several other of Whitman's associates sought safer ground, and they knew that the Tualatin Plains fit the bill. Along the way, Hinman and the others picked up the printing press in The Dalles and brought it to the Tualatin Plains, where it was delivered into the hands of one of the area's earliest settlers, Reverend John Smith Griffin. On June 8, 1848, the printing press that traveled from Boston to Honolulu to Walla Walla, down a Columbia River Gorge cliff, back to Walla Walla, to The Dalles, and then to Forest Grove, printed the first copies of the *Oregon American and Evangelical Unionist*, Oregon's second newspaper. Although the *Oregon American* had a brief life, its short history speaks volumes about the settling of Oregon.

John Smith Griffin was born into a distinguished New England family, and in the 1830s he headed to Ohio and earned a degree from Oberlin College, where he befriended Harvey Clarke. Griffin and Clarke each longed to spread their missionary zeal to the fabled Oregon Territory, and each found their way to Marcus Whitman's mission before becoming two of the first white settlers in the Tualatin Plains. Unlike Whitman, Clarke and Griffin cared little about the Native Americans, instead focusing their efforts on saving the souls of white settlers. Mostly, however, the Reverends Clarke and Griffin battled each other in a feud that created a rift between the eastern and western Tualatin Plains and which led to the eventual rivalry between Hillsboro and Forest Grove, according to a biography by Chemeketa College Professor Steven Richardson in the Winter 1990 *Oregon Historical Quarterly*.

Griffin's *Oregon American and Evangelical Unionist* lasted for just eight sporadic editions, and included some local and national news, but mostly polemics about the murder of Marcus Whitman and his followers. Unlike most people in the Oregon Territory, Richardson writes, the *Oregon American* placed the blame not so much on Native Americans as on the Jesuit missionaries associated with the Hudson's Bay Company. After Griffin shut down the *Oregon American* it would be another 20 years before Forest Grove would have another newspaper, but it would be only five years until Forest Grove had its first great journalist.

Harvey Scott made the trek across the Plains from Peoria, Illinois, in 1852, stopping for a time in Yamhill, Oregon, before proceeding north to the Puget Sound region. Harvey Scott was a hardy fellow, serving as a soldier in the Indian Wars. Scott returned to Oregon, however, because the Puget Sound area did not yet have a college for him to attend. He set out on foot to Forest Grove, just in time to become the oldest student at Tabitha Brown's Tualatin Academy, which just a few years earlier had been expanded to become Pacific University. In 1863, six years after walking to Forest Grove, Harvey W. Scott walked to the podium to accept his diploma as Pacific University's first graduate. After graduating from Pacific, Scott crossed paths with a young man named Henry Pittock, and together the two of them went on to change forever the landscape of Oregon commerce and politics.

Henry Pittock worked at a print shop in Pittsburgh, Pennsylvania, but in 1853 at the age of 17 he set out across the Plains with his brother and some friends, with Oregon their intended destination. Pittock later told biographers that he walked the entire way to Oregon, most of it barefoot after the soles of his boots wore out. Pittock did not walk to Forest Grove, however, settling instead in a river town that had the potential to become another Pittsburgh, the young city of Portland. Rebuffed by Oregon's few newspapers that actually paid employees, Pittock accepted a position with a struggling weekly newspaper called *The Oregonian*. *The Oregonian*'s owner, Thomas Dryer, was more interested in becoming a powerhouse in the Republican Party than he was in becoming a newspaper publisher, and before long Pittock assumed control. Pittock was a printer, not a journalist, so when he met recent college graduate Harvey Scott he saw the ideal editor for his fledgling paper. Their partnership would last for decades, and together they battled and defeated many other better-financed rivals to make *The Oregonian* the biggest newspaper in the Northwest. Along the way, however, they waged many of their most bitter battles against each other, with Scott walking away several times before always returning to an uneasy truce with Pittock.

Scott infused *The Oregonian* with journalistic principles many of his competitors lacked, and also infused it with deeply conservative politics that the paper has embraced through its history. Some of his biggest political battles were against public education and against granting women the right to vote. Ultimately, he ended up on the losing side of both fights, in no small part because of the tireless campaign of *The New Northwest*, a muckraking pioneer newspaper owned by Abigail Scott Duniway, Harvey Scott's sister.

Abigail had made the journey along the Oregon Trail to Yamhill with Harvey, and like her brother made much of the trip on foot. Abigail settled a few miles south of Yamhill in the town of Lafayette, becoming a public school teacher and a fierce promoter of education, particularly for girls. Her disabled husband lost their farm and died, leaving the single mother on her own. She packed up the kids, moved to Portland and did the unthinkable for a woman of her day: She started a newspaper. *The New Northwest* soon was going toe to toe with her brother's *Oregonian*, taking the opposite side of nearly every issue. By now Harvey Scott and Henry Pittock had monied and political elites solidly behind them, but neither had the oratorical and debating skills of the single mother who proudly flouted convention and who developed a passionate following of progressives, particularly women. Abigail Scott Duniway, more than perhaps any other person, is given credit for making Oregon just the seventh state to grant women the right to vote.

Abigail's paper was every bit the intellectual equal of Harvey's but never generated the advertising base it needed to compete. Other rival newspapers battled *The Oregonian* for many years, including the *Portland Bulletin*, edited for a time by none other than Harvey Scott during one of his many snits with Pittock. Ultimately, however, *The Oregonian* won supremacy, in large part because of Scott's vision to be a statewide newspaper, focusing well beyond the Portland city limits that constrained many other editors' views.

Meanwhile, long after Harvey Scott established himself as a journalism heavyweight, the folks back on the Tualatin Plains still waited for another newspaper to replace the pioneering *Oregon American and Evangelical Unionist*. Finally in 1868, with help from Pacific University, the *Forest Grove Monthly* made its debut. The *Monthly* was as much promotional brochure as newspaper, and it too folded after just a few issues. Forest Grove then landed another newspaper, the *Forest Grove Independent*, but quickly lost that one as well, this time to Hillsboro.

Battles between Forest Grove and Hillsboro are nothing new. Since the middle of the 1800s the towns have fought for supremacy in Washington County. The towns battled over which would be the county seat and over which would be the economic hub of the county. J.S. Griffin and Harvey Clarke battled over which town would be home to Pacific University. Against that background, townspeople were stunned on October 15, 1874, when what heretofore had been the *Forest Grove Independent* ran a stunning story. "After due consideration," that story began, "we have decided to move the *Independent* to Hillsboro, the county seat of this connty (sic)." Although this involved a move of only about five miles, the *Independent*'s editors explained their decision in somewhat dire terms. "We do this for the simple reason that the county seat is the best place for a *news*-paper (emphasis in original). The news from the several neighborhoods comes into that place every week fresh from the several precincts and it can be got without trouble." By way of contrast, "At the Grove we cannot get that news without paying heavily for it and this we are not able to do." Fortunately, other publishers had a less dire view of newsgathering in "the Grove," and new newspapers soon popped up. One of the first was the *Pacific Pharos*, whose publisher offered to take "wood, apples or vegetables" as payment for subscriptions. The *Pharos* faded quickly, but other publishers kept trying.

Forest Grove got its first newspaper with staying power in February 1891, when J. Wheelock Marsh, son of Pacific University President Sidney Harper Marsh, took over the struggling *Forest Grove Democrat* and changed its name to the *Forest Grove Times*. In its inaugural issue, Marsh assured readers that the *Times* would provide "the best local news we can find, but such items only that can safely be read in any home." Dr. Charles Large, an obstetrician, coroner and shameless self-promoter, did not like Marsh and longed to open a competing paper. Large was something of a journalist himself, writing about Forest Grove for *The Oregonian*, but operating a newspaper is a full-time job, so Large started looking for an editor. According to Forest Grove historian Eric Stewart, Large found his man in Austin Craig, who arrived in Forest Grove to pursue a degree at Pacific University the year the *Times* began. A few years later, according to Stewart's June 1, 1994, *New-Times* piece, Austin Craig, with his degree and Dr. Large's cash in hand, took over the struggling upstart *Washington County Hatchet*, and in so doing launched Forest Grove's first real newspaper war.

Craig seemingly had everything necessary to be successful. Large built a printshop on land donated by Alvin Smith's nephew. The building was designed to be a statement in itself; black with red trim, the only markings were a bust of George Washington, the word "county" with a snake forming the letter C, and a small wooden hatchet. Craig was a harsh critic of the *Times'* Democratic owners, and promised that the *Hatchet*, by contrast, would be "impartial and uncolored." That claim was somewhat undercut by the Hatchet's slogan: "Readable, Reliable, Republican," and by the fact that the paper's launch coincided with Craig's nomination by the Republicans for the position of Washington County School Superintendent, a position he won. Politics aside, no one doubted Craig's commitment to journalism, and the *Hatchet* was a force to contend with. Craig was tireless in reporting local events, and listed his office hours at the paper as 6 a.m. to 10 p.m. every weekday.

The *Hatchet* and *Times* battled it out in Forest Grove's first newspaper war until at least 1896, but this is when Forest Grove's newspaper history gets murky. We know that in June 1896, J. Wheelock Marsh sold the *Times* to *Hatchet* owner Austin Craig. In June 1899, the *Times* again was independent, with J.B. Eddy announcing that he had bought the paper, while Craig was again publishing the *Hatchet*. Later that year, Eddy and Craig agreed to merge, and things again turned ugly.

With the *Times'* subscriber list in hand, Craig reneged on the agreement and resumed publication, delivering the *Hatchet* free to *Times* readers. The *Times* followed suit, sending its editions free to *Hatchet* subscribers. At that point in 1899, Forest Grove's newspaper wars got even uglier, as Austin Craig decided to go to war against Forest Grove's pharmacies, the only establishments in town allowed to sell alcohol. But if the *Hillsboro Argus* is to be believed, Craig's motive was less about prohibition than it was about extortion. Two of Forest Grove's pharmacists went public with charges that Craig had threatened to ruin their businesses unless they paid $100 each. The *Argus* suggested that the *Hatchet*'s motto should be changed from "Readable. Reliable. Republican" to "Rotten. Rascally. Repulsive." Charles Large sued Craig for breach of contract, claiming that he had reneged on the sale of Large's ownership of the paper. Craig denied all of the allegations, but Forest Grove had had enough of his antics. He lost his job as county superintendent of schools, he lost his newspaper and he was in effect run out of town. Two years later in 1903, the *Argus* reported that "Forest Grove's Angel," as the writers sarcastically called Craig, had moved to the desolate eastern Oregon town of Whitney. No longer interested in the newspaper business, Craig had created a new life for himself as Postmaster and City Recorder for the good folks of Whitney. He also dabbled as representative of a bank and as a mining and real estate promoter. If we believe the Baker County prosecutor, Austin Craig also dabbled as a thief, because he was sitting behind bars, charged with grand larceny.

And then, a few months later, Austin Craig's name mysteriously appeared again as editor of the new *Washington County News*, if only for a few issues, as he staunchly defended his friend, the Rev. Richard Kennedy, against home invasion charges. His boss while he was defending Kennedy was *News* Publisher Will French, whose career was ended that same year by allegations that he blackmailed pharmacists much as Craig had been accused of doing four years earlier, but this time the demand was for only $50, not $100. French and Austin disappeared from Forest Grove, but Austin's distinctive black and red *Hatchet* building survived, at least for a time. The building was painted a drab gray and became a candy store, but its time in Forest Grove lore ended in a ball of flames, when the 1919 arson fire devastated the city.

With the town's most-colorful editor out of the picture, Forest Grove's newspaper scene became relatively tame. The *News* and *Times* continued to compete, joined soon by the *Press*, but the rivalries lacked the intensity of the *Hatchet* days. In 1909, the *Forest Grove Times* merged with the *Washington County News*, becoming the *Washington County News-Times* in 1911. Three years later the *News-Times* purchased its last competitor, the *Forest Grove Press*. The winning publisher announced his conquest with words that foretold what would happen in virtually every other town in America, large or small: "It is the unanimous consensus of the business people of Forest Grove that this city needs but one newspaper and they have so declared themselves to the editor of this paper in a very gratifying way." Despite a brief appearance by the *Forest Grove Express* from 1916 to 1918, the newspaper wars, it appeared, were forever settled in little Forest Grove.

The newly merged *News-Times* was a solid newspaper, but lacked the personality of papers published by Craig, Marsh, French, and activist mayor and editor Walter Hoge. That all changed in 1928, however, when a man came to town who would dominate the town's political discourse for more than 50 years. Hugh McGilvra did not have to walk to Forest Grove, because by the time he was born in 1906 in South Dakota, trains were chugging westward on a regular basis. Hugh's family took the train west when he was a small child, settling in the small Oregon community of Reedville. Hugh loved school and took newspaper routes in both the morning and evening to raise enough money to attend Willamette University in Salem, where McGilvra fell in love with journalism and ended up editing the school's newspaper and yearbook. While at Willamette, Hugh also fell in love with his future wife, Louise, who would become instrumental in his career. When he graduated in 1928, Hugh and his friend Jeeter Gillette scraped together $17,000, according to a 2008 profile in the *News-Times*, and took over the struggling newspaper. A few years later Jeeter left to take over the newspaper in the coastal community of Coos Bay, but Hugh and Louise settled in for a long stay. Jeeter Gillette was supposed to be the business brains behind the operation, but Hugh McGilvra was a visionary and his wife Louise proved to be a master at bookkeeping and management. Hugh McGilvra also had a social conscience and cared deeply about justice. When a series of arsons swept the Hillside district west of town in 1930, he knew that the area was a stronghold for the Ku Klux Klan and helped link the crimes to bigotry against the Japanese farmers moving to the area. Twelve years later, after the attack on Pearl Harbor, in 1942 his was a lonely editorial voice against internment of the Japanese farmers in Forest Grove and nearby Banks and Gaston. If McGilvra had a true passion, however, it was to promote public education.

Born in a tar-paper shack in Draper, South Dakota, young Hugh might have been destined to a life of physical labor like his father, but his mother had a college degree and desired one for Hugh as well. He shared Abigail Scott Duniway's commitment to public education and spent many years on the board of Forest Grove High School and many more on the board of Portland Community College. Although McGilvra professed political independence, he was as Republican as Austin Craig and served in the Oregon Legislature for many years. His political career ended when he was defeated by Les AuCoin, who went on to represent Oregon for nearly 20 years in the United States House of Representatives. AuCoin's victory, however, kept the House seat in the hands of a journalist. The Forest Grove resident and graduate of Pacific University had been a newspaper journalist who had worked at *The Oregonian*. In addition to education and public service, McGilvra also was committed to preserving Forest Grove history, running frequent retrospectives and employing Ellis

Lucia, a journalist and prolific history author of books on the Tillamook Burn and Oregon railroads, among other subjects.

In 1981, McGilvra ended his 53-year ownership of the *News-Times*, selling it to the owners of the *Eugene Register-Guard*. The Baker family, which owned the *Register-Guard*, controlled the second most powerful media corporation in Oregon, and the purchase of the *News-Times* and other suburban newspapers looked like a shot across the bow at the powerful out-of-state Newhouse family's *Oregonian*. Edwin Baker showed that he meant business, assigning his daughter Ann to lead the challenge to *The Oregonian*'s grip on Portland area media, with Forest Grove as a prime battleground. That battle did come, but as it turns out the Bakers were about 20 years too early with their Community Newspapers plan.

To understand the brewing battle for newspaper supremacy in Forest Grove, one must first examine the history of newspapers in Hillsboro, a few miles east of Forest Grove. In 1874, just months after the *Independent* deserted Forest Grove because gathering news from five miles away was too expensive, the *Hillsboro Argus* began publication, in large part to represent competing political interests. The *Argus* struggled mightily for its first 30 years, changing ownership too many times to count, but in 1904 a woman entered the fray who would change forever the newspaper landscape in Washington County. Emma McKinney took controlling interest and ramped up the battle with the *Independent*, finally buying (and promptly folding) it in 1932. The McKinneys held onto the paper for decades, even longer than McGilvra, until 1999, when Walter McKinney sold the *Argus* to the Newhouse family, one of the richest clans in America and owners of the state's largest newspaper, *The Oregonian*. For the next 13 years, the *Argus* operated independently from *The Oregonian*, even competing with it for news and advertising.

But just a year after the Newhouses bought the *Argus*, Robert Pamplin bought the *News Times* and other Community Newspapers from the Baker family. Pamplin didn't have Newhouse-type money, but he was no slouch, either, easily ranking as among the wealthiest Oregonians. He was itching for a fight with the Newhouses, although Forest Grove and Hillsboro were not his preferred battleground. He had his sights set firmly on Portland, and in 2001 launched the free *Portland Tribune*, *The Oregonian*'s first real competitor in many decades. For the next few years, the *News-*

Times and other former Community Newspapers properties now owned by Pamplin served as weapons in the Portland wars by creating something close to what's known as total metropolitan market coverage for large retailers' advertising inserts and by providing profits to support the money-losing *Tribune*.

In 2012, however, several events transpired to shift this battle of the behemoths from downtown Portland to Main Street Forest Grove. In January 2012, *The Oregonian* took total control of the *Argus*, firing staff and turning it into a virtual news bureau, sharing stories between the two papers. With the *Argus* stripped of many of its longtime writers, Pamplin saw an opportunity and launched the *Hillsboro Tribune*, written and sold by his staff at the *News-Times*. A month later, *The Oregonian* fired back with the launch of the *Forest Grove Leader*. It was like old times, with Forest Grove papers battling each other while at the same time battling Hillsboro's papers. At first glance, the moves by Pamplin and the Newhouses seemed spiteful, perhaps even petty. In reality, they might have changed the national media landscape in some very important ways.

In June 2013, *The Oregonian* announced that it was dropping home delivery to four days a week, essentially ending its history as one of the West's great daily newspapers. The personnel cuts made at the time were brutal, including many of the paper's best (and best-paid) journalists. By contrast, the staff of the *Leader* was unscathed. At about the same time, the Newhouses announced the launch of the *Beaverton Leader*, modeled on the fledgling Forest Grove paper of the same name. Suddenly the folks at the *News-Times* and *Leader* looked like the tails wagging the newshounds employed at their Portland parents. More than 150 years after Harvey Scott walked to Forest Grove to become the state's premier newspaper editor, the city once again found itself on the front lines of a newspaper war, with the paper that Harvey Scott built into a juggernaut on one side of the trenches.

Forest Grove probably was destined to be a newspaper town. Harvey Scott was, after all, the first graduate of the university that built the town. The university also was among the town's first newspaper publishers. In a town built on the education industry it's not surprising that the town's best-known publishers made names for themselves as education advocates, albeit in very different ways, with Scott urging the abolishment of post-elementary public education and McGilvra campaigning tirelessly for public high school and college opportunities. Even Austin Craig was briefly a mover and shaker in the field as county Superintendent of Schools, although a cloud of suspicion hung over everything he did; it's probably fitting that his career would fall victim to the city's seemingly never-ending battles over booze.

Newspapers often are called the first draft of history, but Forest Grove's have done more than simply record history. The *Oregon American and Evangelical Unionist,* the *Monthly,* the *Times,* the *Hatchet,* the *News-Times,* and the *Leader* all have been shaped by history and in turn shaped history. While Pacific University's first graduate walked away from Forest Grove at a young age, he shaped, perhaps more than any other person, Northwest newspaper history, a chapter of which was still being written in 2014, in competing downtown Forest Grove newsrooms.

Chapter

11

Forest Grove goes to war

Ryley Gallinger-Long graduated from Forest Grove High School in June 2010. In March 2011 he married his high school sweetheart, Hope. On August 20, 2011, Ryley Gallinger-Long was buried with full military honors at Willamette National Cemetery.

Nine days earlier, on August 11, 2011, Navy Corpsmen Ryley Gallinger-Long was in his first month of duty with his Marine unit in the Helmand Province of Afghanistan, at the time probably the toughest assignment the American military could dish out. That was okay with Ryley, because by all accounts he was about as tough and patriotic a person as America could offer. He had been a cadet with Forest Grove Fire and Rescue and four-wheeled and raised ruckus in his free time. Ryley was someone other young men of Forest Grove looked up to and respected. Yet on the morning of August 11, 2011, he still was just 19, sent half way around the world to do battle in a gruesome war. That morning, one of his colleagues needed medical help on the battlefield, and Ryley raced to his aid. While he worked to save the life of an injured American Marine, the young hero from Forest Grove, Oregon, was shot in the back and killed.

The tragic and heroic nature of Ryley's death touched everyone with a conscience, but it especially touched Forest Grove residents too young to remember the Vietnam War. For many of the younger people, war was in many ways an abstraction. Most under the age of about 55 never had faced the prospect of a draft, and few knew anyone who had died serving their country. For people of a certain age, however, Ryley's death reopened old wounds. Those close to 60 remembered waiting to see where their birthdays would fall in the draft lottery, unless they already had volunteered to go fight. Those yet a little older had fought, or knew someone who had, in the Korean War, World War II or even World War I. The community rallied to build a memorial to honor Ryley and every other Washington County soldier killed in action. The wall ensures that their names will not be forgotten, but the stone is not big enough to list the names of those who managed to come back from war alive, although often not unscarred. No stone is big enough to tell the tales of heroism that these veterans displayed, the tragedy they endured, or the adventure and even in some cases love that they experienced while serving their countries.

By the time of Ryley's death, war had become, quite literally, foreign to most people in Forest Grove and across America. While a select few volunteers journeyed overseas to Afghanistan, Iraq, Bosnia and other distant lands, life back in Forest Grove went on as usual. Such was not the case in World War I and World War II, when virtually everyone shouldered the weight of conflict, enduring rationing, collecting scrap metal and taking on jobs in the defense industry. Even during the Vietnam War, the conflict hit home as every able-bodied young man of draft age knew that his number could be called at any time. But many of the earliest white settlers on the Tualatin Plains had even more up close and personal experience with war. Some had fought on American soil in the War of 1812 or the Civil War. In fact, most of the rugged mountain men who found homes near what would become Forest Grove had fought their way across the Plains and Rocky Mountains in skirmishes of the Indian Wars, and some continued to do battle for years after arriving in the Oregon Territory.

William Roper Barrett was typical of such fighters. Born in Cincinnati, Ohio, Barrett did not fight his way across the Plains. Instead, he sailed to Panama in 1854, crossed the Isthmus and caught a sailing ship

191

up the Pacific Coast to Portland and settled in the hamlet of Greenville, a couple of miles north of Forest Grove. An expert carpenter, Barrett quickly became sought after by other settlers in need of homes, and he built a solid career. Soon, however, Colonel Thomas Cornelius, for whom the town east of Forest Grove is named, sent out word that he needed volunteers to fight the Yakama Nation near what is today Yakima, Washington. The lingering dispute had been brewing since the Champoeg meetings a decade earlier, when settlers sided with the Americans over the British. The British, represented by the Hudson's Bay Company, enjoyed a cordial relationship and trade agreement with the Yakamas, Cayuse and other tribes east of the Cascades, but the Americans had a different relationship. Almost immediately after the Champoeg meetings, a war broke out in the Walla Walla region, resulting in the deaths of Marcus Whitman and others in his party. Many of the Tualatin Plains' earliest settlers had come across the Plains with Whitman or knew him from his visits to the area, including Cornelius, Joseph Meek, Joseph Gale, and Almoran Hill. Many of those men took up arms to avenge the death of their friend. Tensions subsided somewhat for a few years, but in 1855, the American Congress passed the Homestead Act, offering up the vast ranges of the Native American tribes for white settlers to take for free. The Yakamas did not take the loss of their homeland well, and fighting flared anew. That's when Cornelius raised an army, and William Barrett among others eagerly joined the war. In Forest Grove, wives and mothers gathered supplies for the effort and Tabitha Brown, who had intended to be a seamstress when she arrived in town, organized a sewing circle to create an American flag to carry into battle.

Thomas Cornelius spent two years in what he referred to as "Yackimah Country." In letters home to his wife, some of which were printed nearly 90 years later in the *Oregon Journal*, he spoke of his experiences. "We have had a longe tyersome round which I hear below give you a statement of," he wrote in one. He wrote of surviving on horse meat for many days in a fruitless pursuit of Indians, until encountering a small band crossing the Columbia River. His troops, he wrote, "killd two of them the rest of them made their escape ... In hour little fractises with the Indians we have had no damage done by the Indians only one man slightly wounded with an arrow." In closing, he added "I am getting tyred of Fighting Indians unless they were braver and plentyer."

The "Indian Wars" were unlike others in that those who volunteered were, for the most part, expected to furnish their own supplies and received no formal government benefits, such as pensions, like those who fought in more conventional wars. What people fought for in the Indian Wars was land, and many of the fighters were rewarded with grants of 320 acres (or 640 acres for married couples) from the Homestead Act and other such land giveaways. William Barrett became such a beneficiary when he returned to Greenville and met and married Miss Eliza Purdin. Eliza was the daughter of prominent Donation Land Claim owner Ira Purdin. Although he didn't realize it at first, William Barrett and Ira Purdin had much in common. Like Barrett, Ira Purdin had lived near Cincinnati, although earlier, back in a time when much of Southern Ohio was a wilderness. Purdin had moved on to Missouri by the time Barrett was born, but their lives would cross in some mysterious ways. In 1854, Missouri was hit with an epidemic of "ague," an ill-defined term for any number of contagious diseases. Worried for his children's health, Ira Purdin packed up the family and headed to a magical place he had read about with the most salubrious climate imaginable, the Tualatin Plains of Oregon. Ira, Eliza and the other Purdins sailed down the Mississippi and on to Panama, where they crossed the Isthmus and boarded a sailing ship up the Pacific Coast to Portland. Barrett's obituary in the *Washington County News* in 1906 recounted that it wasn't until they met in Oregon that William and Eliza realized that they had made the trip West on the same voyage. Ira Purdin gave the newlyweds part of his land claim, on which to start their lives together.

Not everyone who fought in the Indian Wars was so lucky, of course. Many were ordinary people with no chance of securing a land claim. They volunteered to fight and to supply their own horses, food and even guns. Not everyone wanted to go to war, however, and Cornelius and his lieutenants sometimes put intense pressure on able-bodied men to volunteer. One of the most-committed lieutenants was William Henry Harrison Myers. "Buck" Myers was another Oregon pioneer from Missouri, who drove a team of oxen across the plains in 1852, settling near what today is the town of Gaston. Myers diligently recruited men, and when they balked he asked them to at least lend horses or guns to the cause. Buck Myers didn't like to take "no" for an answer. One legend was that when one reluctant young man refused to offer up his service or weapon and sped off on his horse, Myers engaged him in a high-speed chase on horseback into the forest, eventually overtaking the young man, tackling him and wrestling away his rifle. More than 50 years later, the *Hillsboro Argus* printed the legend in a series of reminiscences about the Indian Wars. Buck Myers saw the story and went to the *Argus* office, not to deny it but to provide further details. He said the young man's name was Bill Merrill, who he said had angered Myers by boasting to friends around town that "no one could get his gun for Indian War service." Myers also proudly added the detail that after taking the young man's weapon he pulled his knife and demanded that Merrill surrender his powder flask as well. He did not say whether Merrill ever saw his gun again.

Buck Myers became more famous for his efforts after the war than for his exploits on the battlefield. Because Oregon was not yet a state in the early stages of the wars, Oregonians officially fought on behalf of the Territorial Government, which promised to pay them for their efforts. There was a problem, however. Because the pioneers of the territory had an aversion to taxation, the government had no money with which to make good on its I.O.U. Myers spent the rest of his life, more than 50 years, trying to rectify the situation for his fellow Indian War veterans. He became the face and voice of the cause, first in Salem and later in Washington, D.C. He had some success, most notably in 1903 when he persuaded the state Legislature to allocate $100,000 to compensate the surviving veterans, whose ranks were thinning rapidly. When that amount came up short of fulfilling all the obligations, he went to the nation's capital for relief. Myers was well off, but he fought for men such as Frances Benefiel, who in 1911 was 66 years old, alone and living in a boarding house in Gaston, scraping out a living by driving a horse-drawn milk wagon. He loved to share stories of his daring adventures as a scout during the Modoc War in California, but lamented the fact that he still had no pension as his health declined and he became too frail for physical labor. Years ticked by, and veterans continued to die. In 1914, William Henry Harrison "Buck" Myers joined them, his cause never fully realized. On November 22, 1921, Frances Marion Benefiel died, single and alone. Without a family and without a pension, he died at the Multnomah County poor farm in Troutdale, which by 2014 had become a trendy brew pub and hotel called Edgefield.

By the time Oregon became a state on February 14, 1859, the nation it joined was tilting toward civil war. California had been admitted to the union in 1850 as a free state, but by 1859 there was talk of secession, and some pro-Union Golden Staters migrated north to Oregon, including a man who would become one of Oregon's first United States Senators, Edward Baker. In many ways Baker was a natural to be sent to Washington, because he already had experience in Congress, having served in the House from his native Illinois, before drifting west to serve in the Mexican-American War. Baker also was extremely well connected; his Illinois neighbor, Abraham Lincoln, was such a close friend that Lincoln named one of his sons Edward Baker Lincoln. Baker headed east to Washington, D.C., determined to help his friend succeed as President. Lincoln's election was the final straw for angry slave-owning Southerners, and within a year the nation was at war. Edward Baker re-enlisted in Lincoln's Army with the rank of general. In October 1861, the South was winning the war, and had pushed perilously close to the nation's Capital. On October 20, Baker and Lincoln sat on the White House lawn lamenting the horrors of war, and hours later Baker led his troops into battle. The next day, Oregon Senator Edward Dickinson Baker became the first, and still only, sitting member of Congress to die on the battlefield.

The Senator's death was Oregon's most notable contribution to the Civil War, but certainly not its only. Perhaps the Forest Grove area's best-known Civil War veteran was Dr. Francis Bailey, who arrived in Scoggins Valley in 1864 while the war still was raging. Bailey was born in Tennessee and earned his medical degree as the war was beginning. He quickly joined the Confederate Army and learned trauma medicine under some of the toughest conditions imaginable. In 1864 he was assigned to a ship heading west on the Missouri River. When the ship reached Kansas City, Bailey just kept going west, arriving in Oregon a few weeks later. He never left, and remained one of the region's most prominent doctors until his death in 1920, after serving several terms as president of the Oregon Medical Association, and several terms as mayor of Hillsboro later in life.

Bailey wasn't the only Southern fighter who landed in Forest Grove. Another was Virginia resident Green Meador Swinney, although he was not a formal part of the Confederacy. Instead, Swinney was a sworn member of a band of guerrillas known as the Flat Top

Copperheads, who swore an oath to fight "the Yankeys." By most accounts, the Copperheads were a brutal and often brutally incompetent band of guerrillas, but after the war, Swinney found his way to Gales City, where he lived out his life.

Most of the Civil War veterans with ties to the region fought for the Grand Army of the Republic and came to Oregon when the war ended. Probably the most noteworthy among them was General Thomas Thorp. Thorp was from New York, and was attending Union College when the Civil War broke out. He became among the first wave of enlistments into the Union Army. Thorp came from a distinguished family and was destined to be a soldier. Both his paternal and maternal grandfathers were heroes of the Revolutionary War, and his brother Alexander enlisted with him. His older brother, Simeon, had long before moved to Lawrence, Kansas, where he served both as State Superintendent of Schools and as a state Senator. While serving in the war, Thomas met and married Mandana Major, the daughter of one of his fellow officers, the aptly titled Captain Major. From there, however, the Civil War would not be kind to the Thorp family.

Things started well. Thomas Thorp proved his valor time after time. But then things changed. He was shot at the Battle of Fair Oaks early in 1862, but a month later he was back in the saddle, only to be shot again at the Battle of Malvern Hill. In 1863, after the Battle of Gettysburg, he was promoted to Lieutenant Colonel and given command of a regiment known as the First New York Dragoons. Within a month, however, his pride turned to anguish as the first of his brothers fell. The casualty was not Alexander, however, who himself was rapidly gaining promotions for his valor, but rather Simeon, the Kansas State Superintendent of Schools. Kansas was a state with loyalty split between the Union and the Confederacy, but the city of Lawrence was staunchly abolitionist and pro-Union, with its townspeople staging guerrilla raids against Confederate forces across the border in Missouri. A Missouri rebel leader named William Quantrill organized an informal but disciplined and savage band of guerrillas motivated by what biographers consider to be revenge, glory, and plundered fortune. Quantrill's surprise raid destroyed the town of Lawrence, leaving most of its men, including Simeon Thorp, dead in what came to be known as "the Lawrence Massacre."

Thomas Thorp had little time to grieve, however, because the First New York Dragoons were among the busiest and bravest regiments in the Union. A biography in the 1893 book *Officers of the Volunteer Army and Navy who served in the Civil War* picks up his story from there. Thorp, we're told, led the Dragoons to victories throughout the winter of 1863 and spring of 1864, until he was shot once again at the Battle of Trevilian Station. In a war in which a battlefield gunshot usually meant death, Colonel Thomas Thorp had now survived three serious gunshot wounds. This time was different, however, because he was captured by Confederate soldiers and sent to a prison camp in Macon, Georgia. Being taken prisoner was not the end of Thomas Thorp's Civil War heroism, however; in many ways it was just the beginning. On the Fourth of July, the still injured Colonel defied his Confederate captors and delivered a fiery patriotic speech to his 1,600 fellow Union prisoners. The speech inflamed passion in his fellow prisoners and fury in the camp warden, who ordered Thorp transferred to a more remote prison. On his journey to the new prison, Thorp broke free and leaped from the moving train, into a swamp. For the next 19 days he foraged for food and survived the miserable summer humidity, but then was recaptured. This time he was sent to the front lines to be used essentially as cannon fodder for his own army's artillery, but Colonel Thomas Thorp escaped once again. While on the lam for three weeks, he missed the news that his other brother, Captain Alexander Thorp, had been killed in action. Thomas Thorp was captured again, this time to be held in maximum security. With Alexander's death and Thomas' third capture, only one Thorp remained on the battlefield: Thomas' young bride, Mandana, who by now had become a hero in her own right as a war-zone nurse. This time there would be no escape for Thomas, but in early 1865, in the waning days of the war, he was released in a prisoner exchange and immediately promoted to the rank of Brigadier General.

Thomas Thorp ended up in Forest Grove for the same reason so many before him had, to pursue a career in education. In the early 1890s, after a stay as an administrator for the Buffalo, New York, schools, Thorp took over as Superintendent of Schools in Forest Grove. In Oregon, he and Mandana sent their son and daughter to Pacific University. Mandana Thorp remained active in the Women's Relief Corps for the rest of her life, leading Oregon's efforts and becoming prominent nationally for her tireless work. Thomas died in 1915, and Mandana followed a year later.

Other Civil War veterans found their way to Forest Grove with less fanfare but with amazing stories of their own. One such unsung soldier was Ambrose Porter, who joined the Union army in Wisconsin and served for three years, until he was honorably discharged on January 4, 1864. The next day he re-enlisted and served until the war ended a little more than a year later. He didn't move to Oregon with his family until 1890, and was still planting beans and potatoes in Scoggins Valley in 1917, when he was 77 years old. His neighbors knew that he was a Civil War vet, but his full story didn't emerge until after he died in June 1919, when his family found a letter written the day after Christmas 1864 from his commander to his mother back in Wisconsin. It seems that after re-enlisting, Porter found himself part of General William Tecumseh Sherman's famous "March to the Sea," from Atlanta to Savannah.

Porter's division was bringing up the rear, the commander, General H.P. Bird, wrote. Porter was a trusted orderly on General H.P. Bird's personal staff. "A more lively, genial, agreeable companion than Porter I have never met," General Bird wrote. Many of the remaining Confederate soldiers had given up the fight and some even had become friendly with the Union soldiers. Bird was so secure of his position that he sent small, poorly armed groups of soldiers off to forage for food. One such foraging party on December 9 included Porter and five other soldiers. The six encountered a band of soldiers still loyal to the Confederacy, and tried to flee. When Union reinforcements arrived, they learned that the rebels "had secured three prisoners, as negroes near tell us, one of whom was, no doubt, your boy." Rumors persisted, Bird wrote, that the prisoners were being taken by train to Florida, and he was making plans to pursue them. In the meantime, Ambrose Porter had entrusted the general with his money and gold watch, and Bird promised to protect the possessions. As it turns out, however, Porter had not been sent to Florida, but rather to the notorious Andersonville Prison in Southwest Georgia. Deplorable conditions had cost the lives of about 13,000 of the 45,000 Union prisoners who had been sent to the prison, many of whom died from diseases caused by living in human waste and drinking from streams contaminated with waste and rotting bodies. Porter spent four months there, but lived to tell about it, although it appears that he rarely did after he settled in for a quiet life as a farmer near Forest Grove.

Many of Forest Grove's rugged mountain men were from the South and had ambivalent feelings about the war. As it turns out, however, most never really had to choose sides, because they were needed at home in their newly minted state. As the war broke out, Lincoln had pulled the Army's regular soldiers from their posts in the Northwest, leaving Oregon unprotected in the settlers' ongoing battles with the native people of the region. Joined by volunteers from California, Oregonians formed militias to take over operation of the vacated forts. Some of the Oregon militiamen soon were deemed ready for battle with the regular Army and headed east to fight, but compared to most states, Oregon survived the war relatively unscathed. Still, the cemeteries around Forest Grove have plenty of headstones bearing the star of the Grand Army of the Republic; still others once bore stars that over the years have been stolen or destroyed by vandals.

Many of the militiamen who stayed also went into battle in what the Army officially refers to as the "Campaign against Indians, Oregon, Idaho, and California," or what the locals called the "Snake War." The war is a mere footnote in history textbooks because the national press had its focus squarely on the Civil War, but for Oregonians the Snake War was much more, ending up as the bloodiest of all the "Indian Wars."

As the wars against the Indians and against the Confederacy faded away, Forest Grove and the rest of America settled into an era of relative peace, except for a conflict of a different kind, the Industrial Revolution, which created a boom and bust cycle that left some Oregonians wealthy and others destitute as financiers and industrialists struggled to find ways to sustain growth and profits. The earliest pioneers in the Forest Grove area had secured large land claims with timber and other resources for a comfortable life, although often with little disposable income. Their children and grandchildren, not to mention later waves of newcomers to Oregon, were not as fortunate. Some found sustenance as tenant farmers and others found backbreaking jobs in the forests and mills. The agrarian nature of those jobs shielded the local economy from the worst of the busts, but also from many of the benefits of the boom cycles. East Coast industrialists were developing machines that turned out steel, clothing, shoes and other goods in ever greater quantities, but residents of Forest Grove and most of the rest of the rural West were too cut off from supply channels, cash, and consumer mentality to be of much help to the industrialists, who soon found that their capacity to produce supply outstripped the ability of the general public to consume their wares. Some of those industrialists desperately wanted new buyers for the things they produced. They found willing supporters among some of the industrialists who produced a product almost everyone wanted and could afford: newspapers. By the end of the Nineteenth Century, these forces helped to create an entirely new kind of war.

The wealthy newspaper owners, particularly William Randolph Hearst and Joseph Pulitzer, depended on ever-growing advertiser revenue, so building demand for the goods produced by their equally wealthy friends in other industries was in their best interest. Just as important was building readership, sometimes with salacious and not-always accurate stories. By 1898, the industrialists concocted a new way to make money; from American taxpayers. The military-industrial complex was born. All the complex needed now was a war. Pulitzer and Hearst settled on an unlikely enemy: Spain. The Spanish long had owned one of the world's most-feared naval forces, which had allowed them to colonize lands around the Globe, from the distant Philippines to lands in North America and the Caribbean. By contrast, the United States had been too consumed with westward expansion to California and Oregon to worry much about the rest of the world, and its mostly unimpressive Navy reflected that priority.

In 1898, Cuban rebels were fighting for independence from the Spaniards, and the American Navy defiantly sent a trouble-plagued battleship, the *Maine*, into Havana Harbor. A few weeks after the ship arrived, it was destroyed by a massive explosion, which killed most of the crew and left few reliable witnesses to what actually caused the blast. The few who did survive told investigators that the thick coal dust that clogged the air in the poorly designed engine room was the likely culprit; the slightest spark could have ignited the dust, turning the vessel itself into a gigantic bomb. But Pulitzer and Hearst did not wait for the investigation, which ultimately never assigned an official cause, before casting blame for the sinking of the *Maine* on the people of Spain. Public outcry and heavy lobbying from industrialists eventually led Congress and the President to do something that heretofore seemed unthinkable. America entered a foreign war.

Because Spain had interests in both the Caribbean and Pacific, the American military put out a call for volunteers on both coasts. Unlike during the Civil War, Oregon held a strategic place in this conflict, in large part because by now America had a growing Navy, and Portland and Astoria stood to become important ports. Oregonians flocked to join the military, but the war would be fought mostly far away in Cuba and was over in a matter of a few weeks, so most never made it into this conflict. Many soldiers on the East Coast did make it into battle, perhaps most notably Teddy Roosevelt, who with his Rough Riders made the Battle of San Juan Hill one of the more famous in American history, thanks mostly to the overwhelming coverage it got in the pages of newspapers owned by Hearst and Pulitzer. By 1901, Roosevelt was President, and he would become the first to view America as a global force. He quickly ordered the construction of the Panama Canal and the Navy's enormous new "Great White Fleet."

Roosevelt also inherited a problem in the Pacific. As part of the truce that ended the brief war in which he had played a starring role, Spain gave the United States its colony in the Pacific, the Philippines. Spain might well have been relieved to rid itself of the islands, because just as in Cuba it was locked in a war for independence with rebel forces. Those rebel forces, as it turns out, didn't like the Americans any more than they liked Spaniards, and the insurrection simmered on, eventually spilling over into all-out war. Like the Snake War, the Philippine-American War is a footnote to most Americans, but in Oregon it marked a turning point in the way people viewed the world.

The West Coast soldiers and sailors who missed out on the Spanish-American War were now the first to be called into battle in the Philippines, marking the first time Oregon sent significant numbers of men onto foreign soil. Back in Forest Grove, anxious friends and relatives awaited any tidbit of information they could get from the boys fighting in the Pacific. Mail was slow and unreliable and press coverage was slim compared with coverage from Cuba. When Oregon newspapers did report on the conflict, editors tended to view it through the prism of the Indian Wars they were familiar with in Oregon. "It is likely," the *Times* opined on July 10, 1902, six days after the war officially ended, "that it will be years before the wild tribes of the islands — many of them far lower in the scales than our American Indians — will be so developed that it will be possible to get along without a large army there."

Large numbers of soldiers did stay in the islands, but with major hostilities ended, mail delivery became more frequent. On September 18, 1902, the *Times* published a letter from Frank Chesmore to his mother back in Forest Grove. Chesmore started off with pleasantries, and not surprisingly for a guy from a city named after trees, he began with a description of the local forest: "mostly mahogany and oak," he said. He marveled at being able to step outside his tent and grab a ripe banana from a tree, and said that while it rained nearly every night, the days were beautiful, if a bit hot. Then, in a matter-of-fact tone, he offered a taste of war. "When we were up by the lake our Sergeant and Lieutenant were walking along the trail when out stepped a boloman with a white flag on a stick, but dropped it as soon as he got a chance to strike a blow, which he did and cut off the Sergeant's right arm at the shoulder."

In March 1903, the *Times* offered a letter home written by Henry Cheney. Henry was assigned to the 28th Infantry, whose duty, Henry wrote, was to build a road through the jungle. He too marveled at the forest he found himself in, so many miles from his home in Forest Grove. "There are some magnificent trees of mahogany and a kind of California redwood," he wrote. "What do you think of using mahogany for fuel and building the cheapest kind of homes out of it?" Much of his letter, however, described a strange race of people he had encountered on the island of Mindanao. These "Mohammedans," he said, were the reason his regiment had been assigned to build a road into the jungle. "The main object in building this road is to get artillery in as it is expected that troops will meet with some resistance, as polygamy is to be busted up, and the Moros are not afraid to fight. They think they will go to Heaven if they die fighting." He said he had never seen a Mohammedan woman close up because they covered themselves from head to toe in cloth. Yet of his fellow soldiers, he said that "there seem to be a lot of fellows who marry native women and seem to be content."

Another returning soldier echoed Chesmore and Cheney's concerns, and told a story that could have come from the Iraq conflict 100 years later. At the time perhaps Forest Grove's best traveled soldier, Walter Buchanan served both in Cuba and in the Philippines. He described to the *Times* the atrocities he had witnessed by Filipino tribesmen using the dreaded bolo knife. Those atrocities, he argued, justified the actions of his commanding officers, who were facing court martial for the way they extracted information from the tribesmen. Those officers had used waterboarding.

Chas. Adkins was another soldier whose trip home from the Philippines opened his eyes to sights he never imagined growing up in 1890s Forest Grove, including stops in exotic locales such as Bombay, India, and Aden on the Yemen Peninsula. All told, however, he wrote to his friend Edward Naylor, "I have had all the army I want. You were wise when you did not go with Teddy and his Rough Riders." Still stuck at a fort in New York, Adkins longed for civilian life back in Forest Grove. "When I get out we will have a good elk hunt on the Salmonberry."

As Adkins and his colleagues returned to Forest Grove, life in Oregon resumed its normal patterns. Young men went elk hunting along the Salmonberry River, farmers plowed their fields and loggers toiled in the forests. Resuming those routine rhythms of life was comforting, but also had put the state's economy in great peril. The great cities of California had embraced the Industrial Revolution and were booming. Even Seattle, until recently Portland's stepchild, had rocketed ahead of the Rose City by focusing on manufacturing. In contrast, Oregon clung stubbornly to its agrarian roots, benefiting from the worldwide industrial boom primarily by exporting its vast natural resources through the Port of Portland. In 1905, Oregon landed the greatest event in its 46-year history, when Portland hosted the first World's Fair on the West Coast of North America, with Pacific University's own Harvey Scott as president of the fair board. The men who planned the fair, officially named the "Lewis and Clark Centennial and American Pacific Exposition and Oriental Fair," had lofty ambitions, including showcasing Oregon's timber industry and Portland's position as the closest port to Japan and other Asian markets. One of the most elaborate pavilions represented the Philippines, including actual Filipinos shipped across the Pacific to be put on display. On the Fair's "Portland Day," Carl Abbott wrote a century later for the Oregon Historical Society, the city highlighted Oregon's fascination with the Philippines by staging an elaborate re-enactment of the Battle of Manila Bay. While Americans were developing a fascination with the rest of the world, and while most people in the major East Coast cities still focused on Europe, Oregonians kept looking west as they always had for new opportunities, watching the sun set over the Pacific and dreaming of prospects in the Philippines.

Yet although the fair's organizers promoted the abundant hydroelectricity potential from Willamette Falls, the emphasis fell mostly on the state's timber resources, and as Forest Grove's soldiers had pointed out repeatedly in their letters home, if there was one thing the Philippines did not need, it was more trees. Meanwhile, Seattle, San Francisco and Los Angeles built up their industrial infrastructures, soon leaving Portland lagging far behind. That strategy doomed most of the state to recession after recession, but served the Forest Grove area well. Farmers kept busy and the timber companies kept even busier, packing off trainload after trainload of lumber to Portland. However, even that prosperity took a hit after 1910 when tariffs were eased on Canadian lumber. Cheap logs from British Columbia helped lower lumber prices for developers on the Eastern Seaboard, but devastated Oregon's economy because of its reliance on timber and lack of other forms of industry. Then came World War I.

By 1914, shipbuilders had embraced steel hulls, but wooden hulls still were cheaper and faster to build. As war spread through Europe, that continent's shipbuilders focused on furnishing vessels for navies, rather than for commercial operators. In addition, Germany's new submarines were exacting a devastating toll on shipping fleets, including passenger ships. In May 1915, the Germans torpedoed and sank the British cruiseliner *Lusitania*, killing 128 American passengers. President Wilson threatened the Germans with war if they did not stop targeting passenger ships, and the Germans yielded to his demands. Attacks on cargo ships, however, continued unabated, and demand for inexpensive wooden ships was high. While other port cities had moved ahead of Portland in metal-hull shipbuilding, no one built cheap, quickly assembled wooden ships better than Portland's shipyards, and no one produced timber for those shipyards better than the mills at the edge of the Coast Range forests in towns such as Forest Grove and Gaston. For the first three years of the war the United States remained neutral, but Forest Grove's economy was starting to shift into higher gear, and for the first time many Forest Grove residents began commuting into Portland for work in factories.

Then in January 1917, with its economy starved by war and its military locked in a stalemate with Britain, Germany decided to take desperate measures, including resuming attacks on passenger ships and attempting to lure Mexico into the conflict with the promise of helping the country regain control of Texas, New Mexico and Arizona. The Germans knew that these moves would draw America into the war, but they were confident that the United States could not raise an Army and Navy fast enough to save its European allies, focusing instead on protecting its border with Mexico. Sure enough, Forest Grove Guardsmen were among the first put into action, sent to guard the border with Mexico in case war broke out. As it turns out, the Mexicans had no interest in going to war against the U.S. or anyone else, but by now the Americans did, and the Germans seriously misjudged just how fast the United States could mobilize for war.

Portland shipyards ramped up production of merchant marine vessels to carry troops and supplies to the war zone and the call went out for men to join the military. Because the military did not have a recruiting station in Forest Grove, the owner of the Palace Barber Shop offered up his establishment for that purpose. On March 29, the *News-Times* reported on recruiting efforts in the city. William Buck, the paper reported, "was enthusiastic to enlist, but his eyes would not pass the test." The other 10 recruits, including the paper's cartoonist, William Thacker, all passed the test and prepared to ship out for training. Before they left, the town's business owners hosted a lavish luncheon in their honor at the Hotel Laughlin, recently rebuilt after two devastating fires. The recruiting sergeant, the paper said, was sure "that the Forest Grove boys will be a fine lot of fellows and that he was sure that the parents of the boys need have no fear of their return." He was sure of American victory. "They will be back home, he declared, in six months and will be greatly benefited by the military training."

On May 3, 1917, the *Forest Grove Express* ran a story at the top of Page 1, announcing that the Army wanted more recruits, and this time the message was a bit clearer. Marshal Joseph Jacques "Papa" Joffre, commander of the French Army, wanted 10,000 American troops on the ground in France as soon as possible, and that 20,000 would be even better. By now Joffre was such a household name in America that the *Express* could refer to him simply as "Marshal Joffre" with no further identification. His exploits on the battleground had earned him the nickname "Papa," and, the American people were told, he soon would force the Germans to surrender. His direct plea for as many troops as America could send might seem to have belied that faith, but the *Express* explained further that the troops were not needed for direct combat. "What is desired is the moral (sic) effect on the French troops of the presence of Americans."

Six months later the first batch of recruits from the Hotel Laughlin luncheon had not returned home as the sergeant had promised. Many of the troops who had been sent to France had discovered that their services were needed for much more than boosting the morale of "Papa" Joffre's fighters. Back home, the military had instituted a draft, and the *News-Times* was running Page 1 lists of dozens of young men from the area conscripted into service. Other lists contained those who volunteered for service.

Patriotic fever swept the area. The Army needed snipers, and the area around Forest Grove was well-known for expert riflemen, dating back to the hunters and fur traders who first settled the region. One of the best marksmen, in fact, was the son of one of the most important Mountain Man pioneers, Almoran Hill. When World War I broke out, Frank Hill was living on his late father's farm near Gaston, across the road from the school and cemetery that bore the family's name, and Frank Hill immediately tried to enlist in the Army as a sniper. The Hills were one of the area's best known and respected families, yet the recruiters refused to allow Frank Hill to enlist. The *Hillsboro Independent* reported that Frank believed that his full beard had caused the recruiter to reject him, so he went home to Gaston and reappeared at the recruiting office clean-shaven, hoping that "the whiskerless face would help." Alas, it did not, and again Frank Hill, despite his expert marksmanship, was rejected. The *Independent* reporter offered a possible problem with the enlistment that couldn't be fixed with a razor; eager recruit Frank Hill was 71 years old.

Although the battlefields of Europe were about as far from Oregon as a war could get, fear gripped the Northwest more than in most previous wars. Residents worried that German submarines, called U Boats, could sneak into the Columbia River, so fishermen kept a watchful eye on the water. Another new technology worried Northwesterners even more. In August panicked residents in the coastal community of Seaside reported lights from what they were sure must be German zeppelins, which were capable of flights longer than any aircraft ever before. The military assured the folks in Seaside, however, that the lights were just a rare visit from the aurora borealis.

In Forest Grove, townspeople did what they could to support the war effort. When the Council of National Defense sent out a call for every woman in America to register in case they were needed to fill civilian jobs of men called off to war, more than 200 filled the Rogers City Library to comply. While they were at the library they heard about the defense council's ambitious plan to raise a million dollars to buy books to send to troops, and organized a committee to figure out how to raise Forest Grove's assigned share of the pot, $100. The county fair was held as usual, but this year featured demonstrations on how to cook without meat, wheat and butter so that more of those staples could be shipped to Europe to feed the hungry troops and American allies, starved by years of warfare. In a boost for the local economy, the Army ordered huge quantities of spruce, which grew in great abundance in the Coast Range forest and which was deemed perfect for the construction of fighter planes for America's first air war.

Meanwhile, local newspapers began to publish letters from soldiers as they trickled in from bases around the country. Richard Wilson wrote of his experience in the Navy, waiting for his ship to be deployed from its port in the Hudson River of New York. Wilson was not impressed with his surroundings. "The weather has moderated and the ice is leaving," he told his parents back in Forest Grove. "You are lucky you don't live here." Oro Davenport wrote from Camp Meade, Maryland. Life at Camp Meade, where he was stationed with the Army Engineers, was "fine and dandy," he reported. "If you see any young fellows who are not willing to join the troops on the firing line, tell him to join the Engineers and work back of the danger zone."

Forest Grove was particularly interested in the exploits of dashing Mark Hogue. One of his earliest letters was published in the *Express*, and explained to his mother and friends back home the roles of various branches of the military and what basic training was like. Hogue explained all this in terms of the islands in San Francisco Bay, where he was stationed. He wrote his letter almost 20 years before the San Francisco Bay Bridge connected some of the larger islands to the mainland. As he wrote, the islands were desolate, often cold and foggy outposts. Yerba Buena Island, he explained, was where "all boys enlisted in the Navy, coming from the Western states, receive their preliminary training." He acknowledged that he knew little what their training consisted of, but after three months they were sent out on ships of various kinds, including exotic submarines. He was stationed two miles away, on Angel Island. Angel Island was perhaps the best known of the islands at the time, because a few years earlier the federal government had established it as an immigration station, similar to Ellis Island in New York, to process the soaring numbers of Asian immigrants in the years since America opened widespread trade with the region. In 1917, the island also was home to the Army's two-month basic training, where Hogue was learning to drill and shoot. Hogue considered himself lucky that he wasn't at the nearby Marine Corps training facility, where basic training lasted seven months, and luckier still that he wasn't on "a small rocky island lying just inside the Golden Gate and a short distance from the fairgrounds." That island, called Alcatraz, had been turned into a prison to house the military recruits who deserted the other islands.

The *Forest Grove Express* folded, but Hogue's letters kept coming and were printed in the *News-Times*. Soon Hogue was writing of places and experiences even more exotic than submarines and an island called Alcatraz. Mark Hogue was in San Diego, training to be one of America's first flying aces. In 1917, America didn't have any pilots with military experience, so his rigorous training came from seasoned French aces. He described a practice bombing run from San Diego to Los Angeles; the "bombs" they dropped were packets of brochures urging people to buy Liberty Bonds. He spoke in awe of the sight of the entire Pacific fleet, all 100 twin-wing airplanes, many built with spruce from back home in Oregon. "It certainly is a great sight to see them all in the air at once, which occurs on many occasions." Mostly he looked forward to his final flying exam. Would-be pilots had only one chance at the exam; those who failed would be sent to the trenches. Mark Hogue did not seem worried about his chances of passing the exam, and looked forward to the $250 monthly salary he would earn once he did. "Of course to you," he wrote a friend, "this might seem a large sum of money, but considering a man's life is always in danger, even here in the United States, flying under the most peaceful conditions, think what it must be compared to battle flying on the front." He closed with this grim statistic from France: "Fifty percent of the aviators are killed."

Guy Aydelott wrote to his "old friends in our beloved Oregon" to tell them of his journey to war through the Panama Canal. He began the letter on January 28, 1918, aboard his ship carrying 1,900 sailors, 240 soldiers, and 400 German prisoners bound for a prison in South Carolina. It would be two weeks before he would arrive at a port from which he could mail the letter, so he added highlights along the way, including impressions of his first taste of a foreign land in Panama, which he reported has "more negroes than whites." In fact, everyone in this sunny climate is "tanned so that they are almost black."

When Forest Grove soldiers began arriving overseas, their letters contained little substantive news of the war, and when they did they were heavily edited by military censors. When James Benoit wrote to someone the *News-Times* identified only as "a young lady friend," he was allowed to tell her only that he was serving in the trenches "somewhere in France." Most of his letter was spent thanking her for writing to him. "Your big, cheery, newsy letter was just what the doctor had ordered for me," he told her. Better yet, it arrived on Thanksgiving Day, just as he was sitting down to a mess hall feast of "turkey, dressing, cakes, salads, mince pies, pudding, dates, raisins, figs, bread, butter and punch." The highlight of the afternoon, he told his young lady friend, was that his team from the Army beat a team from the Marines 12-0, although he neglected to mention what sport was being played. He said most of the time there was not much to amuse the troops except for watching the effects of the local *vin rouge* being consumed "by fellows who are not yet acclimated. Of course I have been here long enough for that, but you know me." Then Benoit slipped up and bragged that the company commander had told them that his regiment "had drawn the most important assignment in France (and) we were to …" The censor cut him off at that point, but allowed a few closing thoughts from "Jimmie" to his young female friend in Forest Grove, hoping that "you girls will appreciate us when we come back from war."

For the first year of America's entry into the war, news trickled back to the homefront, but the residents of Forest Grove were able to breathe a sigh of relief that the local boys were surviving the battles. It appeared that luck would continue as one of the war's worst tragedies unfolded. On the evening of February 5, 1918, the 3-year-old luxury liner *Tuscania* was in the English Channel, approaching its destination of Liverpool with more than 2,000 American soldiers on board. Within sight of both the Scottish and Irish coasts, the soldiers aboard the *Tuscania* felt that they had survived the treacherous journey across the Atlantic, just as every other troop carrier had so far in the war effort. Then, at 6:40 p.m., a torpedo from a U Boat hit the ship, and it began to sink. Other ships from the convoy rushed to help in the darkness, and managed to rescue all but 210 of the ship's passengers. On February 7, news of the sinking hit American newspapers, including the *News-Times*, which assured readers that it was unlikely that any local soldiers were aboard the ship, because it was carrying regiments from the Michigan and Wisconsin National Guard. It was true, the editor assured anxious readers, that the military often assigned stray soldiers from other units to such journeys, but the odds were long that anyone from Oregon would be on the passenger list, let alone among the dead. One week later, the *News-Times* carried the sad follow-up; it turns out that there had been a small contingent of Oregon boys aboard the *Tuscania,* and amazingly 13 of the 210 fatalities were Oregonians. Theodore Lewton, a young Army bugler, was among those on board. Theodore's mother and sister were told of his death at their farm just outside of Forest Grove, while his younger brother, James, got word while stationed with the Army in the trenches of France. A couple of weeks after his brother's death, the *News-Times* ran a poignant letter from James, writing to his mother from a hospital "somewhere in France," recuperating from an undisclosed malady. "I don't suppose you can read this but my hand is still shaky, and this is my first try at writing. Don't worry about me, I feel pretty good and will be ready for duty before long."

Just a month later the *News-Times* ran two letters that summed up another plague haunting the American soldiers: contagious disease. One was from Guy Aydelott, who had completed his journey through the Panama Canal and landed in France, only to be stricken with mumps, requiring quarantine in the hospital. Mumps, measles and other such diseases were not unknown in Forest Grove, but World War I was spurring outbreaks in large numbers among people who had avoided the diseases back home. Between the lines, the letters from Aydelott and the other soldiers were explaining why illnesses that once caused local epidemics were now causing global pandemics. The basic principle was the same one that the white settlers of Forest Grove had helped inflict unknowingly on the Atfalati people back in the 1830s and 1840s. The tribe had no history of small pox, measles and many other diseases common to Easterners, and as such had no immunity. By many estimates, far more native people died of infectious disease than from bullets in the Indian Wars. World War I marked the first time in world history that so many thousands of people moved such long distances in such a short time, mixing with people of many cultures, both of the social and virus varieties. Illnesses spread like wildfire. Many were as lucky as Guy Aydelott, and recovered fairly quickly. Many others were not. The deadliest of all the pandemics was one of the most common illnesses of all: influenza. The strain of flu afflicting the World War I troops was virulent, and the mass movement back and forth across the Atlantic caused the disease to spread across the civilian population of the United States, killing many thousands of Americans who never ventured within 3,000 miles of a war zone. Newspapers of the day carried stories of doctors tracing the spread of the flu from the cities of the East Coast, hoping that the pandemic would dissipate as it reached the more sparsely populated Midwest and then be blocked completely by the Rocky Mountains. The story next to the one about Aydelott pinpointed the futility of that hope. This story was about Forest Grove native Frank Lloyd Smith, who had joined the Army and within a few months rocketed to the rank of sergeant. Now stationed at Fort Lewis near Tacoma, Smith eagerly awaited his turn to go to the frontlines to replace those who had completed their tours of duty. As those troops returned from France, some carried the flu virus, which then spread quickly through the tightly cramped barracks at Fort Lewis. Frank Lloyd Smith never made it to the frontlines, succumbing to his illness within a few days. His death was classified as the second line of duty death of someone from Forest Grove. His promotion papers had not yet arrived when he died, so they were forwarded to his parents instead. By now, one Forest Grove church had 42 silver stars on its wall, each bearing the name of a church member serving in the military, including Guy Aydelott. The church changed one of them to a gold star, this one bearing the name of Frank Lloyd Smith.

Usually word of a loved one's death was delivered quickly, but other times the folks back in Forest Grove spent months worrying about the boys overseas that they had not heard from. Usually the silence ended with good news; sometimes letters had been lost in the mail, or the soldier was deployed on a mission so dangerous or secret that no mail was allowed. But in December 1918, when Glendora Carpenter had not heard since October from her Marine son, Oates, she wrote to the American Red Cross. Other boys were coming home after the official end of hostilities, but she had heard nothing from Oates. She received a telegram from the Red Cross just after Christmas saying that his name did not appear on any casualty list. He was, apparently, in transport home. But two months later she received a letter from his commanding officer, informing her that Oates had been killed in a trench somewhere in France on November 5, while trying to carry a wounded comrade to safety.

By contrast, the parents of Pacific University chemistry graduate Egbert Bishop learned of his death within days. Egbert grew up in Forest Grove and went on to earn his doctorate in chemistry from Clark University in Massachusetts. He enlisted in the Army immediately after the war broke out, and was assigned to the Army's Picatinny Arsenal laboratory in New Jersey. The Americans did not trust completely the armistice that the British and French signed with Germany, and work continued apace to build bigger and better bombs, just in case. In a letter to Bishop's father in Forest Grove, the arsenal's commander, Lieutenant Colonel Roland Pinger, explained the events of May 29, 1919. Pinger said that he had walked with his four-year-old son through the building in which Bishop was working, unaware of any special danger. A few minutes later, however, he heard a muffled explosion and one of his aides told him that there had been an explosion in the laboratory. Racing to the scene, Pinger found the lifeless body of one of his top chemists, Egbert Bishop. Although Pinger was unaware of the dangerous experiment Bishop was working on, Bishop himself knew just how volatile the mixture of hydrogen and oxygen really was. He had told his assistants and co-workers to evacuate the area while he checked the pressurized shell in the lab. The shell casing was the strongest variety in use, made of hardened vanadium steel. The casing had been tested to withstand 80,000 pounds per square inch of pressure, and the last time Egbert had checked, pressure was at 4,000 pounds and falling. Because he entered the concrete bunker alone, no one saw exactly what happened, but the force of the explosion demolished the shell casing and the machine used to fill it. The blast was so powerful it blew a hole through the concrete wall of the bunker. The remains of Dr. Egbert Bishop, one of Pacific University's brightest graduates, were put on a westbound train to his native Oregon for cremation.

Back home in Forest Grove tensions were rising among some of the many Germans who had come to the area to grow flowers in Blooming or to work in the forests, not all of whom had left their allegiance to the Kaiser back in their homeland. A conductor on the Southern Pacific line from Hillsboro to Gaston was arrested by federal agents after he was alleged to have been collecting money from like-minded people and shipping it to Germany to support the war effort. Many other suspicious activities were linked to the local German population, albeit usually with little or no evidence to support the conclusion. One of the most serious accusations came in February 1918, days after the *Tuscania* sank and the newspapers ran headlines with such phrases as "Hun Atrocities." Some boys playing near the Southern Pacific tracks south of town discovered a large box of dynamite on the tracks. After discovering that the dynamite was war-grade and not of the type used in local construction, police immediately announced that although they lacked evidence, they suspected German involvement in the case.

The war had been tough on German-Americans. In 1918, President Woodrow Wilson ordered anyone who still retained German citizenship to register with the Department of Justice, which labeled them "alien enemies." According to research by Kimberly Jensen in the Winter 2013 edition of the *Oregon Historical Quarterly*, there were a lot more suspected "enemy aliens" in Oregon than one might expect: 3,729 to be exact, according to archives at the Oregon Historical Society. That's a lot of suspicion cast on a lot of Oregonians. In April 1918, United States Attorney for the Oregon District Bert Haney went a step further and ordered all "unnaturalized German women" to stay away from railroad depots and the docks of Portland and Astoria, or risk being arrested and held until the war ended. Although many German immigrants publicly pledged their support for their new country, and few if any crimes were ever pinned on the alleged "anarchists," the rumors continued even after the war ended.

On July 18, 1919, the "Chautauqua" came to Forest Grove. Chautauguas were festivals that moved from town to town, and included musicians and other performers, but also educational lectures. In 1919 Forest Grove, the Chautauqua was a major event, attended by most of the town. This year the keynote speaker was William Jennings Bryan, three-time Democratic and Progressive Party candidate for President. Bryan was a dynamic public speaker who had been the biggest draw for years at Chautauquas around the country. He also was a leader in the national Prohibition movement, and as such was a hero to many people in dry Forest Grove. Attendance for Bryan was so great that organizers nearly doubled the anticipated revenue for the event. Bryan was such a draw on Friday night that other speakers on the weekend long schedule garnered little or no publicity. One of those speakers was Arthur Gibbons, a young Canadian soldier who had spent seven months as a prisoner of war in Germany. Exactly what Gibbons told the crowd on Saturday night was not mentioned in the news accounts of Bryan's speech, but we know he railed against the evils of the Kaiser and Germany in general.

The next day about noon, just as church crowds had returned home, a fire started that quickly consumed most of the downtown core. Firefighters immediately suspected arson, but had few clues. Monday morning, as Forest Grove was reeling from the worst fire in the city's history, George Paterson, a downtown business owner and former mayor, collected his mail. Among the letters was one dropped at the Post Office sometime over the weekend. "Mayor Paterson," the letter began, "if you want to let a liar come to town just to disgrace the German people as that black devil did Saturday night, your business and all the rest will go up in smoke." The anonymous writer made many threats, but did not specifically take credit for igniting the fire that destroyed so much of the town the day before. The letter was signed "The Other One and I," so perhaps it was the other one who did it. Either way, the arson never was solved.

By late 1918, most of the brave men who went off to war from Forest Grove began returning from their posts around the world. Not all stayed in Forest Grove, however, including Mark Hogue, the pioneering pilot whose correspondence from San Diego enthralled his friends back home. It seemed likely that Hogue was destined to live elsewhere from the day he graduated from Forest Grove High School and prepared for his studies in mining engineering at Stanford University. A brilliant student, Mark Hogue also was athletic and sported a broad toothy grin.

When the war broke out he interrupted his studies after a year at Stanford to enlist in the Army, and was sent to flight school. As he confidently predicted after studying with his French instructors, he aced his final exam, but did not become a flying ace in Europe. Instead, the Army deemed him too important for that role, and made him an instructor in the States. Mark Hogue was a flying superstar.

After the war, Hogue returned briefly to Forest Grove, but then set off to become one of the country's first famous "barnstormers," performing aerobatic acts at air shows and fairs across the country. When the United States Postal Service implemented air mail, he again became a pioneer, joining the likes of aviation legends Charles Lindbergh, James Dewitt Hill and Lloyd Wilson Bertaud among the first pilots. Hogue's route was one of the most important and took him back and forth between Washington, D.C., and Philadelphia. His friends back in Forest Grove eagerly awaited tales of his adventures, of which there were many. In one episode, Hogue took off from Philadelphia with World War I Army ace Richard Wright as his co-pilot. After 15 miles and at about 1,700 feet altitude, Hogue's plane caught fire. According to a dispatch in the April 10, 1920, *Oregonian*, Hogue stayed at the controls as Wright climbed out onto one of the bi-plane's wings to prepare to jump. Hogue got the plane to within 200 feet of the ground, at which time it nosedived into the ground. Although Hogue was injured, Wright took the brunt of the collision, breaking both legs and an arm, among many other injuries. Hogue managed to carry Wright to a nearby hospital. Later that same month, Hogue took off again from Philadelphia and encountered an unexpected thunderstorm. He steered his plane out of danger, but with his first fuel tank depleted by the maneuvers, Hogue switched over to his auxiliary tank, only to find that his ground crew had forgotten to fill it. For the second time in a month Mark Hogue crashed, and once again he walked away with minor injuries.

Soon Mark Hogue was lured into private enterprise, moving to Boston and creating an air charter service with his brother from Forest Grove, Harry. Before long, they expanded to New York, and the wealthiest people of the day availed themselves of his passenger service. In December 1924, Mark married the beautiful debutante Marguerite Bisco of New York City. On July 23, 1925, a proud Anna Hogue was at her Forest Grove home, planning a trip to Boston to visit her son Mark and Marguerite. By now she might well have forgotten the words her son had written to her eight years earlier: "A man's life," he wrote, "is always in danger, even here in the United States, flying under the most peaceful conditions." The conditions on July 23 were about as peaceful as a pilot could hope for as Mark took off from his private airfield near Boston carrying one of that city's richest real estate moguls, George Burroughs. Harry saw his brother lift off into the clear skies. Other witnesses saw Mark's plane "freeze" in midair a few moments later and crash headfirst into a railroad trestle. Both Burroughs and Forest Grove's most-famous man of the era, Mark Hogue, died instantly.

At the time Hogue died, one of Hogue's aviation pioneer friends had just bought a farm south of Forest Grove, on which he planned to settle. Before he settled down, however, James Dewitt Hill planned to become the first man to fly solo across the Atlantic. Lindbergh won that race, landing in Paris in May 1927. But Hill, who at 42 was among the oldest pilots of his day, still wanted one more shot at glory before retiring to his property in Patton Valley. Lindbergh had set the record, but Hill believed that he could break it by adding several hundred miles to his flight, landing in Rome instead of in Paris. Hill found a backer in one of America's richest men, newspaper publisher William Randolph Hearst. Hearst owned both the *New York Daily Mirror* and an airplane that he believed could beat Lindbergh's record. He asked Hill and the editor of the *Daily Mirror*, Philip Payne, to make the journey, with Lloyd Bertaud as a back-up pilot. On September 6, 1927, James Dewitt Hill took off from Old Orchard Beach, Maine, in William Randolph Hearst's *Old Glory* with Payne as a passenger to record every inch of the historic flight. Payne's breathless account of the departure scene included tales of women cooing over the only single man involved, James Dewitt Hill, even adding the detail of Payne's own wife telling Hill that although he had no woman to see him off, "you are a fine fellow and we all love you." Within hours the plane sent a distress call that was picked up by the *Transylvania*, the identical twin sister ship to the *Tuscania*, upon which Theodore Lewton had become Forest Grove's first World War I fatality. The *Transylvania* never found the *Old Glory* nor the bodies of Hill, Bertaud and Payne. James Dewitt Hill was mourned in the national press as one of America's most courageous pilots and most eligible bachelors. Back in Forest Grove, a mysterious woman sold the Patton Valley farm that Hill had planned to retire to. America had not known that he had a woman in his life, nor did most people in Forest Grove know that one of America's best-known aviators had planned to become their neighbor.

World War I opened the eyes of Forest Grove residents and all Americans to world events that most never had considered. In nearby Cherry Grove, Levi Lovegren, scion of the wealthy family that founded the small community and now a Baptist missionary, left for China to spread the word of God. Forest Grove resident and pharmacist Ross Reder, meanwhile, departed for Siberia with the Red Cross to take part in another major war, the Russian Revolution. The Americans had thrown their support behind the Tsar and royal family, known to Americans as White Russians, in their battle against communist rebels known as Red Russians. Ross Reder cared little about the politics, but cared desperately about the plight of the Siberian people. By May 1919, hostilities in Europe were fading and Forest Grove residents turned their rapt attention to dispatches from Reder as he arrived in exotic Russia, sending letters back home written on a portable Corona typewriter his sister bought for him in Forest Grove.

The port city of Vladivostok, he told readers, reminded him of his home in Forest Grove, with mountains, green valleys and even pheasants like those he knew in Oregon, only in much larger numbers. The city was well protected by America's allies, the Japanese. He was put on a train protected by French, British and American troops, which, he assured readers, meant that he was well guarded, even if he did have to extinguish all lights after dark to hide the train from the Reds. Soon he told of arriving in the frigid inland areas of Siberia, where temperatures often hit 40 below zero. He told of piling on layers of blankets to stay warm, but he had few fears as his wood-burning, steam-powered train chugged for weeks along its 4,000 mile route to Omsk, which had become the capital of White Russia. Having run Forest Grove's primary pharmacy, Reder was put in charge of distributing medicine to the city's hospitals. "All the common work," he wrote, "is done with Austrian prisoners. All that the American personnel do is oversee and manage the work." Things, he wrote in early August 1919, were running smoothly. Then Ross Reder, mild-mannered pharmacist from Forest Grove, seemingly dropped off the face of the earth. His wife moved from Forest Grove to live with her family in Vancouver, Washington, and found work as a bank teller.

By now, Americans knew part of what was happening in Omsk. The Red Army was winning the war and the Japanese were sending tens of thousands of troops into Vladivostok and other coastal cities. The Americans, worried that the Japanese had ulterior motives, concentrated their efforts on monitoring the Japanese in these coastal regions. Americans knew little of their fellow countrymen, such as Ross Reder, stranded in the middle of Russia as the Red Army advanced on them.

In April 1920, Forest Grove's own Ross Reder was among the first to shed light on what happened to these hapless Americans. In the eight months since anyone back home had heard from the stranded Americans, Ross had written and attempted to mail many letters to his wife and mother. Those letters had become lost in the Allies' retreat from Russia, and arrived in a batch as Spring spread across Oregon. The letters told the travails that Reder had suffered in the previous Fall and Winter in Siberia. The letters revealed that the Americans had fled Omsk at about the same time as Reder's last missive hit Forest Grove. As the American military shifted its attention to the coast, Reder was left under the care of the Polish army, and boarded a train back to Vladivostok. The Red Army pursued the train Reder was on, and he described the scenes he saw along the way, such as the city of Achinsk, where bombs had killed 1,500 men, women and children, whose bodies had been laid out in a line along the railroad tracks to freeze in temperatures colder than Oregonians ever had experienced. He knew as he wrote that his letters might never make it to Forest Grove. In one, he wrote "God only knows if this letter or I will ever reach you." Then he wrote, "well, dear mother, I hope you never got the word that the Reds had captured us ... tell sis that I hated to lose my Corona typewriter and that swell case." Ross Reder had spent months as a prisoner of the Red Army and finally escaped with no thanks due, he said, to the Polish army. He and a couple of his friends had been "hoboing" it for several weeks, jumping 14 trains, warming themselves by dancing around and rubbing their hands in front of bonfires set inside rail cars as the temperatures reached 30 below zero. Finally they found safety in the coastal forces of the American Army and safe passage home.

After the First World War, Forest Grove rode a rollercoaster through the booming Roaring Twenties, the gloomy Great Depression and two horrific fires in the Tillamook Forest. World events again faded into the background as troubles at home took precedence. Unfortunately, trouble also was brewing nearly everywhere else in the world as well, from South America to China. Things got so bad in China, for example, that lumber-baron-turned-dam-engineer-turned-missionary Levi Lovegren returned to Oregon as Russia's Communist Revolution toppled the Tsar and revolution spread into neighboring China. Adolf Hitler was raising concerns in Germany, but Americans had mixed feelings about whether he was a good or bad guy, although in 1936 he briefly created a consensus around Forest Grove that he was bad, at least for one of the area's biggest industries: Prunes. According to a story in the April 16 *News-Times*, Germans consumed nearly half of Forest Grove's prune harvest, so farmers were devastated financially when Hitler announced his distaste for prunes and cut off imports. Soon after, harsh judgments subsided as Hitler yielded to his citizens' passion for prunes and allowed limited exports to once again flow into Germany. Meanwhile, Oregon Governor Charles Martin and others wrote of their admiration for Hitler and the way he crushed labor unions and moved against Germany's minority populations. Animosity toward the Germans had waned since the last war, as many in rural Oregon turned their attention toward what they saw as a new threat, the Japanese.

Just as it had before World War I, America remained officially neutral when in 1939 Hitler provoked war in Europe, but Forest Grove began feeling the effects almost immediately. The military draft was reinstituted, and a call went out for young men to join the National Guard, just in case war came to America. Forest Grove's quota for the first round of enlistments in October 1939 was 20 men, but 23 men answered the call of duty. In 1940, Pacific University started a course in civil aviation to train pilots; as students signed up they learned that they must pledge to join the military upon successful completion of the class. Federal work programs and vocational training shifted from the New Deal agencies to the Defense Department, and pressure mounted to end the many strikes and slowdowns at local lumber mills, most notably the giant Stimson operation south of town.

The reason for these moves became clear in early 1941, when Franklin Roosevelt poked a giant hole in the illusion of neutrality by implementing the Lend-Lease program that sent vast amounts of supplies and armaments to our allies in Europe and Russia with which to battle Hitler. Forest Grove's lumber mills soon buzzed with activity, turning out wood for such things as railroad ties with which to rebuild Europe's damaged railways. Henry Kaiser, the West Coast's major shipbuilding magnate, ran out of capacity at his California shipyards and shifted operations to Portland. The shipyards needed timber in enormous quantities, for everything from scaffolding to the ships themselves. The Depression by now was over in Forest Grove; instead of unemployment lines or picket lines, just about anyone willing to work was standing in line for a paycheck.

Despite the United State's official neutrality, however, people in Forest Grove and everywhere else realized that war was a distinct possibility. Soon Forest Grove's National Guard unit was 106 members strong, and was sent to California for military exercises. As the months passed in 1941, more preparations were made, including a visit by Defense Department officials to the local Veterans of Foreign Wars chapter. The veterans were told that the government would not allow a repeat of the tragedy that unfolded after World War I as soldiers and sailors were cast out of the military with little or no help returning to civilian life. If war did indeed break out again, the officials pledged, Forest Grove would be given resources to provide vocational training to returning vets and help for those left disabled, medically or emotionally.

In October 1941, the town buzzed in anticipation of the opening celebration for the Wilson River Highway, but the celebration had to be delayed because although rainfall in the Fall of 1941 was below normal, the dirt portion of the highway had turned to foot-deep mud. Rescheduling the opening, however, soon took a backseat to more urgent matters in preparation for possible war. On Halloween night, the Army was planning a mock air raid on Washington County to test preparedness, just in case the Japanese tried a sneak air raid over the area. More than 100 fighters, bombers, and military surveillance planes would fly over the county, prepared to drop flare "bombs" over any city in which even a single light stayed on. Batteries of anti-aircraft artillery would blast blanks into the night sky to add to the realism.

On Halloween, dozens of volunteers, including the town's Boy Scout troops, mobilized to stop traffic and go door to door if anyone failed to turn off the lights. Similar parties were organized in other villages in the area, including Cherry Grove, much of which even a year earlier would not have had lights to turn off, but by now the Rural Electrification

Administration had brought power back to town. Across the county, residents braced for the air raid sirens to blare in Forest Grove, Hillsboro, Gaston and several other towns. The sirens let out their screech just after 10 p.m. Lights went off across the county, as Boy Scouts roamed the streets looking for violators. Forest Grove, officials were proud to report, had not a single light on for the 30 minutes or so until the sirens sounded the all-clear. No flares were dropped on the city by bombers that night. The rest of the county's cities reported similar success, and only three problems were reported during the massive operation.

First, people living on some of the more remote farms in the area could not hear the sirens, so they didn't know when to turn off their lights. Second, only one scofflaw was found in the county's towns and villages; a family in Cherry Grove had ignored the siren. Family members said that after trick or treaters had finished their rounds, they fell asleep in easy chairs and the sirens had failed to arouse them. No "bomb" flare was dropped over Cherry Grove, however, because of the third problem that Halloween night: Fog. The fog was so dense on Halloween night, 1941, that pilots could not see to fly, and the entire fleet of nearly 150 aircraft sat grounded during the air raid drill.

No air raid sirens sounded over Forest Grove less than six weeks later on the night of December 7, 1941, but the next morning the town awoke to the same dreadful news that rocked the rest of the country. The Japanese had bombed Pearl Harbor, leaving a horrific death toll among the American military personnel stationed there. The aftermath was chaotic and communication systems failed. Anxious families back on the mainland awaited word on the fate of their loved ones. One such household was the Burki family farm on Spring Hill Road near Gaston. Their son, Frank, was born on the farm and had grown up to play football at Forest Grove High School and then for Pacific University. In November 1941, in the middle of the football season and his freshman year of college, Frank Burki quit school to join the Navy. In less than a month he was stationed at Pearl Harbor. Days before Christmas, the Burki family got the awful news from the Navy. Their son Frank was among those killed on December 7. It had not taken long for this war to hit home in Forest Grove. Christmas was a somber one across town, particularly at the Burki home.

The day after Christmas, the Burkis received a letter written by Frank. Mrs. Burki looked at the letter with dread. She opened it and started reading. The letter had been so heavily edited by military censors that deciphering it was difficult, until she got to a line that had not been blacked out. Frank reported that he had come through the December 7 attack "without a scratch." He went on to apologize for not sending Christmas gifts home, but the attack had delayed his first paycheck from the Navy. "Oh, but I have my Christmas present," Mrs. Burki told the *News-Times*. "My son is alive!" As the fog of war cleared, it turned out that Frank Burki was not a casualty of war. His friends in town and at college were joyous. Frank Burki survived World War II and returned to Oregon, where he enjoyed a comfortable life as a carpenter before dying at the age of 83 in 2007.

The Burki family was not the only one across the country that received erroneous news of a loved one's death in the chaos of Pearl Harbor. With many bodies washed away or trapped in sunken ships, mistakes were made. The Burkis were lucky, but as time passed and the casualties were confirmed, other families were not as lucky and instead were told that their loved one had perished. On January 29, the *News-Times* ran the story of one such shock. David Edmonston had joined the Navy in 1940 after graduating from high school. He was assigned to be a baker aboard the World War I vintage battleship *Oklahoma*. He came home on leave to Cornelius in the Fall of 1941 and hung out with friends, before returning to Honolulu. He was one of 429 sailors who went down when the *Oklahoma* sank on December 7.

After Pearl Harbor many of Washington County's Japanese residents enlisted to fight for the United States, but soon efforts were started to send the remaining population to internment camps. Forest Grove was selected as one of the major processing centers for internees. As reported in the May 21, 1942, edition of the *Washington County News-Times*, "Pathetic cases were not missing in the wholesale shuffling of families. One boy, deferred from service until he had completed high school work, asked only to join his two brothers in the country's service, but had to be refused as the date for enlistment of Japanese had passed." Thus the young man was spared dying in the war but instead was sentenced to years of frigid winters and stifling summers behind the fences of an Eastern Oregon "camp." Meanwhile, as their families languished in internment camps in Oregon and California, soldiers from an all-Japanese-American regiment went on to free the survivors from the German concentration camp at Dachau.

Almost weekly, the *News-Times* published letters from local people in the military. Just as in World War I, most of the letters were chatty and hopeful. William Purdin, grandson of pioneer Ira Purdin, wrote in July 1942 from Sheppard Field in Wichita Falls, Texas, where he was enjoying aircraft mechanic school in the stifling heat, and added "we wouldn't mind it, however, if you could arrange to send a little Oregon weather to us."

As America went to war, folks back in Forest Grove tried to get back to some sort of routine, although "routine" took on new meaning for many. Reverend Edwin Kellogg of the Congregational Church organized the Forest Grove chapter of the Aircraft Warning System, along with businessman Art Brodersen. Volunteers staffed a makeshift shelter atop the First National Bank Building 24 hours a day, through heavy rain, bitter cold and extreme heat throughout the war. The Reverend Kellogg, with his relatively flexible work schedule, took many of the shifts himself, day and night, with an eye to the western sky on the lookout for Japanese planes. With nearly every able-bodied young man now off to war, the farms, shipyards and lumber mills faced severe labor shortages, and filling those shortages would bring changes that would forever alter the face of Oregon's workforce. One of the biggest shifts seemed distant from Forest Grove, but had far-reaching implications for the local economy. To supplement Oregon's limited supply of experienced factory workers, Kaiser brought hundreds of workers and their families west from the Midwest and the Deep South to work in his shipyards in Portland and nearby Vancouver, Washington. All of those workers needed homes, and all of those homes were built of wood, much of it from Forest Grove and Gaston. Even more significantly, many of the workers Kaiser imported were black, and nearly all-white Portland and Vancouver were not particularly welcoming. By 1943, an entirely new city was built in the floodplain of the Willamette and Columbia rivers, away from white neighborhoods. The city, named Vanport in honor of the cities that didn't want the workers, needed an entirely new infrastructure to keep it segregated, so wooden schools and other public buildings rose, built with fir from the Tillamook Forest. Within months, Vanport's population exploded to 40,000, making it the second-largest city in Oregon. An effort of that magnitude uses a lot of lumber.

Closer to Forest Grove, labor shortages were taking a toll in the farms and fields around the county. By May 1942, with the Japanese-American farmers in internment camps and many young men off to war, the strawberry crop was in deep peril. Farmers feared the loss of an entire year's harvest of one of the region's most important crops. *News-Times* editor Hugh McGilvra hatched a plan, and before long nearly every school in Washington County had agreed to cancel classes and send their students out into the fields to pick the berries. To make the farm labor situation even worse, the Japanese owned much of the berry crop in Forest Grove and Banks, and most of the huge onion crop in Gaston. Gaston was especially hard-hit, because nearly a quarter of its population was Japanese, now suddenly lost to internment or military service. With so many farms left unattended, an urgent plea went out for Mexican migrant laborers, who were rare at the time in the Northwest. The next year, to encourage more reluctant Mexicans to come to Oregon, Governor Earl Snell signed a letter, translated into Spanish, to be run in Mexican newspapers. "We hope that your associations here have been congenial and that you have found it to be as profitable to you as it has been for us," he wrote in part. "We would consider it a privilege to welcome you back to this state." Farmers sent out urgent pleas for more Mexican families to make the trip north, and eventually they came to work the fields.

The effect that wars had on Forest Grove had changed immensely since the city's earliest days. Whereas the Civil War had relatively little impact on day-to-day life in the prettiest town in Oregon, World War II consumed it. No longer an isolated outpost, Forest Grove now felt the weight of the world upon it. Those changes came slowly, over many decades, over several generations of soldiers. Hardly a person alive in the Civil War could have ever imagined the changes those intervening decades would bring, although there were exceptions. On September 5, 1942, the people of Forest Grove received jarring news about perhaps their favorite soldier, Dan Daffron. By 1942, Daffron was in many ways the face of local military members, although he no longer was on active duty. In fact, in 1942 it had been 77 years since "Uncle Danny" Daffron had seen combat. In May, local groups gathered for

Daffron's birthday when he turned 96 and presented him with a large, hand crocheted American flag. Marking the birthday of Washington County's last surviving member of the Grand Army of the Republic had become a community celebration in Forest Grove, with family, friends and the American Legion turning out to celebrate. Because of the war, the 1942 celebration was a bit more subdued than previous birthdays, especially the barn-burner for his birthday on Monday, May 2, 1938, which doubled as a bon voyage party for his trip to a huge reunion of Union and Confederate veterans at Gettysburg, Pennsylvania, a few days later. The celebration actually began the previous Saturday as friends and family arrived from out of town, but the major festivities were reserved until Monday. The *News-Times* described the day's activities. "Feet Most Nimble at Clogging and Voice Above the Rest During the Singing," the sub-headline on Page 1 said. The singing and dancing commenced in the morning, along with the first of eight giant birthday cakes that would be consumed that day. Festivities paused in the afternoon as some of the state's last few members of the Grand Army of the Republic arrived for a ceremony. The party really started up again that evening as members of the American Legion got off work and showed up by the carload. The revelry didn't end, the story said, until several hours after midnight, with 92-year-old Danny Daffron still going strong after a nearly 24-hour party in his honor.

When he returned from Gettysburg later in the summer of 1938, Daffron had been dubbed "The G.A.R. Kid" by the national media for his antics at the reunion. He had been called a kid his entire life because of his five-foot-five frame, on which he carried barely 100 pounds. The name rankled him for most of those years, especially when he signed up to fight in the Civil War, only to be relegated to bugle boy because of his size. He spent most of the war at Fort Leavenworth, Kansas, far away from actual combat, until his unit was called upon to drive Native Americans from the Plains. He spent a year on horseback, engaging in fighting all the way to Montana, proving that he was more than a kid. By September 5, 1942, Danny Daffron wore the moniker "The G.A.R. Kid" with pride.

On that Saturday morning, the G.A.R. Kid was a passenger in a car driven by his daughter, cruising down Baseline Street in nearby Hillsboro, light years away from his days on horseback pursuing Indians across the Plains. Suddenly, at the intersection with First Street, the car they were in collided with a truck. Their car was demolished. The truck driver was injured enough to be taken to the hospital for observation. Daffron's daughter, however, was rushed to a Portland hospital for possible amputation of her mangled limbs. That left Danny Daffron, who had chased Indians on horseback and danced for hours at the age of 92. Witnesses rushed to help him, but it was too late. He already had jumped out of the car and exclaimed "You young fellers play too rough for me!" After his daughter and the other driver had been rushed to emergency rooms, Daffron was persuaded to make the six-block trek to Jones Hospital, just to be sure he was as healthy as he said he was. Doctors found two broken ribs and worried that he might have suffered internal injuries, so he was admitted. On Tuesday morning he took a sudden and dramatic downturn, and doctors told his family that he had only about an hour to live. As they gathered at his bedside to say their goodbyes, Daffron suddenly regained consciousness and pronounced that he was "chipper as ever." Sadly, that was not the case, with "'Taps' sounding at 4:15 p.m.," the *News-Times* reported. Like Tabitha Brown, Dan Daffron had come to Forest Grove from Missouri, and like "Grandma Tabitha," "Uncle Danny" came late in life, at the age of 65. The mark he left was not as significant as Tabitha Brown's, but nonetheless he danced and sang his way into the hearts of Forest Grovers, and reading about his death didn't do anything to help the somber mood that hung over the city as World War II dragged on.

Just as it had in World War I, the military conducted a census of women willing to do jobs traditionally done by men, including tasks such as welding in Portland's shipyards, or running saws in Forest Grove's lumber mills. The government set up a welding school in Forest Grove, and the first class filled quickly. Margaret Steinbach of Cornelius proved to be an ace student and was the first to be hired at the Swan Island shipyards in Portland. She reported that she loved her job. The city was jolted a few months later, however, when another shipyard worker from Cornelius, Jane Schneider, mother of two small children, was crushed between a crane and the ship she was working on. The first *News-Times* story reported that while she was in "very critical" condition at Portland's Emanuel Hospital, she was showing some signs of improvement. Two weeks later, she had improved enough to return home by ambulance, and eventually she was able to walk again. Her story drove home the fact that women who took physically demanding wartime jobs in the shipyards, which were working at breakneck speed to supply the Navy, were very much in harm's way. Jane Schneider's story also drove home another point: Forest Grove-area women were tough as nails. About two months after being critically injured, she returned to work at the shipyard.

The timber unions dropped all labor activity and the women and older workers ran shifts 24 hours a day, turning out lumber for the shipyards in Portland. With steel in short supply because of its need in tanks and armored vehicles, huge quantities of wood were needed to build scaffolding and for use on the ships themselves. Even airplanes still used wood in the early stages of the war, and when the military sent out an urgent request for designs for a fleet of enormous cargo planes, far larger than any ever before imagined, the request was for the planes to be made entirely without metal. Henry Kaiser, the industrialist who owned most of Portland's shipyards, was one of the few who believed that such a scheme was possible, and he knew just the non-metallic substance that would work, namely wood. Henry Kaiser also knew where to find strong, flexible, lightweight wood, because he already was buying huge quantities of it from the mills around Forest Grove. Kaiser enlisted the help of aviation pioneer Howard Hughes, and the "Spruce Goose" was born, although most of the wood was fir rather than spruce and Hughes hated the name. The woods and mills around Forest Grove had become vital to national security. By 1943, supplies of lumber were running so short that the military started a campaign of brochures and newspaper and radio ads, urging anyone with logging experience to quit any job not related to timber and go back into the forests and sawmills. "Every skilled job in the woods and mills," the ads said, "is, in every sense, a battle station. Every tree 'of fighting age and size' is wanted in the Battle of Freedom." Eight years after being attacked by former Oregon Governor Charles Martin and others as treasonous Bolsheviks when they protested for higher pay and safer working conditions, local millworkers were being hailed as "front-line fighters in this conflict."

The Tillamook Forest was so vital, in fact, that the military knew it was a prime target for the Japanese. The Oregon Coast is the closest mainland point to Japan, and the Tillamook Burns of 1933 and 1939 had shown the Japanese that the forest was a place in which they might cause tremendous damage with minimal risk or effort. Ignited in the right place at the right time, even a small incendiary device could touch off a fire that might devastate the forest and drain precious resources to fight it. It would turn out that this scenario was not purely hypothetical. Oregonians lived in mortal fear of a surprise air raid, and mistaken reports of Japanese planes along the Coast were not uncommon. The first real attack came from the sea, not the air, when one night in June 1942 a Japanese submarine emerged long enough to lob a few shells at Fort Stevens on the Oregon Coast near Astoria. The fort's commander ordered a blackout, and the sub's crew ended up inflicting little property damage. The emotional damage to the psyches of Oregonians was more severe, and erroneous sightings of Japanese planes became even more common. On September 9, fire lookouts in southern Oregon spotted what they thought was a Japanese plane and reported it to the military, which promptly dismissed their concern. The lookouts could have been mistaken, because they were on edge from 24 hours of watching a thunderstorm in the forest. A short time later, the lookouts spotted a small column of smoke and called out firefighters. The split tree at the fire's origin was consistent with the presumed cause of the fire: a lightning strike. The firefighters discovered some metal fragments at the scene, and took them back to the nearby military base. Only when the local military commander examined them was it discovered that they were fragments of a bomb with Japanese writing on them. Word leaked out of this first and still only aerial bombing on the continental United States, and soon panic spread well beyond Oregon. It turned out that most of the rest of the country had nothing to fear, because the plane that dropped the bomb was a tiny wooden plane launched from a submarine with a range of less than 100 miles. Still, after the national furor the bombing created, military censors vowed to keep any future attacks hidden from public view if possible.

That decision ended up causing the only civilian wartime deaths on the mainland, and again, Oregon took the hit. By 1944 it was clear that the Japanese were losing the war. They came up with a desperate scheme to launch balloons into the jetstream, which tended to flow directly over Oregon. The balloons would soar to 30,000 feet and were designed to gradually lose their lighter-than-air gases until they fell to Earth over Oregon, igniting forest fires with the small bombs they carried. The plan was a fiasco, with most of the balloons falling harmlessly into the Pacific or drifting hundreds or even thousands of miles off course, nearly always failing to explode when they hit ground. Although the Japanese military told the war-weary readers of that nation's newspapers that the balloons were wreaking havoc on America and turning the tide of the war, most American newspaper readers remained blissfully unaware of the balloons, as military censors managed to quash news of the rare incidents before panic spread across the country. That ignorance proved fatal near Bly, Oregon, when a young minister and his wife took five children out for a picnic in the woods. The minister dropped off his passengers and went to find a place to park. His wife and the five children saw a deflated balloon on the ground and picked it up to examine it. The resulting explosion killed all six of them. Back in Forest Grove, the third devastating Tillamook Burn erupted, its cause reported as undetermined; only later would unsubstantiated rumors swirl that it was caused by a Japanese balloon bomb.

Overseas, Forest Grove boys were managing to stay alive remarkably well, until May 28, 1942, when Alan Detrick of Cornelius died. Detrick had learned to fly at Pacific, and perished when the plane he was piloting crashed during training in Alabama. On January 22, 1943, the city suffered another death. Brooks Taylor, a graduate of Forest Grove High School and a freshman at Pacific University when he joined the Army, was killed in the South Pacific. Few details of his death were revealed because of the nature of the mission he was on, but his presumed place of death was New Guinea; his father accepted a posthumous Silver Star for his son's gallantry. Forest Grove's Jack Hopper died a few months later in a Texas plane crash, just hours from being certified as a fighter pilot. In the nearby community of Timber, the Shipley family was sent reeling when two of their sons became prisoners of war within weeks of each other. Edwin was injured and recuperating at a Dutch hospital in Indonesia when Japanese forces overtook the medical center and imprisoned the American patients. Soon after, his brother Marion was a turret gunner in a B-26 shot down after a bombing run over North Africa on June 18, 1943. Other bomber crews reported seeing six parachutes deploy over the Mediterranean Sea, and his family was told he had been taken prisoner by the Italians. When the war ended, the Italians said that none of Marion's crew had been captured, and that all had died at sea. On December 3, 1944, his mother, Martha, was given the medals he had earned in combat, including a Purple Heart for his death in combat. In October 1945, Martha Shipley received better news, when she learned that her son Edwin was back safely in the United States, at a New York hospital.

Just days after Marion Shipley's death in 1943, another Forest Grove bomber pilot, Wayne Hutchens, disappeared over the Mediterranean. Three months earlier, Hutchens had earned a Distinguished Flying Cross after the B-17 he was co-piloting was hit by heavy gunfire, knocking out three of its engines and most of its controls. On that April day, Hutchens was able to crash land the battered B-17, saving his crew. On July 8, he was attacked again, and this time there was nothing he could do to save the plane or his crew. Because he went down at sea, the military held out hope that he had been taken prisoner, but on December 6, 1944, three days after Martha Shipley received her son's medals, Orval Hutchens, owner of the Forest Grove Shoe Store, was given Wayne's Distinguished Flying Cross and nearly a dozen other medals he had earned for bravery. His status remained Missing In Action.

William Purdin, the grandson of one of Forest Grove's earliest settlers who had yearned for a little Oregon weather while training in Texas, was now in the South Seas, flying missions as a tail gunner. On October 10, 1943, Purdin was making his seventeenth bombing raid when his plane was shot down. The pilot and co-pilot were killed, but the other eight crew members survived the crash. The Purdins received a letter a week later telling them that William was recuperating at an Army hospital. An agonizing month passed with no further word on his condition until two letters arrived at the Purdin home on November 20. One was from another member of Purdin's crew, expressing sympathy to the family for the loss of their son. He assured the Purdins that while William had briefly survived the crash, his injuries were such that he likely did not suffer. The second letter was from a flight surgeon. "Due to an error," the surgeon said, the first letter they received after the crash said that William was still alive, when in fact he was not. About the same time, Forest Grove lost its first female enlistee when physical therapist and recent Pacific University graduate Mary Selfridge was listed as a line of duty death at her base in New Orleans, with no other explanation given to the *News-Times*.

Tales of heroism kept arriving in Forest Grove. On August 20, 1944, Fern Prickett Hutchens eagerly opened a letter from her husband, Army Captain Donald Hutchens, which he wrote on August 10. The young wife read the news that her husband had been nominated for a Silver Star for his bravery that day during a fierce battle with the Nazis in France. Such bravery was nothing new for Donald Hutchens, whose regiment was among the first to storm the beaches of Normandy on D-Day. But Fern Hutchens did not know as she read his letter on August 20 that Donald Hutchens was dead, killed in action three days earlier. That horrible news would not arrive in Forest Grove until September 4.

The *News-Times* published as much news from the front as it could get, including a photo of a sword taken from a dead Japanese soldier by Raymond Strong of Gaston after an American victory. Two weeks later, the paper ran the story of Sergeant Raymond Strong's combat death in New Guinea.

A Pacific University student, Edwin Fisher, became a star when he shot down three German warplanes in one hard day of work, but that single day hardly defines the heroic life of Edwin "Bill" Fisher. Fisher was an Oregonian born and bred. He joined the Oregon National Guard in 1936, and pursued his education at Pacific. When the war broke out, he was among the first to volunteer for active duty. He was chosen to pilot a P-47 Thunderbolt. The P-47 was not a great fighter airplane because of its weight, but it could carry nearly as many bombs as the B-17 bomber, albeit for much shorter distances. That made the P-47 a good aircraft for supporting ground troops, because it was able to bomb enemy artillery and strafe machine gun installations. In the capable hands of Bill Fisher, however, the P-47 could do much more. In just a few short weeks of combat in 1944, Fisher compiled an astonishing record as an ace in the skies over Europe. Fisher's heroics began on May 10, when he was sent to bomb a German air base. His plane absorbed a barrage of gunfire, nearly crippling it, yet he managed to deliver his payload and return to safety in his battered P-47. Bill Fisher earned a Silver Star for valor on that mission, but he had not begun to show what he was made of. After the Allied invasion on D-Day, Fisher was assigned to provide air support for American bombing missions, and to drop bombs and attack German ground forces in France with the 50-caliber machine guns on his plane's wings. At the same time that Fisher was sent to France, however, the

Germans unleashed a devastating new weapon, the jet-powered V-1 "Buzzbomb," a precursor to the modern cruise missile. While Bill Fisher was escorting American bombers, the Germans were launching their new V-1s across the English Channel at London. The American bombing runs were so successful that Fisher often had many rounds of ammunition left over for the return trip, and the enterprising Pacific University student decided to use them to disable the devastating Buzzbombs. In his first few days over France in June, Fisher managed to maneuver his slow, propeller-driven P-47 into position to intercept three of the missiles, battering them with machine gun fire until they exploded harmlessly in mid-air.

July 5 would be the day that Bill Fisher secured his place in Army Air Corps history. He and his 377th Squadron were supposed to have a day off, but were instead called into action to lead a team of three other pilots over France. That morning, the four American pilots suddenly found themselves under attack by nine German Messerschmitt 109s. With his wingman taking heavy fire, Fisher circled around and blasted one of the German planes out of the sky. The other German pilots scattered, but not before downing one of the planes in Fisher's squadron. Undaunted, Fisher and the others proceeded on their mission. On the way, Fisher saw a V-1 racing across the sky and intercepted it, slicing it in half with machine-gun fire. He was so close to the explosion that "the concussion rocked my plane gently like a swing," he said later. But Fisher's day was not over yet. That afternoon, he found himself under attack by 15 German Folke-Wulf 190 fighters. He promptly blasted one of the German fighters out of the sky and he and his squadron sent the rest scattering for safety.

By August 9, Fisher shot down three more German planes, earning himself a place in the *Military Times* Hall of Valor. After the war, Fisher decided to stay in the military rather than return to Pacific. While working as a trainer at Andrews Air Base near Washington, D.C., on March 28, 1947, Edwin "Bill" Fisher was at the controls of a AT-6F fighter when it crashed and burned in a Pennsylvania farm field. United States Army Captain Edwin O. "Bill" Fisher's remains were returned for burial in Oregon a few days later. He was 29 years old.

As the war wound down another Forest Grove pilot, Ken Miller, was awarded the Distinguished Flying Cross, an award made more special because the Lieutenant Colonel who made the presentation was actor Jimmy Stewart, the Hollywood superstar who enlisted when the war broke out. When well-known Marine Sergeant Jack Nemeyer was killed in action, the story was just two paragraphs, buried beneath items about the prune harvest, high school football team tryouts, and a list of new teachers for the upcoming school year. J.M. Kirk, well-known as manager of the gas station at the corner of Pacific Avenue and College Way, got only three paragraphs when he was killed on just his second day on the battlefront in Germany.

As the war slowly ground to a halt, military censors eased restrictions and let Forest Grove residents in on some of the secrets local soldiers had been keeping. Through the story of James Fuiten, *News-Times* readers learned more about the brutal fighting in the Philippines. Fuiten had been awarded the Silver Star, one of the military's highest honors, for actions he took when his squadron was surrounded by Japanese forces and suffered horrendous casualties; Lieutenant Fuiten used a brilliant flanking maneuver to lead his men out of almost certain doom. More remarkably, it was one of two Silver Stars Fuiten earned for his bravery during the war. After returning to Forest Grove, he established the town's largest mortuary and Metro West Ambulance company. Through the actions of Marine Corps Captain Julius Lemcke, readers learned about the battle for Iwo Jima. Lemcke was not one of the Marines shown raising the American flag in triumph in the iconic image, but he certainly contributed to making that triumph possible. Lemcke commanded a tank company during the assault. Months later, Marine Corps correspondent Harold Breard told Lemcke's story to his hometown newspaper. One of the tanks under Lemcke's command took a direct hit from Japanese mortars, with one piercing the tank's armor. Three of the tank's crew members, one of whom was badly injured, managed to escape from the tank and find refuge in a crater left by a large explosion. With the injured Marine too weak to continue, one of the survivors made his way back to the command post to tell Lemcke what happened. The survivor led Captain Lemcke through ferocious enemy fire toward his fallen comrades in the tank, eventually taking machine gun fire to his leg. Lemcke sheltered him in another bomb crater and continued to the stricken tank to rescue his men. He climbed on top of the tank, which was still running, and attempted to climb inside to find the two crew members who had not made it out with the first three. Suddenly, 23-year-old Julius Lemcke, who just a few years earlier had been a student at rural Forest Grove Union High School, found himself the target of a focused attack in the middle of one of the most brutal and famous battles of the war. Then another mortar hit the tank, blowing up its engine and throwing Lemcke to the ground. By now other Marines had made it to Lemcke's side and detonated a round of mortars to create a smokescreen. Under cover of that smokescreen, Lemcke climbed inside the stricken tank, only to find the two crew members inside dead. He and his colleagues retreated, collecting the wounded along the way. That evening, under cover of darkness, Marine Captain Julius Lemcke, still little more than the kid he was when he lettered in football at Forest Grove Union High School, sneaked back to the tank and recovered the bodies of his two friends. Five fellow Marines and a Navy corpsman would raise the American flag to note the victory, but the story of Lemcke's heroism would not reach his proud friends and neighbors back in Forest Grove until several months later, after being cleared through military censors.

When Julius Octav Lemcke was born on April 1, 1922, few would have guessed that he was destined to become an American war hero. After all, he was born in Germany, although he came to Forest Grove with his parents when he was just 11 months old. Once in Oregon, he and his brother Al became all-American kids. While the kids back in Germany played soccer, Julius and Al Lemcke played football, first in high school and then at Pacific University. Both Julius and Al joined the Marine Corps, but Al's frequent letters home showed little interest in following his brother to the battlefield. On March 3, 1943, Al Lemcke wrote from his base in the Finger Lakes region of New York, which he said reminded him very much of Forest Grove. He was in no hurry to enter the war zone. "I hope I get to stay here for quite some time," he wrote, "as I hope to spend spring, summer and fall here if Uncle Sam sees fit." Al Lemcke worried about his brother Julius, whom he called Octav, who had been sent to the Pacific front, into the heart of combat. In another letter, Al Lemcke mourned the loss of his friend Brooks Taylor, a fellow football star, who had died under mysterious circumstances while fighting in New Guinea; Al had not yet heard of the Silver Star that Brooks would receive posthumously. Al also didn't know as he wrote his letters that his brother

Julius would go on to win the Bronze Star in Guam and the Navy Cross for his bravery at Iwo Jima.

The easing of military censorship brought other, more horrific news as well. "So they fooled you guys on the news about it being over over here," Staff Sergeant Arthur Goodrich wrote to his friends in Forest Grove in a letter dated April 21, 1945. Goodrich revealed he had been assigned to help liberate a Nazi concentration camp. "I sure saw it all," he wrote. "The torture chamber where they beat them to death. The gallows where they hung them. The furnaces where they burned the bodies and some unburned parts were still there. Outside were bodies half-naked stacked up like cordwood." Goodrich wasn't done. "Never have I seen such inhuman, uncivilized, uncalled for treatment of humans." He added a warning: "Nobody at home ever wants to tell me that the Nazi were human or I'll go up for second degree murder." Arthur Goodrich never went up for a charge of murder, although his return home was not the one he deserved. After winning a slew of awards for meritorious service, Goodrich returned to his pre-war job at Forest Grove Light and Power. He married and had two sons, but he spent almost two years in the hospital before dying at the age of 35 on December 3, 1952. The once strapping young Staff Sergeant was laid to rest next to his grandmother at Mountain View Cemetery in Forest Grove.

Yet even as tales of victory and bravery kept coming in, spirits in Forest Grove were beginning to flag. War bond sales were not meeting goals, tin can drives were coming up empty. By New Years Day 1945, Forest Grove was growing weary of war. Fortunately, the war was nearly over. Forest Grove was preparing for the homecoming of its troops, but worried that many of the programs promised for returning vets were slow to materialize. Communities prepared for the return of Japanese internees, although not everyone was happy about such a turn of events. In an editorial, the *News-Times* worried about how, or even if, the Japanese would be accepted back in Forest Grove. Another concern was about the black workers brought to Oregon to work in the shipyards. "To our way of thinking, these Negroes are apt to create a bigger post-war problem than the Japs," the editorial said. "What are we to do with them? Should we try to fence them in or drive them out?" The writer acknowledged, however, that neither the Japanese nor the black workers should be blamed for being who they were. "They didn't choose their parents," he wrote, "which seems most unfair, for had they been given that opportunity they would have been born smart, white and goodlooking." Others were even more blunt: "We must deport the Japs," attorney George Crandall thundered at a Forest Grove meeting of the Japanese Exclusion League. "Get rid of them. There is no place in America for them!" An overflow crowd had been anticipated for the meeting at the high school, but the *News-Times* reported that the auditorium was less than half full and the response was less than enthusiastic. With the exception of a few hotheads, few in Forest Grove wanted to keep fighting. They were tired of war, and by summer, the war was over. By fall, sawmill workers went back on strike. Farmers demanded that the Mexican laborers, whom they had begged to come, go home. Women who had taken classes to learn welding and carpentry were sent packing. Life was returning to normal in Forest Grove. Many of the black families in Vanport left the region for good when, on May 30, 1948, a levy on the Columbia broke and the river reclaimed its floodplain, wiping away all traces of what once was Oregon's second-largest city, and what today is its largest ghost town.

But World War II left many loose ends, diplomatically and in many other ways, and in the next few years Forest Grove and environs would be thrust into the international spotlight several times. One such tale involves a lovesick soldier, daring adventures on the high seas, strange foreign lands, and an exotic black-haired beauty; so compelling was this tale that it was chosen by editors of the *News-Times* as Forest Grove's top news story of 1948. William "Pat" Cody was a Forest Grove lad who joined the Army in World War II. Trained as a cook, he was shipped to a base in Iran. In 1943, he was on leave in Tehran when he met a beautiful waitress named Soghra. Pat and Soghra spent the night talking and before long he had been absent without leave from his unit for a week. When he returned, he was thrown into the brig for two weeks and then forbidden to leave the base. A few weeks later, he broke his glasses, and he was granted permission to travel to Tehran to have them replaced. While there, he had a secret rendezvous with Soghra. "After that I went to Tehran as often as I could break my glasses," he told the *News-Times* in 1948.

When the war ended, he told his commanders that he had secretly married Soghra on one of his frequent trips to the optometrist in Tehran, and he asked to have her accompany him back to Forest Grove.

The Army refused to recognize the marriage, and the lovers were torn apart. Back in Oregon and discharged from the military, Pat Cody longed to be reunited with his bride in Tehran, but post-war travel restrictions prevented them from reuniting. Eventually, Cody hatched a plan. He would join the Merchant Marine, catch a freighter to the Far East, jump ship and somehow make his way to Iran. At first the plan worked, because he was assigned to a Japan-bound ship leaving from Vancouver, Washington. The trip did not go well, however, as he suffered a severely burned foot while at sea in the Pacific. Arriving in Japan, he prepared to go AWOL for a second time, but slipped and fell, breaking his arm in eight places. Instead of going to Tehran, he ended up being shipped back to a hospital in Seattle. Once healed, he hitchhiked to ports up and down the West Coast, trying to find a ship sailing to Iran. While he was on the road, Soghra finally got permission to leave Iran, and headed to be reunited with her husband.

Unaware of this, a dejected Pat Cody had decided to rejoin the Army at Fort Ord, hoping to be sent back to Iran. When Soghra made it to Ellis Island in New York, she could not reach Cody and immigration officials labeled her as "unclaimed" and ordered her deported. At the last minute, Cody heard of Soghra's arrival. Back in Forest Grove, his mother, Margaret, received a letter from him telling her that he had joined the Army, been granted emergency leave and was hitchhiking to New York. Weeks passed with no word, until Margaret picked up *The Oregonian* and saw a national newswire photograph of her son with his bride, whom he had hastily re-wed in New York. Within a week, Soghra was living with Margaret in Forest Grove and Pat was back on duty, this time at Fort Lewis in Washington. Soghra adopted the American name "Irene," because it sounded like "Iran." Pat and Soghra's love story made headlines in Forest Grove and around the country for a brief time, but then the historical trail went cold.

While Pat and Soghra's drama was unfolding, a Forest Grove military hero was writing a new chapter to his legend down the coast near San Diego. Julius Octav Lemcke never was content to rest on his laurels. Having earned the Bronze Star and the Navy Cross for his heroism on land during the Battle of Iwo Jima, after the war Lemcke asked for and received a transfer to the Marine Corps Aviation division. Piloting an airplane is very different from driving a tank, but Lemcke mastered both, and before long he was engaged in mock dogfights over the California desert. On March 9, 1948, Julius Lemcke was still just 25 years old, but far removed from his years growing up on Stringtown Road in Forest Grove, let alone his birth in Germany. Julius Lemcke was on his way to becoming a flying ace. Becoming a pilot, however, requires extensive training, and as Mark Hogue pointed out 30 years earlier, it also involves great risk, even in perfect conditions over American soil in peacetime. On March 9, 1948, two Marine Corps fighters collided in mid-air while in training over California. One pilot ejected and rode his parachute to safety. The other pilot was Julius Octav Lemcke of Forest Grove, immigrant from Germany, football star, and winner of multiple medals for bravery. Julius Lemke died on March 9, 1948, as his fighter plunged into the California desert east of Riverside.

Meanwhile, in an exotic land far from Forest Grove, rumors persisted that American POWs from World War II were being held in a jungle prison. This particular land, China, was by now under the Communist control of Mao Zedong, and Americans had severed all ties with his regime. Few Americans knew much about China, but Levi Lovegren was a notable exception. Lovegren had built the dam that promised to make Cherry Grove a major city and then became a Baptist missionary to China after his dam and dreams broke in a winter deluge. Lovegren knew China about as well as anyone, and government agents approached Lovegren's superiors at the Baptist Missionary Association to ask if they would send Levi back to China with a group of people the government had assembled to accompany him. Everyone agreed, and Lovegren returned to China for the first time in years. He never found the supposed POWs, at least in part because he and his crew were soon arrested as spies and thrown into a Chinese prison, where they remained for five years until Swiss intermediaries, acting on behalf of President Dwight Eisenhower, persuaded the Chinese to release them in 1955. Levi Lovegren returned to Cherry Grove, where he died in 1983, 70 years after his dam broke.

Perhaps Forest Grove's strangest encounter in post-war intrigue, however, involved two seemingly naïve Pacific University students who went to Vienna for a year to study abroad. Before long, their story involved an alleged international spy ring and murder on the Orient Express. The story begins in February 1950 in Budapest, when Robert

Vogeler, ostensibly a mild-mannered vice president of International Telephone and Telegraph, was convicted by the Communist government of Hungary of spying for the United States and thrown into prison for 15 years. Perhaps by happenstance, Vogeler's best friend, Navy Captain Eugene Karpe, also was living in Europe, serving as the Naval attaché to Romania. Karpe rushed to Vienna, where Vogeler had been living before his imprisonment, to comfort Vogeler's wife. Karpe then jumped aboard the Orient Express and headed back to his native Louisiana.

Also on board the Orient Express was a 21-year-old Pacific University student named Russell McKichan, who also was beating a hasty retreat from Vienna. McKichan, who grew up on Ash Street about three blocks from the Pacific campus, had traveled to Austria with Vernonia native and fellow Pacific student Doug Culbertson. They planned to spend a full year at the University of Austria. After one semester, however, McKichan tired of life under communist rule and caught the Orient Express for home. He and Karpe struck up a friendship as the train rolled across Europe, sharing meals and generally avoiding the other passengers. On February 23, 1950, McKichan and Karpe enjoyed first breakfast and then lunch together aboard the train, then retired to their compartments, the Pacific student told reporter Ellis Lucia when he got home to his parents' house on Ash Street.

What happened between the time the two said their goodbyes at 1:30 p.m. and McKichan finally making it home to Ash Street had the young man's name splashed across newspapers and newsreels around the world. At about 8:30 that night, French police officers boarded the train. Unable to understand French, McKichan needed an English speaking officer to explain what was going on. "Your American friend has been killed," the officer told him. "He has had his throat slit." The time of Captain Eugene Karpe's death was pegged at 1:30 p.m. By the time the Orient Express arrived in Paris, McKichan was surrounded by police and investigators from the American government. Austrian newspapers already were printing accusations that the boy from Ash Street had been sent to murder Karpe, an American spy. Austrian police, however, were jumping to no such conclusions. Although McKichan told Lucia that he was not aware the train was in a tunnel as he and Karpe parted, they were in fact in a very long, curved tunnel. It was inside that tunnel that a railroad worker later stumbled upon Karpe's body, so mutilated that police could not begin to settle on an exact cause of death; they labeled it either an accident or a suicide. Authorities in Paris were inclined to believe that McKichan was innocent as well, and allowed him to board the *Queen Mary* to return to America. Within days, he was bombarded with calls and telegrams from reporters, and ended up hiding in the cabin of a friend to avoid other reporters on board the ship. When he arrived in New York, agents from the United States and Austria grilled him for eight days before finally allowing him to board a train for Oregon.

No one will ever know exactly what happened aboard the Orient Express that day. Eugene Karpe was buried with full military honors at Arlington National Cemetery. McKichen's friend, Doug Culbertson, who had stayed behind in Vienna, offered his version of events when he arrived back at Pacific in September. It seems that Austrian and American investigators had questioned him in the immediate aftermath of Karpe's death, and the Austrians publicly accused him of being a spy. He dropped out of the University of Vienna, but stayed in Vienna working for the United States Special Services. He denied being in any way connected to spying or to Karpe. Under intense international pressure, the Hungarians released Robert Vogeler from prison just 14 months into his 15-year sentence, and he went to his grave denying that he was a spy. In 1952, Swiss police arrested an alleged Romanian spy, and charged him in the murder of Eugene Karpe.

By the time the Korean War broke out in 1950, Forest Grove was war-weary. Enlistments were slow, and try as they might, city leaders could not find volunteers to man the air-raid observation towers. Spirits were dampened further when the city suffered an early combat death. Marine Lieutenant J.D. Sharp had enlisted in World War II and spent three brutal years fighting in the South Pacific. When the war ended he did not return to Forest Grove, but rather to Washington, D.C., to study law at George Washington University. Law degree in hand, he went to work as a trial lawyer for the federal government. In September 1950 he was drafted back into the Marines and shipped to the front lines, where his previous combat experience earned him command of a mortar section. Within a month, he found his unit surrounded. What he did next earned him a Bronze Star for valor. An expert rifle marksman, the trial attorney from Forest Grove picked off several enemy soldiers, opening what he hoped would be a big enough hole for him to slip through and summon help. His sprint drew the attention of the enemy forces. Brilliant young attorney J.D. Sharp was shot and killed in the jungles of the South Pacific. His unit took advantage of the diversion to fight its way to safety. Eighteen months later, just before Memorial Day, Mrs. Elmer Sharp was given her son's medal at their home on 24th Avenue, Forest Grove, Oregon.

Like it always had, Forest Grove mourned its dead and celebrated the heroism of those that returned, but by now not with the fervor it had demonstrated in previous wars. The military still had most of its naval and aviation stock. By now the planes and ships that were being built were made of steel and aluminum, not spruce and fir from the Tillamook Forest, so there was no surge of employment, at least not in rural Oregon. Faraway lands no longer seemed as exotic as they did when people awaited word of Bolo tribesmen and the Battle of Manila Bay, and the exact rationale for the Korean War seemed less clear than for the World Wars.

Overall, the country was as war-weary as at any time since the end of the Indian Wars, and just like the Indian War soldiers, veterans returning from Korea would have been justified if they felt they didn't always get the credit and glory they deserved. On March 22, 1951, one such soldier, James Wilson Smith, died. Smith had lived in North Plains and Forest Grove for many years, but little was known about him until intrepid reporter Ellis Lucia interviewed him for a Page 1 profile in *The Oregonian* on July 8, 1946, on the occasion of Smith turning 103 years old. Smith had only three months of formal education, but had lived an interesting life. Born in Missouri like so many other Tualatin Plains pioneers, he crossed the Plains as an infant with his parents, who settled on a Donation Land Claim near North Plains in 1846. Smith spent much of his life roaming the West on horseback, from the forests of Canada to the deserts of Mexico, once in a while striking gold as a prospector and eventually winding up back in Forest Grove. He told Lucia of his secret to long life which, he said between puffs on his pipe, was abstaining from alcohol. Oh, and he mentioned that he was a Civil War veteran. After years of stories about Dan Daffron's status as Washington County's last surviving veteran of that war, this news confused many in Forest Grove, but there was an explanation. Daffron was the last surviving member of the Grand Army of the Republic, when he died in the midst of World

War II, but Smith could stake a legitimate claim to the title of oldest Civil War veteran. In 1864, Smith served a stint with Olney's Detachment of Oregon Cavalry, a rag-tag group of men loosely affiliated with the Union army, who roamed Oregon fighting Indians and by some accounts anyone else who got in their way, including each other. His time with Olney was short, but the Sons of Union Veterans of the Civil War honored the 108-year-old Smith with a plaque on his headstone as the last surviving Civil War veteran in Oregon. Smith lived out the last few years of his life on the meager pension he earned for fighting in the Indian Wars, a tribute to the efforts of Gaston's William Henry Harrison "Buck" Myers.

The Korean War years were brutal on Forest Grove. The normally rainy city experienced a major multi-year drought. In 1951, yet another Tillamook Burn erupted west of town, following the six-year cycle started by the first fire in 1933 and continued in 1939 and 1945. The hills around the city were so dry that wildland fires raged until nearly December. Water levels dropped so low throughout the Northwest that dams could not create enough electricity, resulting in emergency brownouts. Mandatory water rationing soon followed. Timber from the forests had lost its role in armaments, so the mills didn't enjoy any special boost.

When a Korean truce was signed in July 1953, Forest Grove finally had something to cheer about, and waited for its sons to return from war. For some families, the wait was a short one. The September 10, 1953, *News-Times* tells of a much longer wait for one mother, Mrs. Albert Evers. Two of her 11 sons had entered the military at the height of the war. Edmund had been sent to the relative safety of Germany to work at a hospital, and Eugene joined the Air Force as a camera technician and was sent to Japan. Gene Evers' strange, twisted, tragic story didn't become fully public until 60 years after the armistice was signed to end the Korean Conflict, when he related his experience to reporter Mike Francis of *The Oregonian* in a story published March 30, 2013. A camera on a B-29 bomber was not functioning properly, so on July 3, 1952, Evers was assigned to fly with the crew to investigate. On a bombing run over Korea, Russian MiGs shot down the bomber. Several crew members were killed by the MiGs attack, and Evers was knocked unconscious. The surviving crew members parachuted from the plane, leaving him because they thought he was dead. He regained consciousness before the bomber crashed and leaped from the plane. Never trained in the use of a parachute, however, his leap did not go well and he landed face-first in a rice paddy. He spent the Fourth of July wandering, lost and with a fractured vertebrae, through the Korean countryside. On July 5, he was captured by North Korean troops and sent to a prison operated by the Chinese. The North Koreans would not tell anyone what had happened to Evers. First he was reported as killed in action, later changed to missing in action.

Evers told reporter Francis that for the first seven months, he was kept outdoors as Chinese interrogators harangued him about his presence in Korea. He was not a formal member of the flight crew, so the Chinese accused him of being a spy. After seven months, he was transferred to another prison, where he was held for seven more months in solitary confinement. For 14 months Mrs. Evers awaited word, but none came. After the truce other mothers welcomed their sons home, but still Mrs. Evers waited. In the interim, two more of her sons enlisted in the military. One of those sons was stationed at Fort Ord, California, where released prisoners of war were being treated before being sent back into society. Finally, Mrs. Evers got a telegram. Eugene had been found alive at a communist prison camp. He would be returning home, by way of Fort Ord. When he got home to Forest Grove, he was under orders to eat light meals while he recovered from severe malnutrition. A reporter was at his mother's farm when he arrived, and Eugene obliged with a short interview. Then he sat down to a bowl of apple sauce made fresh from his family farm's trees, and a big glass of fresh milk from one of the farm's cows. The 11 Evers boys finally all were accounted for. Gene Evers suffered physical pain and nightmares for many years, but went on to raise a family and work as a cabinet maker and dairy farmer. On April 20, 2013, Eugene Evers was honored at an All-Star Salute in Portland. His brother Edmund was not as fortunate, dying in an automobile accident in 1956, shortly after his return to Forest Grove.

By 1960, American soldiers were stationed in Vietnam, although not as official combatants, but rather as advisers to the South Vietnamese. The situation was confusing to the American public, as it was to many of the brave men stationed in Southeast Asia. One of those brave men was from Forest Grove, and he offered some candid assessments of the war in the August 6, 1964 *News-Times* while home on leave. Foy Leatherman joined the Army to become a military police officer. His first assignment as an MP was in Vietnam, but within months he was transferred to a helicopter crew. His role as an adviser would be to use heavy machine gun fire against suspected Viet Cong fighters on the ground. His MP training had focused on the use of small arms, and he got little training before being sent out on his first combat mission.

"I enjoyed the flying," Leatherman said, "but I did not enjoy what I had to do." Reporter Fritz Meagher picks up his story: "One of the most worrisome things about the strange combat was telling foe from harmless bystander. 'Someone standing by a (Viet Cong) might be an innocent villager,' Leatherman pointed out, but gunners couldn't afford the luxury of guesswork. Anyone in a Viet Cong combat area was considered to be the enemy. 'We had no choice …' he said, indicating clearly that the 'no choice' was a difficult one."

The choice of whether to volunteer to fight was a difficult one for many people this time around, but some people did. Soon busloads of young men were headed off to war, most of them called by the draft. One man who did volunteer, Cornelius resident Gene Goeden, quickly became a Navy pilot. In 1967 his A-1 Skyraider was hit by enemy fire, and he became the first local fatality of the Vietnam War, leaving behind two young daughters. Walter Sargent of Gales Creek was next. Then came Marine Corporal Arthur "Garry" Schauermann. Schauermann's death on April 29, 1968, was nothing out of the ordinary by war standards. He was riding in a vehicle that struck a land mine about 25 miles south of Da Nang. But for the families of those killed in action, no death is ordinary. In the case of Marine Corporal Garry Schauermann, we know that he was much more than just a passenger in a vehicle that struck a land mine 25 miles south of Da Nang. Among other things, he was the son of a prominent local businessman, Arthur Schauermann Sr., a partner in Forest Grove's major insurance brokerage. Garry was destined to inherit the business at some point after returning from Vietnam. We know that Marine Corporal Garry Schauermann loved his parents, because a few days before he died, he mailed a letter to them, expressing his excitement about seeing them on May 3 during his leave in Hawaii. His parents received his letter on the day that he died, riding in a vehicle that struck a landmine. Instead of seeing their son on May 3 in sunny Hawaii, the Schauermanns buried him with full military honors in rainy Oregon on

May 13. By 1968, Americans on the homefront were not as personally affected by foreign conflicts as they were in the World Wars, at least not directly, but Garry Schauermann's death illustrates how war can affect communities in unseen ways for generations to come. Garry's cousin, Tim, was working for Boeing after graduating from Pacific University when Garry was killed. "May he have died to make a better world," Arthur Schauermann wrote of his son in a letter published in the May 9, 1968, edition of the *News-Times*. But Schauermann urged readers to do more than just wish for a better world. "Couldn't we all contribute to a better country in which to live and rear our children? ... I have dedicated myself to serve to this end." Nephew Tim took the message to heart, quit his job at Boeing and returned to Forest Grove to become his uncle's business partner. For the next five decades, he became one of the best-known local advocates for young people. In 1993, for example, he received an award from the Forest Grove Chamber of Commerce honoring his years of work with the local economic development council, West Tuality Habitat for Humanity, and Rotary Club scholarship committee. He also volunteered with the Concours d'Elegance car show and as a Pacific University trustee and donor.

Other families were notified that their sons or husbands had been captured by the North Vietnamese, but their stories rarely made the newspaper, because the military exerted heavy pressure on them to not publicize their loved ones' plight, fearing that doing so would just inflame opposition to what already was an unpopular war. A Forest Grove woman, Darleen Sehorn, made headlines when she went public in March 1970 with the story of her husband, James. Darleen knew little about her husband's fate, other than that the plane he had been piloting was shot down over North Vietnam on December 14, 1967. Given the circumstances of the crash, he was presumed to have survived. The Air Force asked Darleen to keep this information private. That would not be easy, because James Sehorn had been born in Forest Grove, went to school in Forest Grove, and except for his four years at Oregon State University, had lived in the town his entire life. He had many, many friends. Still, Darleen complied with the Air Force's request, even changing her telephone number to preserve privacy. But by March 1970, more than two years since she had received word of her husband, Darleen grew restless. She had two small daughters, one of whom remembered her father, and one so young that she did not. With the help of the American Red Cross, families of other presumed POWs connected. Of the 32 such men from Oregon in that category, two were from Forest Grove; James Sehorn and Douglas Condit. Douglas Condit, it turned out, had a lot in common with James Sehorn. Condit had grown up in Forest Grove and also went to Oregon State, where he became an electrical engineer. Condit was an F-4 Phantom fighter pilot, and had been shot down just 12 days after Sehorn went missing. Condit's mother, Eva, who with her husband were well-known as owners of the local feed store, also had obeyed orders from the Air Force, as had Douglas's older brother, James, in the Air Force himself.

Thousands of letters to the North Vietnamese government sent as a result of the Red Cross effort brought results. In May, after more than two years without any word from her husband, Darleen Sehorn received a letter from James. The handwritten note was just six lines long, the maximum his North Vietnamese captors would allow, but at least she could tell his daughters that he still was alive. She kept up the pressure, leading a delegation to Paris to press the North Vietnamese to provide better treatment for POWs and to allow greater communications. She testified before Congress, then led another delegation to Geneva, Switzerland. Finally in March 1973, Darleen Sehorn heard the news she had been waiting for, a truce in Vietnam. That same week she was named Forest Grove's citizen of the year for her efforts on behalf of POWs.

On March 30, 1973, James Sehorn arrived home to a spectacular welcome. Rain poured down on Forest Grove as a crowd gathered downtown, listening to their transistor radios as KUIK broadcast the progress of the motorcade making its way from Portland International Airport with the homebound hero, accompanied the entire way by a police escort. After five and a half years in a Vietnamese prison, James Sehorn waved to the crowd and wiped away tears, but didn't speak. He wanted just to get home to his family. "It was just as if he had never been away," Darleen said a couple of days later. "Everything is so natural and normal."

Long after her divorce from James, Darleen Sehorn remained committed to the Red Cross, becoming an employee and travelling the world wherever she was needed. After several years in Korea, in 1998 she found herself as Red Cross team leader in war-torn Bosnia. Her job was to help the soldiers, but she said it was the orphans of war that touched her heart the most.

James Sehorn's friend and fellow pilot, Douglas Condit, did not return to a hero's welcome. When the war ended, the North Vietnamese denied that he was a POW. For years, teams of Americans searched for those missing in action, with a surprising degree of cooperation from the Vietnamese. Finally in 1979, the Air Force gave up and switched Douglas Condit's status from missing in action to killed in action. Still, there was no proof that he was dead, and Eva Condit "kept hope alive even though she was faced with the evidence," her son James told *News-Times* columnist Jim Hart in 1993. Eva Condit died in 1990, never knowing for certain the fate of her pilot son. In 1992, a dog tag was found in the dense jungle of Vietnam, and nearby was a skeleton. The dog tags belonged to Douglas Condit, and so did the skeleton, as confirmed by dental records. On Saturday, July 24, 1993, Douglas Condit finally got the welcome home he deserved when four F-15 fighters flew overhead in formation as he was laid to rest at Forest View Cemetery, next to the grave of his mother.

Not every hero from the Forest Grove area who went off to fight for his country got the welcome home he deserved. Norman Lien is a prime example. Norman Lien was a kid from Banks who got straight A's in high school. Norman Lien was a star athlete and a member of the Banks High School debate team that won the state championship in 1941. Norman Lien graduated at the age of 16 and enrolled at Oregon State College. When he turned 17 he joined the Navy, which transferred him to the University of Colorado, where he won national honors in mathematics. The Navy had high hopes for Norman Lien from Banks High School, but Norman had other ideas. Norman Lien asked several times to be sent to the front lines, and in 1943 the Navy complied. He spent time at the Chicago Naval Yards and at Treasure Island, California, before being shipped to the front lines in the South Pacific in 1945. On February 13, just weeks after Norman Lien arrived in the war zone, his parents received a telegram informing them that their son was dead. The message was cryptic, saying only that Norman's death involved a shotgun and an accident. Forest Grove would never learn the details. The telegram said that he was buried on a South Pacific island, the location of which would not be divulged until the war ended. Indeed, after the war his parents learned that he had died on Samar Island, and his remains were sent home to Oregon. But Forest Grove residents would never learn the details of the death of one of its best and brightest, and will never know what he might have become had he not volunteered to fight for his country.

Forest Grove will never know what Ryley Gallinger-Long would have become, either. Or Julius Octav Lemcke. Or Jack Nemeyer, Mary Selfridge, William Purdin, Frank Lloyd Smith, Douglas Condit, Oates Carpenter or any of the others who died serving their country. Any one of them could have become pillars of their community, like Thomas Thorp and Thomas Cornelius did. Any one of them could have brought joy to their little corner of the Earth, like Dancing Danny Daffron did.

We do know a few things. We know that for better or worse, wars have shaped the economy and character of Forest Grove. We know that the names of the dead were etched in stone by a community that does not want to forget their sacrifice. And we know that there are countless others, including military veterans and courageous civilians such as Jane Schneider who risked their lives in service to their country.

Chapter

12

Gay Old Times

Walk along Gay Nineties Way between Pacific Avenue and Twenty-first Avenue on some hot July weekend evening and you'll feel almost as if you're stuck in a time warp, suspended somewhere between the past and present.

The buildings are old and made of bricks formed from the local clay, just as they were a century ago. You can almost hear the dulcet tones of a barbershop quartet wafting in the air, which is appropriate, given that you strolled past the "World's Tallest Barber Pole" just a few blocks back, planted in honor of Forest Grove's famous ballad contest. Step inside almost any of the buildings, however, and you'll be reminded that your feet are planted firmly in the present. One dead giveaway? In about half the buildings you'll find restaurants, pizza joints and wine bars, all serving alcohol. That's not something you would have seen back in the 1890s, the decade for which the street is named, just a block away from Pacific University and its ironclad rules banning the demon rum. Another clue? The only modern building on the block is a sleek Congregational Church, which bears no resemblance to the wooden chapel with its towering steeple that dominated the skyline more than a century ago.

The fact that Gay Nineties Way and the sidewalks are paved is yet further evidence that you are not in Nineteenth Century Forest Grove, with its muddy, rutted streets and wooden sidewalks. Yet there's no sign of railroad tracks in the street; no sign of the streetcars that Forest Grove fought for at the dawn of the Twentieth Century. As dusk settles in, bright street lights kick on, another sure indication that you're not in the streetcar era. In fact, you must be in at least 1918, because there's a 1918 Chevrolet roadster cruising down the block, carrying a happy couple dressed in clothes of the era. To add to the confusion there's also a 1929 Duesenberg, and a 1966 Mustang, and a 1942 Packard, and a 2012 jacked-up Dodge pickup ...

This portrait of a July evening is confusing but all true, except for the Gay Nineties Way part. Everyone knows that there's no such street in Forest Grove, although there would have been if the Gay Nineties festival committee had its way on January 16, 1961, when members asked the Forest Grove City Council to consider changing the name of Main Street to Gay Nineties Way. The rationale was that nearly every town in America has a Main Street, but only Forest Grove would have a Gay Nineties Way. The city balked, and the committee that suggested the change suggested just adding the Gay Nineties Way sign under the Main Street sign. With the city leaders still unconvinced, the committee suggested adding the signs below the Main Street signs only during the Gay Nineties festival. Main Street never was renamed Gay Nineties Way. That does not mean that the people of Forest Grove were not very serious about the Gay Nineties festival, however.

The festival was started in 1947 by a group known as SPEBSQSA, or the Society for the Preservation and Encouragement of Barber Shop Quartet Singing in America. The Forest Grove chapter, called the Gleemen, put together the All-Northwest Barber Shop Ballad Contest as a way, in the words of one of its founders, to bring back the good old days of the 1890s to escape their worldly cares. None of the group's members was old enough to appreciate that the 1890s were anything but carefree in Forest Grove, considering the lack of a railroad and sewer, frequent bank panics and epidemics of communicable diseases, and only sporadic electricity and drinking water. In fact 10 years after the first festival, local author Lester Mooberry wrote a book about the hardships of the 1890s around Forest Grove, which he called *The Gray Nineties*. Nonetheless, nostalgia won out and soon the Barber Shop Ballad Contest was wrapped into a larger festival called "the Gay Nineties." The celebration brought Forest Grove attention it never had enjoyed before. By 1950, NBC televised the finals of the singing contest live across the nation, except on the West Coast, where it was tape delayed. The *News-Times* put a happy face on the delay, however, pointing out that locals could attend the concert live and race home in time to watch it again on television. By 1954, the *News-Times* was touting the festival as the nation's premier barber shop competition. Each year on the festival's first day, every person in town was encouraged to dress in 1890s attire, or at least what they believed to be 1890s attire. The school day was devoted entirely to learning about the 1890s through songs and essays. Businesses throughout town decorated their windows and let employees off work for events. The annual parade drew entries from throughout the region, including bands and old automobiles, although most of the cars were from the 1920s and '30s, rather than the 1890s. Before long, the name "Ballad Town" adorned a number of local businesses and even one of the city's first shopping centers.

As beloved as the festival was, however, it was not without its share of controversy. Before Aldie Howard finally broke through the booze ban in 1970, he was chairman of the festival committee, and asked City Council to allow a beer garden in one of the vacant brick buildings along Gay Nineties Way, or rather Main Street. The request was denied. After Howard was elected to the Council himself, he played a pivotal role in another controversy, this one involving the "World's Tallest Barber Pole." The pole actually was not created to stand in Forest Grove, at least officially, although it was the brainchild of Forest Grove resident Chuck Olson. It seems that Olson, a balladeer himself, got wind that San Antonio, Texas, laid claim to the title of world's tallest barber pole, reaching 40 feet into the sky. Olson felt that justice demanded that the honor should more properly belong in Oregon, the land of tall timber. With the national barbershop quartet competition returning to Portland in 1973, he hatched a plan to not only eclipse San Antonio's record but to double it. He arranged with a regional bank and a local electric utility to transform a wooden power pole into his dream, to be displayed at Portland's Memorial Coliseum during the national championships.

When the singing competition ended, the pole was removed and taken to the electric utility's storage yard. Olson, who worked for the Forest Grove School District, and Aldie Howard, by now a City Council member, arranged to bring the pole to Forest Grove, and suggested placing it near the entrance to the city on Highway 8. Other Council members were unimpressed with the idea of an 80-foot log with a Styrofoam ball on top as the first thing visitors to the city see, and said no. The pole went back into storage. Then, a few months later at a March 1974 City Council meeting, Ora Faye Thogerson posed a question to her fellow Council members. "Who put the 80-foot barber pole up in the middle of Lincoln Park," the *News-Times* quoted her as asking, in what the reporter described as "wry disgust." It turns out that Mrs. Thogerson did not have the facts straight; after being placed in a hole in the ground at Lincoln Park, the pole was a mere 72 feet tall. It was, however, towering above Lincoln Park as she spoke. New City Manager Anthony Baldwin acknowledged that, caught up in the spirit of the Gay Nineties Festival, he had told the city's electric utility to install the pole. The Council discussed options for dealing with the pole. "Some spoke darkly of a chainsaw," the *News-Times* reported. In the end, the Council members did what their predecessors had done so often a generation earlier during fights over water, electricity and sewers. They voted to consider the matter further. "I told you we'd rue the day we brought that thing to Forest Grove," the reporter quoted Aldie Howard as saying at the meeting. The paper did not report whether Howard and his co-conspirators retired to his Coffee Grinder Restaurant after the meeting to plot their next steps over cocktails that were now legal because of one of his earlier battles. It took two years, but ultimately Howard prevailed again. The pole was formally welcomed to the city in July 1976, as a centerpiece of the city's celebration of the nation's Bicentennial, when civic leader Helene Stites christened it by smashing a bottle of hair tonic against it.

The barber pole still stands in Lincoln Park, which has been transformed in the Twenty-first Century into a state-of-the-art athletic complex for the city and for Pacific University. The celebrations for which it stands, however, are all but forgotten. Just about the time that the pole was raised in what seemed like a coronation for the Gay Nineties

Festival and Ballad Town Barbershop competition, societal changes were sweeping over Forest Grove. By the early 1970s, Forest Grove's transformation from a regional center to commuter bedroom community was well underway. For most of its history, Forest Grove leaders had fought for better transportation options, under the assumption that they would bring people *to* the city; the obvious corollary is that those same transportation options can ferry people *from* town just as easily. By the early 1970s, the railroad that the city had coveted in the 1860s no longer carried passengers to within 30 miles of Forest Grove. The electric trolleys that the town coveted in the early 1900s came and went in a heartbeat; today light-rail "trolleys" are back, but their trip from Portland ends in Hillsboro, six miles short of Forest Grove. By the 1970s, cars ruled the day, and they whisked Forest Grove's residents to and from work and shopping outside of town. With their lives increasingly focused beyond city limits, the residents of Forest Grove gradually lost the sense of community that fueled the Gay Nineties.

With that in mind, perhaps it is fitting that the parades of vintage cars that visitors still see along Forest Grove streets each July began in 1973, at the height of the intrigue swirling around the "World's Tallest Barber Pole." The Concours d'Elegance draws classic cars from throughout the West for one of the region's more prestigious automotive events, including cars from before 1910, when automobile trips to Forest Grove were all but impossible and entirely unwelcome, in the eyes of many. In 1903, the few cars that made the treacherous journey were referred to as "Red Devils" by the editor of the *Times* because they spooked horses and kicked mud and dust onto the faces and clothes of Forest Grove residents. In 1973, those same cars were being venerated in what has become perhaps the city's most-famous celebration.

The cars stretch the imaginations of many Forest Grove residents back into history almost beyond comprehension, but not nearly as far back as to when Tabitha Brown and Harvey Scott had to walk to town, or for that matter even to when the President of the United States had to walk to Forest Grove to pronounce it the prettiest town in Oregon, or at least something to that effect. Most of the folks who ogle a shiny 1910 Oldsmobile probably have no idea that when the car was built, raw sewage flowed in the streets of Forest Grove and children died of communicable diseases now thought to belong only in Third World countries. In many ways the Concourse d'Elegance is no more true to Forest Grove's history than the Gay Nineties Festival was to the reality of Lester Mooberry's *Gray Nineties*. Still, the Concours d'Elegance is held on the beautiful grounds of Pacific University, under the shade of one of the most impressive groves of old oak trees anywhere. On a sunny afternoon, viewing the historic cars, few would argue that Forest Grove is at least a worthy contender for the title of Prettiest Town in Oregon. Likewise, few would argue with the goal of the event, which is to raise money to help educate the children of Forest Grove and the students of Pacific University; that was, after all, the goal of the city's founders.

Forest Grove's major festivals through the years have tended to glorify its storied past. More to the point, as Lester Mooberry pointed out long ago, the festivals celebrate a sanitized vision of the past, sometimes quite literally so; after all, the Concours d'Elegance cars don't have to plow through raw sewage in the streets. People still gaze up at the World's Tallest Barber Pole, but more out of amusement than amazement at what it represents. The timber industry that the pole commemorates remains an important part of the local economy, although Forest Grove residents are as likely to go off to work today in a quest to build the world's fastest microprocessor. The sense of communal gaiety the pole also suggests is lost on many today as well. While there never was a time in the 1890s that the town was full of roving bands of barbershop quartets bursting into song, there really was a time when entertainment consisted of local lasses singing "Three Little Green Bonnets" and "You'll Get Heaps of Lickings." Before there were movie houses, before there were televisions, before there were even roads to bring travelling entertainers to town, Grovers made their own merriment, gathering to share their joy. Today, people tend to seek entertainment in their own homes, often not even sharing their fun with their own families; the microprocessors that produce so many jobs also produce devices that allow Dad to watch a game in one room, Mom to watch the news in another, Sister to engage in social media, and Brother to play video games. In the sanitized version of history, this is a recent development, but only if we forget that as early as 1950 families were staying home to watch national coverage of their own local festival on television rather than walk a few blocks to share it in person with their neighbors.

Forest Grove no longer is a dry town. Far from it; wine and beer are now mainstays of the economy. In reality, Forest Grove never was dry, and at least now there aren't bootleggers kidnapping local cops, or druggists selling morphine to cure vague "woman problems." Forest Grove no longer has just one "Chinaman," one "Oriental," one "Celestial" that everyone knows by name. Today the city has a large and diverse Asian population, with Chinese food, Sushi, Thai food, and even a sakery. Far from trying to drive the culture out of town, today Forest Grove's Pacific University pulls at least a quarter of its undergraduate student body from Hawaii, and one of the few events people still attend in large numbers is the school's annual Luau, celebrating the cultures of the Hawaiian Islands, China, Japan, Fiji, Samoa, the Philippines and other faraway lands.

Forest Grove still sends some of its best and brightest young people off to war, just as it always has, and still grieves as some are sent back home for military funerals in their honor. Even so, the nature of the wars those sons and daughters go off to fight has evolved. We no longer have to wait weeks for word from the frontlines in Eastern Oregon to trickle back to the Grove, or months for word from far off battlefields in exotic lands such as the Philippines. Today we can watch military campaigns unfold live on television from the safety and comfort of our homes, virtually untouched by the reality of the war we're watching. We tend to sanitize that part of history as well, forgetting that for most of Forest Grove's history, going to war meant that every person in town would know someone over on the frontlines, and by the time a war was over, almost everyone in town knew at least one person who had died in battle. Even those who didn't know anyone personally knew there was a war going on, without even having to pick up a newspaper or check the internet to find out. Nearly everyone sacrificed in some way, whether through rationing, volunteer work, or by taking on a grueling job they never imagined having to do.

It's easy to look back and believe that the past was full of people gaily singing in harmony. Nothing could be further from the truth, with constant fighting between the Wets and the Drys, between those who wanted public power and those who wanted private companies to control electricity, and between those who wanted a public sewer and those who wanted to be left alone to dump their feces into an open ditch. In the early days, most people resented government intrusion of any kind. Some were happy living in a virtual No Man's Land, protected by both the British and the Americans but beholden to neither. The only taxes most were willing to accept were those to pay bounty hunters to rid their fields and forests of wolves and coyotes so they could bring cattle to the territory. Decades later, settlers agreed to pay taxes for fire protection, although it would be many more decades before they were willing to ante up enough to actually pay the men who fought their fires for them. Many still believed into the Twentieth Century that private enterprise was best equipped to provide other services, including water and even law enforcement, leaving it to the Pinkertons and the Law and Order League to catch criminals. Yet Forest Grove emerged as a stalwart of public utilities.

More than most cities, however, Forest Grove has preserved the most important elements of its heritage. The natural beauty and "salubrious" climate are still here. It's only through the undying effort of townspeople that the city has not fallen victim to the bland suburban sameness that has overtaken many other small towns in exurban America. Joseph Meek, Thomas Naylor, Joseph Gale and the other rugged Mountain Men who settled the area knew that Forest Grove was about as far as one could go to escape the hustle and bustle of encroaching East Coast culture. They wanted to preserve as much of the Wild West culture as possible, while picking and choosing what elements of modern culture to accept. Among other things, they wanted wild, open hunting grounds, but also carefully cultivated farmlands and city streets lined with flowers and trees to make Forest Grove a warm, welcoming oasis in the wilderness to attract others to follow in their footsteps.

The importance of the Mountain Men of the Tualatin Plains too often is underplayed. They were rugged, and could be uncouth. Most were poorly educated, and some were illiterate. Yet while Oregon City, Astoria, Vancouver, Salem, and Portland get most of the attention in tales of the early Oregon Territory, the Tualatin Plains produced many of the most important participants at the Champoeg meetings that formed the basis of the modern state of Oregon. Joseph Meek's role as the de facto Father of Oregon is well-known, but Joseph Gale, Alvin Smith, Harvey Clarke, William Doughty, and others played important roles. William Doughty's name, for example, is nearly lost to history. In fact, on the monument to the state's founders at Champoeg, his name is etched as "Daugherty." Doughty was an archetypical Mountain Man, living in a remote cabin at the base of the Chehalem Mountains south of Forest Grove and continuing to earn a living trapping and hunting after many of his colleagues had turned to farming. Doughty was such a great hunter, in fact, that he was given the first important assignment at the Champoeg meetings, which were called the "Wolf Meetings" because they took place ostensibly to create a bounty system to rid the territory of wolves. Doughty was chosen to administer the bounty system. But Doughty was more than a hotshot Mountain Man. He was a founding member of the Congregational Church on the Tualatin Plains, and as the Champoeg meetings progressed he was elected as one of the first nine legislators, given charge of the ways and means committee to create a budget, and asked to help write what would become the state's Constitution, all at the tender age of 31. Yet like so many of his neighbors on the Plains, Doughty shunned the limelight. He never chased fame and fortune in Portland, Salem, or Washington D.C., choosing instead to live a quiet, useful life on the Tualatin Plains. Forest Grove was the only city he needed.

Doughty, Meek and some of the other Mountain Men personified the dichotomy of early Forest Grove, creating a bridge to those who created the city's most lasting legacy. Many of the second group of settlers who ever walked to Forest Grove had little interest in the area's wilderness. Their interest was in leading the Mountain Men, or at least their souls, out of the wilderness and into the light of Christianity. Biographers tend to agree that the Reverend Harvey Clarke did not cross the Plains with the specific intent to create a university. Like several other early missionaries, biographer Steven Richardson points out, Clarke was a bit of a lost soul himself when he walked across the Plains. Likewise, it's clear that when Tabitha Brown set out on foot from Missouri she had no idea that someday she would be known as the "Mother of Oregon." Neither Clarke nor Brown set out for Forest Grove, because when they hit the Oregon Trail there was no such place; in fact when Clarke ventured west there was no such thing as the Oregon Trail. Their paths converged on the Tualatin Plains only because by happenstance Tabitha's son, Orus, had a Donation Land Claim there.

Tabitha Brown had a dream of nurturing and educating every child in her known universe, and while Harvey Clarke wanted to help her nurture that dream, all he had to offer in way of support was a ramshackle cabin. Together that wasn't much, but it was enough to lure George Atkinson to town while he searched for a site for a Congregationalist college. It was enough to stir the souls of Alvin Smith, Elkanah Walker, Thomas Naylor and others into believing in their cause. It was enough to entice Harvey Scott to walk all the way from the Puget Sound to share the dream, and enough to encourage Rutherford B. Hayes to shed the privileges of the American Presidency and walk to Forest Grove to see the seeds of what they had planted in what would become the prettiest town in Oregon.

It's sad that the Gay Nineties festival didn't survive, and it's nice that the Concours d'Elegance has. As fun as such festivals are, however, neither begins to capture the magic that happened back in the 1840s, long before barbershop quartets or automobiles. A few simple words from a petite grandmother who had just walked much of the way across a continent sparked a miracle at the end of the Oregon Trail. A small miracle, to be sure, but one well worth writing about.

Afterword

The history of the Oregon Territory usually is told from the perspective of Portland, Astoria, Oregon City, Vancouver and Salem.

But while those cities competed with each other for commerce, no town contributed more than Forest Grove to shaping the cultural and intellectual future of the wild Northwest.

The list of early settlers on the Tualatin Plains is a who's who of the first provisional government. Joseph Meek and Joseph Gale were the flashy ones who craved the formal titles and prestige, but William Doughty, Alvin Smith, David Hill, John Griffin, Harvey Clarke and others all quietly played vital roles in the creation of the territorial government.

All of those men were as rough and tough as any man in the West, but in many ways they all take a back seat to a small, gentle woman named Tabitha Brown, who earned the title "Mother of Oregon" by making Forest Grove the unofficial educational capital of the Oregon Territory.

The missionaries who supported her efforts, including Harvey Clarke and George Atkinson, stifled the city's commercial growth with their sometimes self-righteous piety. But they also helped to preserve the rural, agrarian flavor that still pervades Forest Grove, where the economy remains more intellectual than industrial.

The quiet, unassuming nature of the city's founders persists in other ways as well. While the other early centers of the Oregon Territory proudly proclaim their role in history, Forest Grove tends to shun the spotlight.

Yet while the city's history rarely is told, it is well-preserved. This book would not be possible without support from the people at the Pacific University Archives, Friends of Historic Forest Grove, the University of Oregon Microfilm Archives, and the library systems of Washington and Multnomah counties.

Most of all, however, this book is possible because of one of the city's many treasures, the Forest Grove City Library. The library staff has provided incredible support and encouragement for this project over the past several years, and they have our eternal gratitude.

Because of my background as a print journalist, Kris and I rely heavily on newspaper archives when doing research. Over the years, the editors of the two papers we relied on most heavily for this book, *The News-Times* and *The Oregonian*, have employed excellent reporters in Forest Grove and have exhibited a keen interest in history. We owe a special debt of gratitude to two particularly fine journalists, Hugh McGilvra, who owned the *News-Times* for decades, and Ellis Lucia, who reported for both newspapers in addition to writing many books about local events.

I have learned over the years that the more I know about a subject, the more I realize how little I really know about it. Forest Grove is no exception, and this book barely skims the surface of the city's past, present and future. With that in mind, Kris and I already are working on a second volume of stories about this wonderful and vastly underrated city.

Over the years, I have visited almost every city in Oregon, and I have too many favorites to say with certainty that Forest Grove is the prettiest. However, I wholeheartedly agree with the travel writer who in 1888 wrote that the city "impresses the stranger with a sense of its enlightened and homelike pleasantness … so cozy a nook as Forest Grove is a gem that would be esteemed in any land where enlightened people dwell."

- *Ken Bilderback*
Laurelwood, Oregon
March 9, 2014

About the authors

Ken Bilderback grew up near Detroit, Michigan, and graduated from the University of Dayton. He spent 30 years as a journalist at newspapers across the country. His autobiographical novel, *Wheels on the Bus: Sex, Drugs, Rock 'n' roll and Life in 1974*, chronicles the wild cross-country trips that eventually landed him in Oregon, which has been his home since 1980. Ken also served several stints at the Freedom Forum Media Studies Center at Columbia University and the University of California. He is a National Fire Protection Association certified Public Information Officer and holds certificates in many aspects of emergency Incident Management and Command.

Kris is a graduate of the University of Washington and spent her career in administration at the UW, Bastyr University and at Pacific University. From 1998 to 2011, Kris served as the Executive Assistant to the President and Board of Trustees at Pacific University during the administrations of Dr. Faith Gabelnick, Dr. Phil Creighton and Dr. Lesley Hallick. After her departure from higher education, Kris joined Ken in launching a new career publishing stories about Washington County's incredible history.

Index

Bibliography

Abbott, Carl. *Portland, Gateway to the Northwest.* Northridge, CA: Windsor Publications, Inc., 1985.

Abbott, Carl. *Portland: Planning, Politics, and Growth in a Twentieth-Century City.* Lincoln, NE: University of Nebraska Press, 1983.

Abbott, Carl. *The Great Extravaganza: Portland and the Lewis & Clark Exposition.* Portland, OR: Oregon Historical Society Press, 2004.

Amato, Lisa, Mary Jo Morelli, and the Friends of Historic Forest Grove. *Images of America: Forest Grove.* Charleston, SC: Arcadia Publishing, 2010.

Andrews, Ralph W. *Historic Fires of the West: 1865 to 1915 – A Pictorial History.* Seattle, WA: Superior Publishing Company, 1966.

Applegate, Shelton P. State of Oregon Department of Geology and Mineral Industries. "A Large Fossil Sand Shark of the Genus *Odontaspis* from Oregon." *The Ore Bin.* 30.2 (February 1968): 32-36.

Atkeson, Ray. *Oregon, My Oregon.* Portland, OR: Graphic Arts Center Publishing, 1998.

Azuma, Eiichiro. "A History of Oregon's *Issei* 1880 – 1952." *Oregon Historical Quarterly* 94.1 (Winter 1993 – 1994): 315-367.

Bagley, Clarence B. "Pioneer Papers of Puget Sound." *The Quarterly of the Oregon Historical Society* 4.4 (December 1903): 365 – 385.

Ballou, Howard Malcom. "The History of the Oregon Mission Press." *The Quarterly of the Oregon Historical Society* 23.1 (March 1922): 39 – 110.

Bates, Henry L. "Pacific University." *The Quarterly of the Oregon Historical Society* 21.1 (March 1920): 1-12.

Baun, Carolyn M. *A Changing Mission: The Story of a Pioneer Church.* Forest Grove, OR: The United Church of Christ (Congregational), 1995.

Baun, Carolyn M. *This Far-Off Sunset Land: a Pictorial History of Washington County, Oregon.* Virginia Beach, VA: The Donning Company/Publishers, 1999.

Beckham, Stephen Dow. National Park Service. *Cultural Resources of Patton Valley, South Fork of the Tualatin River Oregon.* McMinnville, OR: n.p., 1975.

Beckham, Stephen Dow. *Stimson Lumber.* Portland, OR: ARCUS Publishing, 2009.

Beckham, Stephen Dow. *The Indians of Western Oregon: This Land was Theirs.* Coos Bay, OR: Arago Books, 1977.

Benson, Robert L. *Pioneer Landmarks of Washington County, Oregon.* Hillsboro, OR: Washington County Historical Society, 1966.

Bevan, Dane. "Recruits at the Forest Grove Indian School." *ohs.org.* Oregon Historical Society: The Oregon History Project, 2004. Web. October 2013.

"Boos Quarry, Yamhill County." Oregon Bureau of Mines and Geology. *The Mineral Resources of Oregon.* 1.2 (February 1914): 29-31.

Brauner, David R., and William Robbins. *The Archaeological Reconnaissance of the Proposed Lower Tualatin Sewer Project, Washington County, Oregon.* Corvallis, OR: Oregon State University, 1976.

Brown, Tabitha. "A Brimfield Heroine – Mrs. Tabitha Brown." *The Quarterly of the Oregon Historical Society* 5.2 (June 1904): 199 – 205.

Carey, Charles H. *A General History of Oregon.* Vol. 2. Portland, OR: Metropolitan Press, 1936.

Clarke, S. A. "The Oregon Central Railroad." *The Quarterly of the Oregon Historical Society* 7.2 (June 1906): 133-144.

Clock, Paul Michael. *Punk, Rotten & Nasty: the Saga of Pacific Railway & Navigation Co.* Portland, OR: Corbett Press, 2000.

Collins, Dean. *The Story of Tillamook: the Little County that Became the Big Cheese.* 1933. Reprint. Portland, OR: The Oregon Journal, 1961.

Corbett-Atterbury, Vivian. *The Oregon Story.* Portland, OR: Binfords & Mort, 1959.

Cressman, Luther S. "Petroglyphs of Oregon." *University of Oregon Monographs, Studies in Anthropology.* Eugene, OR: University of Oregon, 1937.

Curtis, Mildred, ed. *Laurel Echoes Yearbook.* Laurelwood, OR: Laurelwood Academy, 1928.

Davis, Wilbur A. United States Department of Interior, National Park Service, and Oregon State University. *Scoggin Creek Archaeology Final Report.* Corvallis, OR: Oregon State University, 1969.

Decker, Doyle D., and Wilbur A. Davis. United States Department of Interior, National Park Service, and Oregon State University. *Survey of Impacts on Prehistoric Resources Tualatin Project, Second Phase.* Corvallis, OR: Oregon State University, 1976.

Delamarter, George Guy. *The Career of Robert Newell, Oregon Pioneer.* 1951. Reprint (Master's Thesis for the University of Oregon, Department of History). Saint Paul, OR: Newell House Museum, 2005.

Dobbs, Caroline C. *Men of Champoeg: a Record of the Lives of the Pioneers who Founded the Oregon Government.* Portland, OR: Metropolitan Press Publishers, 1932.

Dodds, Linda, and Carolyn Baun. *Portland Then and Now.* San Diego, CA: Thunder Bay Press, 2001.

Doorways to the Past: a Tour of some of Forest Grove's Finest Historical Homes. Hillsboro, OR: Washington County Historical Society, 1987.

Drury, Clifford Merrill, ed. *On To Oregon: The Diaries of Mary Walker and Myra Eells.* 1963. Reprint. Lincoln, NE: University of Nebraska Press, 1998.

Duniway, Abigail Scott. *Path Breaking: An Autobiographical History of the Equal Suffrage Movement in Pacific Coast States.* 1914. Reprint. New York: Schocken Books, 1971.

Dutro, Jean, ed. *The Laurel Yearbook.* Laurelwood, OR: Associated Students of Laurelwood Academy, 1942.

Edwards, G. Thomas and Carlos A. Schwantes, eds. *Experiences in a Promised Land: Essays in Pacific Northwest History.* 1986. Reprint. Seattle, WA: University of Washington Press, 1990.

Eisenberg, Ellen. "'As Truly American as Your Son': Voicing Opposition to Internment in Three West Coast Cities." *Oregon Historical Quarterly* 104.4 (Winter 2003): 542-565.

Engeman, Richard H. *The Oregon Companion: An Historical Gazetteer of the Useful, the Curious, and the Arcane.* Portland, OR: Timber Press, 2009.

Faubion, William. *Treasures of Western Oregon.* Medford, OR: Morgan & Chase Publishing, Inc., 2005.

Fletcher, Randol B. *Hidden History of Civil War Oregon*. Charleston, SC: The History Press, 2011.

Frachtenberg, Leo J., Albert S. Gatschet, and Melville Jacobs. *Kalapuya Texts*. Seattle, WA: University of Washington Publications in Anthropology, Vol. 11, 1945.

Friedman, Ralph. *In Search of Western Oregon*. Caldwell, ID: The Caxton Printers, Ltd., 1990.

Friedman, Ralph. *Oregon for the Curious*.1972. Third rev. ed. Caldwell, ID: The Caxton Printers, Ltd., 1979.

Fulton, Ann. *Banks, A Darn Good Little Town*. Banks, OR: Friends of the Banks Community Library, 1995.

Gaston, Joseph, and George H. Himes. *The Centennial History of Oregon 1811 - 1912*. 4 Vols. Chicago, IL: The S. J. Clarke Publishing Co., 1912.

Gaston, Joseph. "The Genesis of the Oregon Railway System." *The Quarterly of the Oregon Historical Society* 7.2 (June 1906): 106-132.

Gaston, Joseph. "The Oregon Central Railroad." *The Quarterly of the Oregon Historical Society* 3.4 (December 1902): 315-328.

Gaston, Joseph. *Portland, Oregon: Its History and Builders*. 3 Vols. Chicago, IL: The S. J. Clarke Publishing Co., 1911.

Gatschet, Albert S. "Oregonian Folk-Lore." *The Journal of American Folklore* 4.13 (April – June 1891): 139 - 143.

Gatschet, Albert S. "The Kalapuya People." *The Journal of American Folklore* 12.44 (January – March 1899): 212 - 214.

Hall, Lisa Shara. *Wines of the Pacific Northwest*. London, GB: Mitchell Beazley, 2001.

Himes, George H. "Beginnings of Christianity in Oregon." *The Quarterly of the Oregon Historical Society* 20.2 (June 1919): 159 – 172.

Himes, George H. "History of the Press of Oregon 1839 – 1850." *The Quarterly of the Oregon Historical Society* 3.4 (December 1902): 327 – 370.

Hodge, Frederick Webb, ed. *Handbook of American Indians North of Mexico*. 2 vols. New York: Pageant Books, Inc., 1959.

Holmes, Kenneth L., ed. *Covered Wagon Women: Diaries and Letters from the Western Trails, 1840 – 1849, Volume I*. 1983. Reprint. Lincoln, NE: University of Nebraska Press, 1995.

Hult, Ruby El. *Lost Mines and Treasures of the Pacific Northwest*. Portland, OR: Binfords & Mort Publishers, 1957.

Hult, Ruby El. *Treasure Hunting Northwest*. Portland, OR: Binfords & Mort Publishers, 1971.

Hussey, John A. *Champoeg: Place of Transition, A Disputed History*. Portland, OR: Oregon Historical Society, 1967.

Jeffries, Jessie, Robert L. Benson, and Mrs. John Gates, ed. *A Centennial History of Washington County Oregon*. N.p.: Extension Study Groups of Washington County, n.d.

Jensen, Kimberly. "From Citizens to Enemy Aliens." *Oregon Historical Quarterly* 114.4 (Winter 2013): 453 – 473.

Jensen, Vernon H. *Lumber and Labor*. New York: Farrar & Rinehart, Inc., 1945.

Johnson, Brian K., and Don Porth. *Images of America: Portland Fire & Rescue*. Charleston, SC: Arcadia Publishing, 2007.

Juntunen, Judy Rycraft, May D. Dasch, and Ann Bennett Rogers. *The World of the Kalapuya: A Native People of Western Oregon*. Philomath, OR: Benton County Historical Society and Museum, 2005.

Keller, Clyde. *Pioneer Landmarks of Washington County, Oregon*. Hillsboro, OR: Washington County Historical Society, 1978.

Kemp, J. Larry. *Epitaph for the Giants: the Story of the Tillamook Burn*. Portland, OR: The Touchstone Press, 1967.

Laemerman, Anne, comp. *The Hayward Story*. N.p.: n.p., 1996.

Lampman, Evelyn Sibley. *Wheels West: the Story of Tabitha Brown*. Garden City, NY: Doubleday & Company Inc., 1965.

Land of Tuality. Vol. 1. Hillsboro, OR: Washington County Historical Society, 1975.

Land of Tuality. Vol. 2. Hillsboro, OR: Washington County Historical Society, 1976.

Land of Tuality. Vol. 3. Hillsboro, OR: Washington County Historical Society, 1978.

Lenox, Edward Henry. *Overland to Oregon: In the Tracks of Lewis & Clark.* Ed. Robert Whitaker. 1904. Reprint. Fairfield, WA: Ye Galleon Press, 1993.

Linenberger, Toni Rae. United States. Bureau of Reclamation History Program. *The Tualatin Project.* Denver, CO: Research on Historic Reclamation Projects, 2000.

Lloyd, Francis E. "Petroglyphs in Patton's Valley." *The Oregon Naturalist* 3.6 (June 1896): 84 – 85.

Lucia, Ellis, ed. *This Land Around Us: A Treasury of Pacific Northwest Writing.* Garden City, NY: Doubleday & Company, Inc., 1969.

Lucia, Ellis. *Don't Call It OR-E-GAWN: A View of Oregon Today.* Portland, OR: Overland West Press, 1964.

Lucia, Ellis. *The Big Woods: Logging and Lumbering, From Bull Teams to Helicopters, in the Pacific Northwest.* Garden City, NY: Doubleday, 1975.

Lucia, Ellis. *The Saga of Ben Holladay: Giant of the Old West.* New York: Hastings House Publishers, 1959.

Lucia, Ellis. *Tillamook Burn Country: A Pictorial History.* Caldwell, ID: The Caxton Printers, Ltd., 1984.

Lucia, Ellis. *Wild Water: the Story of the Far West's Great Christmas Week Floods.* Portland, OR: Overland West Press, 1965.

Lyman, H.S. "Recollections of Grandma Brown by Jane Kinney Smith of Astoria." *Oregon Historical Quarterly* 3.3 (September 1902): 287-295.

Mackey, Harold. *The Kalapuyans: a Sourcebook on the Indians of the Willamette Valley.* Salem, OR: Mission Hill Museum Association, 1974.

MacReynolds, George. *Place Names in Bucks County Pennsylvania.* Doylestown, PA: Bucks County Historical Society, 1955.

Mallery, Garrick, and James Gilchrist Swan. United States. "Pictographs of the North American Indians, A Preliminary Paper: Rock Carvings in Oregon and in Washington." *Fourth Annual Report of the U.S. Bureau of Ethnology to the Secretary of the Smithsonian Institution 1882 - 1883.* Washington DC: U.S. Government Printing Office (1886): 25-26.

Mallery, Garrick. United States. "Picture-Writing of the American Indians: Oregon." *Tenth Annual Report of the U.S. Bureau of Ethnology to the Secretary of the*

Smithsonian Institution 1888 - 1889. Washington DC: U.S. Government Printing Office (1893): 104-105.

"Matching Stone Found for Pacific's Marsh Hall Rebuilding." Nov. 4, 1975. Pacific University.

McArthur, Lewis A. *Oregon Geographic Names*. 1928. Third ed. Portland, OR: Binfords & Mort Publishers, 1952.

Miranda, Gary, and Rick Read. *Splendid Audacity: the Story of Pacific University*. Seattle, WA: Documentary Book Publishers, 2000.

Mooberry, Lester C. *The Gray Nineties*. Portland, OR: Binfords & Mort Publishers, 1957.

Moreno, Bill, ed. *The Laurel Yearbook*. Laurelwood, OR: Associated Students of Laurelwood Academy, 1945.

Morrison, Dorothy Nafus. *Ladies Were Not Expected: Abigail Scott Duniway and Women's Rights*. 1977. Second ed. Portland, OR: Oregon Historical Society Press, 1996.

Murrell, Gary. "Hunting Reds in Oregon, 1935-1939." *Oregon Historical Quarterly* 100.4 (Winter 1999): 374-401.

Murrell, Gary. *Iron Pants: Oregon's Anti-New Deal Governor, Charles Henry Martin*. Pullman, WA: Washington State University Press, 2000.

Nelson, Donald R. *Progressive Portland II – Stop and Go*. Portland, OR: D. Nelson Books, 2006.

Nixon, Birgetta, and Mabel Tupper. *Cherry Grove: a History from 1852 to the Present*. N.p.: n.p., 1977.

Norris, William G. United States. Department of Agriculture. *The Details of the Tillamook Fire from its Origin to the Salvage of the Killed Timber*. Portland, OR: Forest Service. 1935.

Olsen, Deborah M. *Minthorn House Boyhood Home of Herbert C. Hoover Thirty-First President of the United States of America*. Newberg, OR: The Herbert Hoover Foundation of Oregon, 1979.

Pacific University. Records of the Board of Trustees 1848 to 1857. Pacific University Archives. Forest Grove, OR.

Peter, Susan, Shirley Ewart, and Barbara Schaffner, eds. *Exploring the Tualatin River Basin: a Nature and Recreation Guide by the Tualatin Riverkeepers.* Corvallis, OR: Oregon State University Press, 2002.

"Petroglyphs in Oregon." *The Oregon Naturalist* 3.4 (April 1896): 56 – 57.

Pintarich, Dick, ed. *Great and Minor Moments in Oregon History.* Portland, OR: New Oregon Publishers, Inc., 2003.

Pitz, Ray. *Images of America: Tualatin Valley Fire & Rescue.* Charleston, SC: Arcadia Publishing, 2012.

Powell, William H., ed. *Officers of the Volunteer Army and Navy who Served in the Civil War.* Philadelphia, PA: L. R. Hamersly & Co., 1893.

Richardson, Steven W. "The Two Lives of John Smith Griffin." *Oregon Historical Quarterly* 91.4 (Winter 1990): 340-370.

Robertson, James R. "Origin of Pacific University." *The Quarterly of the Oregon Historical Society* 6.2 (June 1905): 109 – 146.

Robertson, James R. "Reminiscences of Alanson Hinman." *The Quarterly of the Oregon Historical Society* 2.3 (September 1901): 266 – 186.

Ross, John R., and Margaret Byrd Adams. *The Builder's Spirit: the History of the Stimson Lumber Company.* Portland, OR: John Ross and Associates, 1983.

Rykowski, Thomas Jon. "Preserving the Garden: Progressivism in Oregon." Ph.D. dissertation, University of Oklahoma, 1981.

Saalfeld, Rev. Lawrence J. *Forces of Prejudice in Oregon 1920 – 1925.* Portland, OR: University of Portland Press (1984).

Schuck, Walter. "Gaston Petroglyphs." *Oregon Archaeological Society Screenings* 6.8 (August 1957).

Seaburg, William R., ed., and Pamela T. Amoss, ed. *Badger and Coyote were Neighbors: Melville Jacobs on Northwest Indian Myths and Tales.* Corvallis, OR: Oregon State University Press, 2000.

Seaman, N. G. *Indian Relics of the Pacific Northwest.* Portland, OR: Binfords & Mort Publishers, 1967.

Sevetson, Donald J. *Atkinson: Pioneer Oregon Educator.* North Charleston, NC: CreateSpace, 2011.

Smith, Jane Kinney. "Recollections of Grandma Brown." *The Quarterly of the Oregon Historical Society* 3.3 (September 1902): 287 – 295.

Snell, Earl, comp. *The Oregon Blue Book 1935 – 1936.* Salem, OR: State Printing Department, 1935.

Snyder, Eugene E. *Early Portland: Stump-Town Triumphant.* Portland, OR: Binfords & Mort Publishers, 1970.

Stearns, Marjorie R. "The Settlement of the Japanese in Oregon." *Oregon Historical Quarterly* 39.3 (September 1938): 262-269.

Steere, Margaret L. State of Oregon Department of Geology and Mineral Industries. "Fossil Localities of the Sunset Highway Area, Oregon." *The Ore Bin.* 19.5 (May 1957): 37-46.

Sullivan, William L. *Oregon's Greatest Natural Disasters.* Eugene, OR: Navillus Press, 2008.

"The Metropolis of the Pacific Northwest: Some Attractions of Forest Grove." *The West Shore.* Number 5, (May 1888): pp. 270 – 272.

Thomas, Lowell. *The Wreck of the Dumaru.* New York: P. F. Collier & Son Corporation, 1930.

Trollinger, Jr., William Vance. "Forgotten Flames." *University of Dayton Magazine.* Winter 2013 – 2014: 34 – 39.

Verboort Centennial 1875 – 1975 of Visitation Blessed Virgin Mary Church. Provo, UT: Community Press, 1975.

Vestal, Stanley. *Joe Meek: the Merry Mountain Man.* 1952. Reprint. Lincoln, NE: University of Nebraska Press, 1963.

Washington County Wanderings. Hillsboro, OR: Hillsboro Junior Women's Club, 1970.

Welton, Bruce J. State of Oregon Department of Geology and Mineral Industries. "Fossil Sharks in Oregon." *The Ore Bin.* 34.10 (October 1972): 161-166.

Wentz, Walt. *Bringing Out the Big Ones: Log Trucking in Oregon 1912 – 1983.* Salem, OR: Oregon Forest Products Transportation Association, 1983.

West Union 145 Years. Hillsboro, OR: The West Union Community Club, 1995 – 1996.

Williams, George C. *Alanson Hinman – Pioneer of 1844: A Story of Old Oregon.* N.p.: n.p., 1994.

Winther, Oscar Osburn. *The Old Oregon County: A History of Frontier Trade, Transportation and Travel.* 1950. Reprint. Lincoln, NE: University of Nebraska Press, 1969.

Workers of the Writers' Program of the Work Projects Administration in the State of Oregon, comps. *Oregon: End of the Trail, American Guide Series.* Portland, OR: Binfords & Mort Publishers, 1940.

Yuskavitch, Jim. *Mysteries and Legends Oregon: True Stories of the Unsolved and Unexplained.* Guilford, CT: Morris Book Publishing, 2010.

Zimmerman, Gordon N. *A Song of Yamhill.* Portland, OR: Binfords & Mort Publishers, 2005.

Newspaper Archives:
Forest Grove Democrat 1890 to 1891
Forest Grove Express 1916 to 1918
Forest Grove Independent 1873 to 1874
Forest Grove Leader 2012 to present
Forest Grove Monthly 1868 to 1869
Forest Grove News-Times 1981 to present
Forest Grove Press 1910 to 1914
Forest Grove Times 1891 to 1909
Forest Grove Venture 1887
Gaston Herald 1918 to 1920
Gaston Star 1920 to 1921
The Oregon American and Evangelical Unionist 1848 to 1849
The Oregonian 1856 to present
Washington County Hatchet 1895 to 1899
Washington County News 1903 to 1911
Washington County News-Times 1911 to 1981
Washington Independent Hillsboro 1874 to 1875

Made in the USA
San Bernardino, CA
25 March 2014